The Post to Come

European University Studies
Europäische Hochschulschriften
Publications Universitaires Européennes

Series XX
Philosophy

Reihe XX   Série XX
Philosophie
Philosophie

Vol./Band 668

PETER LANG
Bern · Berlin · Bruxelles · Frankfurt am Main · New York · Oxford · Wien

Jane Mummery

The Post to Come

An Outline of Post-Metaphysical Ethics

PETER LANG

Bern · Berlin · Bruxelles · Frankfurt am Main · New York · Oxford · Wien

Bibliographic information published by Die Deutsche Bibliothek
Die Deutsche Bibliothek lists this publication in the Deutsche
Nationalbibliografie; detailed bibliographic data is available on the Internet at
‹http://dnb.ddb.de›.

British Library and Library of Congress Cataloguing-in-Publication Data:
A catalogue record for this book is available from *The British Library*, Great Britain,
and from *The Library of Congress*, USA

ISSN 0721-3417
ISBN 3-03910-218-4
US-ISBN 0-8204-6873-8

© Peter Lang AG, Europäischer Verlag der Wissenschaften, Bern 2005
Hochfeldstrasse 32, Postfach 746, CH-3000 Bern 9
info@peterlang.com, www.peterlang.com, www.peterlang.net

Printed in Germany

Table of Contents

Acknowledgements

This book would not have been completed without the support of a number of people. I am glad to have the chance to acknowledge at least some of them here.

I would like first of all to acknowledge the support and help of Marnie Nolton who has read countless drafts in unfailing good humour and who has been my mainstay in much more than just the lengthy process of developing this book. I also wish to thank Christine Honegger at Peter Lang for all her patience with my missed deadlines. My thanks also go to Niall Lucy and Peta Bowden who have provided ongoing encouragement throughout this project, and to Claire Colebrook, Tony Thwaites, Linnell Secomb and again to Niall Lucy for all their suggestions on preparing the manuscript for publication. My thanks to my colleagues at Murdoch University, who have been very supportive, and especially to Lubica Ucnik who came to the rescue at a late stage.

Above all I am grateful to Carolyn Abbs, Debbie Rodan, Reece Plunkett and Katrina Ironside who have read, listened, given feedback, and provided constant encouragement and friendship.

Finally I wish to thank my family who have always supported me in all of my choices.

Introduction: On Beginning Where We Are

For what is put into question is precisely the quest for a rightful beginning, an absolute point of departure, a principal responsibility. (Derrida, 1982a: 6).

In a counterbalance to the above problematic – which has been taken to mean that indecision and arbitrariness cannot be overcome – Derrida has also proffered the advice that '[w]e must begin *wherever we are*' (Derrida, 1976: 162). In this case, with regards to the following project, this means to begin in the midst of that 'Post' which has been at the forefront of much of the thinking that is associated with post-structuralism and postmodernism. Now this 'Post' is not, of course, a homogenised concept, tending rather to have different meanings or functions for different disciplines, and indeed for different approaches within disciplines. Nonetheless, in its most general form it stands for a notion of having moved beyond any belief in transcendental principles or verities. Following Nietzsche, Saussure, Heidegger and Wittgenstein, the 'Post' presupposes the dismissal of the possibility of there being any foundationalist or mind or context-independent truths. In this line of thinking we are supposedly 'post' any number of concepts. Not only have we apparently overcome metaphysics, but we are also supposed to have moved beyond the constraints of foundationalist beliefs in rationalism, teleology, or indeed ethics.

To begin in the midst of this 'Post', then, means beginning with the desire to escape the conditions and constrictions of delimitative metaphysical thinking. Given this context, we have, for instance, Jean-François Lyotard's proposed replacement of metaphysical delimitation and homogeneity with the excess and incommensurability opened by his theory of agonistics, the differend and justice. Secondly, there's the Deleuzean projection of a thinking that unfolds and maps a rhizomatic logic of the 'and' rather than that of the ontological

9

'is'. Thirdly, Emmanuel Levinas wants to clarify what he sees as the transcendentally determined irreducibility of difference and alterity – an irreducibility he sets out in terms of an ethical witnessing of the infinite, the Absolute Other. And, lastly, there is Jacques Derrida's deconstructive reinterpretation of closed metaphysical difference and logic into the logic of 'différance' and 'undecidability'.

However, in view of what can be seen as a common desire to escape or deconstruct transcendental ideals and grand narratives – a desire that Heidegger sees as a necessary 'overcoming' of metaphysics – such discourses have often been perceived by various critics as flirting, dangerously, with relativism, free play, and a free-floating politics of desire and nihilism. Furthermore, to be post-metaphysical is supposedly also to be post-ethical insofar as some of the moves made by the 'Post' seem to suggest that we have moved beyond the very possibility of ethical discourse and practice. As the argument goes, if there are no truths independent of human minds and human contexts, then there can be no foundation beyond their specific contexts for ethical principles.

Ethics and ethical practice, then, can only be context-specific, meaning that any attempt to argue for universal or transcendental principles needs to be seen in terms of cultural imperialism. On this view the 'Post' is indeed unsympathetic to ethics, promoting instead an oft deplored 'anything goes' approach to questions of ethics and politics. In addition, even if projects of the 'Post' have proclaimed themselves as ethical, they have still tended to be attacked for their perceived inability to extricate themselves from paradox or apparent inefficacy – for their lack of moral fibre if you like.

The 'Post' it seems cannot win. In terms of ethics, all it seems to be able to offer is either complete relativist dissipation or ineffectual practices that can't cut it in the real world. These sorts of dismissals thus manifest not only in the form of commentators describing the 'Post' as being 'condemned to infinite deconstruction' and relativism (Ferry & Renaut, 1997: vii), but as those questions that have been directed to many of the proponents of a 'Post'. For instance Jacques Derrida was asked: '[A]fter deconstruction, what is to be done? How do we act?' (Derrida, 1999b: 65). We also have Richard Kearney asking Emmanuel Levinas whether 'the ethical obligation to the other [is] a purely negative ideal, impossible to realize in our everyday being-in-the-world?' and whether his ethics is 'practicable in human society as we know it?' (Levinas, 1986: 64). And we have Gilles Deleuze and Félix Guattari being asked in a conversation with Catherine Backès-Clément on *Anti-Oedipus* not only about the 'book's unity but of its practical implications' (Deleuze, 1995: 18). In her words the important question is that 'if nothing can prevent "fascist investments," if no force can contain them, if all one can do is *recognize* they're there, [then] where do your political reflections get you, and what are you actually doing to change anything?' (18).

What is seen as characteristic about the 'Post' here, then, is its perceived inadequacy when faced with the real world. In this view the overriding question is whether or not any thinking of the 'Post' can provide what Simon Critchley calls an 'adequate account of political life' (Critchley, 1993: 102). The theories of the 'Post' don't appear to tell us what to do, so we ask for further clarification and help.

The point of this book is thus to rethink these assumptions, arguing for a possibility for ethical engagement whilst accepting that we are indeed 'post' to a particular conception of metaphysics. Although any extra clarification and help is of course useful, I don't believe that we need the 'Post' to knuckle down and get serious, to do what Heidegger was once asked to do: get over these provisional beginnings and write an ethics.[1] This book, therefore, will instead show that the so-called 'Post' versus ethics opposition itself rests on a particular confusion about the 'Post'. Regardless of its rejection of foundationalist truths, the 'Post' should not be regarded as antithetical to ethics. In an important sense, then, this book is intended to reintroduce ethics into the 'Post', showing that the 'Post' is actually no stranger to ethical thinking and practice and that, like Heidegger, it has been doing ethics all along.

---

1   See Heidegger's 'Letter on "Humanism"' (1998: 239–276) for this question and his response to it.

Now whilst a proposal for a post-metaphysical ethics is not itself new, what distinguishes this approach is twofold. Firstly is a matter of scope insofar as this projection of a possible post-metaphysical ethical engagement considers in detail both Heidegger's oeuvre and a wide range of its associated projects in continental philosophy, including phenomenology, deconstruction, pragmatism, the newer French liberalism and post-structuralist aesthetics and theology. Secondly, this book argues that fundamental to the notion of a post-metaphysical ethics, is a distinction between the non- and post-metaphysical. Indeed it is the making of this distinction that enables readers to see that ethical thinking within the 'Post' is not a contradiction per se and hence that the proclamation of any such so-called contradiction is not a good enough reason to dismiss the thinking of the 'Post' as irresponsible and amoral.

This, then, marks out the ground and aims of this book. However, far from starting a discussion of this 'Post' through the contrast of the work of various of its proponents as being more or less paradoxical, I propose that this ideal of a post-metaphysical ethics needs first of all to be traced via an exploration of the work of Martin Heidegger. Indeed I suggest that it is this work that grounds many of these contemporary configurations of the 'Post' and that the possibility for any sort of viable and effective post-metaphysical ethics needs to be mapped with regards to its instantiation within Heidegger's work. It is only through this mapping in terms of Heidegger that it becomes possible to consider whether a post-metaphysical ethics can hold, and, if so, what form it might take and what it might then be able to effect.

Hence I have two main objectives. In the first instance, I am concerned to situate the possibility for a post-metaphysical ethics within the work of Heidegger, arguing that Heidegger's work sets forth the conditions of possibility for any and every attempt aimed at 'overcoming' metaphysics. Secondly, I aim to demonstrate that although many of these attempts exemplify a misreading of certain of Heidegger's disclosures and thereby reach an impasse, other possibilities develop an outline of a 'Post' that does not collapse into paradox or remain at an impasse. Finally it is through the development of this latter possibility and its implications that I argue for the non-abandonment of the 'Post', a view which contrasts with those of many other commentators of the 'Post', who argue, in various ways, for some sort of 'return to reason'.[2] Such a return is of course predicated on the rather problematic assumption that as the thinking of the 'Post' has abandoned reason (along with ethics) so too it must be abandoned in turn.

Very briefly, the methodology and structure of the book can best be understood in terms of the 'hermeneutic circle' that, for Heidegger, constitutes the model and function of a radicalised and radicalising interpretation. Hence my argument progresses in the form of a spiral, where points are begun and followed, and then rebegun and refollowed. Beginning with Heidegger and the question of the 'Post' – 'what is post-metaphysics?' – the first section outlines the impasse reached by several of the contemporary attempts made to configure this 'Post'. Starting again with Heidegger, the second section suggests another reading of both Heidegger and the question and possibility of the 'Post'. This 'new' beginning thus aims to set forth a 'way' out of the impasse outlined in the first section. In its turn, the afterword again picks up and asks the question of the 'Post'. In other words, this book marks an attempt to map the hermeneutic and ethical situation of the 'Post'. It is an attempt to come into and respond to the question of the 'Post' in, as Heidegger stresses, 'the right way' (1995a: 195; 1996: 143).

In a little more detail, then, the first section starts with considering both Heidegger's own aims and strategies, and some of the more recent attempts to overcome a delimitative metaphysics. The following two chapters comprise a detailed elaboration of these attempts, outlining them as attempts to configure a 'Post' that is constitutively irreducible to and other than Heidegger's depiction of metaphysics as

---

2   See, for instance, Luc Ferry and Alain Renaut's *Why We are Not Nietzscheans*, Charles E. Scott's *The Question of Ethics: Nietzsche, Foucault, Heidegger*, and Anthony J. Steinbock's 'The origins and crisis of continental philosophy'.

enframing and delimitative. The final chapter in this first section draws these various issues together, discussing these configurations of the 'Post' in terms of their relations with Heidegger, metaphysics, and a desired otherness. In concluding this section, this last chapter demonstrates that these configurations and their various relations culminate in a series of impasses – demonstrating that the question of the 'Post' is itself caught in an impasse with regards to its relation with its other, metaphysics.

Beginning again with these considerations, the second section aims to open a way that leads out of at least some of the impasses depicted in the previous section. As such it begins again with Heidegger, mapping his logic of anxiety that, I suggest, potentially unfolds a way for the 'Post' that remains both open and ethical. The remaining chapters of section two argue that this way and its logic have been at least in part developed by the interaction between the work of Jacques Derrida and that of John D. Caputo. Borrowing, then, a term used by both Derrida and Caputo, this interaction can be instantiated, for example, as a 'jewgreek' thinking, a 'jewgreek' justice.[3] Now, by this I mean, following Caputo, the possibility of a minimally metaphysical justice, and it is this that I suggest constitutes a provisional outline of a post-metaphysical ethics which is neither constrained nor confounded by the impasse within both metaphysics and non-metaphysics, nor paralysed with indecision before the demands of the real world.

Lastly, it remains for me to consider the possibilities and implications of such an instantiation of the 'Post'. The afterword thus comprises a series of speculations as to what such a 'Post' might enable and effect, and how it might then be configured and projected. Here, I suggest that despite its inability to prescribe or legitimate any actual institution or programme, jewgreek justice suggests and opens a new notion of tolerance, a new democracy and another notion of

---

3   Derrida uses this term in his discussion of Levinas's project in 'Violence and metaphysics' (Derrida, 1978b: 153), and a similar one – 'Judaeo-Greek' – in his 'Force of law: the "mystical Foundation of authority"' (1992a: 56). Caputo, in his turn, uses it throughout his work to describe the possibility of a minimally metaphysical justice.

community. In other words, it opens the way for what might be called a new enlightenment. It is this possibility, then, that I believe not only opens up some room for speculation on future directions in contemporary continental philosophy, but shows that the question of the 'Post' is not solely of academic interest. Indeed I would suggest that this vision of the 'Post' holds positive significance and implications for our conceptions of ethics and ethical practice in the 21st century.

Part I

Getting Beyond Heidegger and Metaphysics

1. Interpretation and the Questioning of Metaphysics

> Do we in our time have an answer to the question of what we really mean by the word 'being'? Not at all. So it is fitting that we should raise anew *the question of the meaning of Being*. But are we nowadays even perplexed at our inability to understand the expression 'Being'? Not at all. So first of all we must reawaken an understanding for the meaning of this question. (Heidegger, 1995a: 1).

Although stated in *Being and Time*, Heidegger's first major publication, the above aim can of course be seen as driving all of Heidegger's writings.[1] At the same time though it also marks out the site of his much-touted dispute with metaphysics: his famous 'overcoming' of metaphysics. For Heidegger, then, we have forgotten the question of Being. Worse, we have forgotten both that we have forgotten about the question and that we have forgotten how to question. Heidegger suggests that all this forgetfulness is a direct result of the style of our metaphysical conceptualising where Being is translated over and over again as beingness: 'What is being?' asks philosophy; 'beingness' answers metaphysics and then goes on to define exactly what is meant by a particular notion of 'beingness'. It is a mode of translation or an-

---

1   As Günther Neske and Emil Kettering elaborate: 'Throughout his life, Heidegger understood thinking to be a path, as being underway in asking the *one* fundamental question around which all of his writings circle: the "question of Being", or, more precisely, the question on the nearness between Being and human beings, on the *belonging* together of Being and human beings in turn, and their origin in the happening' (Neske & Kettering, 1990: 33). Hence, Heidegger's first major publication *Being and Time* had the aim of unfolding the question of Being through the horizon of temporality. Although this project was never completed as such, the relations between Being, Dasein, temporality, and history have remained pivotal and in question throughout the entirety of Heidegger's work.

swering that represents both the gradual loss or concealing of this question, and the associated concealment (via a predetermination) of Being. The question as question is forgotten in the answer. Hence to overcome our forgetfulness and perplexity and to reawaken our propensity towards questioning, Heidegger suggests that we interrogate and in fact overcome metaphysics, and by metaphysics he means the overall historical progression of the various translations or definitions of beingness.

Metaphysics as he sees it, then, despite being comprised of different definitions of beingness, is united through its desire to ascertain and ground a specific answer as opposed to sustaining and developing the question itself:

> The more this question becomes the guiding question, and the longer it remains such, the less the question itself becomes an object of inquiry. Every treatment of the guiding question is and remains *preoccupied with the answer*, preoccupied with *finding* the answer. (Heidegger, 1991b: 190).

Heidegger thus sees metaphysics overall as the delimitation of the question as question, insofar as metaphysical configurations seem to use their translation of beingness as an a priori conditioning (and delimiting) of their possibilities. It is this preoccupation with beingness or the answer rather than with the question of Being that Heidegger sees as the problem with metaphysics. In each case the question, posed automatically, recedes as a question. This mode of a priori conditioning – itself perhaps the 'proper' of metaphysics (e.g. 1991b: 187–188) – is thus the context for Heidegger's interpretation of metaphysics as a tradition which has gradually closed over its question, resulting in our forgetfulness and its thoroughgoing neglect. Heidegger thereby delimits metaphysics into its unfolding as its tradition, considering metaphysics *as* its various historical configurations – as, in fact, something that has been in some senses, having situated and forgotten its question and ground, completed. In his view, 'Metaphysics – treatment of the guiding question – is at an end' (1991b: 205).

Now it is from this 'ending' that Heidegger sets his imperative – the necessity of starting over again with a thinking that escapes these various delimitations.[2] Heidegger thus sees his role as one of developing a contrasting treatment of this guiding question, a radicalising treatment which concerns itself with developing – reawakening – the question (and questioning) itself. In response to the question 'What is being?', Heidegger wants to propose another radical response, that of a post-metaphysics. However rather than starting from scratch, Heidegger suggests that this radical development can itself be drawn from a transformative interpretation of all those sundry historical answers to the question that comprise the tradition of metaphysics.[3] Such an interpretation, as both an unfolding and a violent re-reading of these configurations,[4] would necessarily be both disruptive and transforma-

---

2   Interestingly it is also on this basis that John McCumber argues that 'Heidegger's thought' is 'the twentieth century's most important challenge to oppression', where oppression marks the practice of metaphysics (1999: 13, 14).

3   Although Heidegger's overriding focus is to distinguish the progression of metaphysics 'proper' from the not-yet thought question of Being itself – metaphysics being unable in his view to 'bring the history of Being itself, that is, the Origin, to the light of its essence' (1975: 81) – he is nonetheless careful to stress that they must not be seen as unrelated. Focused on disclosing the essential ambiguity inherent in any thinking (metaphysical or otherwise) concerned with Being itself, Heidegger thus considers Being as its ambiguous 'sending', as *Geschick*: 'When speaking of the *Geschick* of being, "being" means nothing other than the proffering of the lighting and clearing that furnishes a domain for the appearing of beings in some configuration, along with the contemporaneous withdrawal of the essential provenance of being as such' (1991c: 88). Further, 'As such a *Geschick*, being essentially comes to be as a self-revealing that at the same time lasts as self-concealing. The history of Western thinking is based in the *Geschick* of being' (1991c: 75). In other words, then, when disclosed as its doubled history, Being both reveals and conceals itself in a happening relation which Heidegger considers variously, for example, as *Geschick*, *Ereignis*, 'difference', '᭼', 'the mystery', and *aletheia*.

4   See Joanna Hodge's *Heidegger and Ethics* (1995: 118–120, 149–150) for further discussion of the violence inherent in Heidegger's dealings with the losophical tradition. Hodge argues, in regards to this violence, for the use of

tive – and, paradoxically, rigorously faithful in Heidegger's vision – in its radicalising of that metaphysical conceptualising it unfolds.

Having briefly outlined the context for the Heideggerian imperative re metaphysics, my aim now is to draw out some of the strands and implications of this extremely complex dialogue between Heidegger and metaphysics. As this book stresses, however, this dialogue is not just of interest with regards to an enhancing of our general understanding of the Heideggerian project (something that has been done with far more detail than I can offer here). Rather I suggest that this dialogue has had profound and far-reaching implications for contemporary continental philosophy, specifically for what has become known as postmodernism and post-structuralism or, more broadly, as the thinking of the 'Post'.[5] Now although many individual thinkers of the 'Post' have acknowledged and explored their relationship to the Heideggerian project,[6] the overall interaction of the 'Post' with this project needs much more elaboration. On the basis, then, of a forthcoming discussion of Heidegger's famous 'overcoming' of the rigidified and rigidifying tradition of metaphysics, I hope with this chapter to begin to clarify what I see as the formative relation of the 'Post', that stretching between the Heideggerian imperative and the philosophy of the 'Post'. As such, I want to explicate what I see as the dwelling of the 'Post' within Heidegger's peculiar 'overcoming' of metaphysics – that is, within the Heideggerian imperative to start again with thinking.

---

the term 'reading' rather than that of 'interpretation' in that Heidegger thoroughly disrupts 'the boundary between interpretation and text' (Hodge, 1995: 119).

5   Although I follow here Niall Lucy's distinction between postmodernism and post-structuralism in his *Postmodern Literary Theory*, focusing on the overall project of the 'Post' allows for the inclusion of philosophers such as Derrida in my discussion.

6   For instance, Derrida comments that it is Heidegger's work that comprises the site of 'what, today, are for me the *open questions* – questions opened by Heidegger and open with regard to Heidegger' (Derrida, 1989b: 7; cf. 1995c: 223).

Beginning the Heideggerian Dialogue

Along with his consideration and critique of metaphysics in terms of its history, and in line with his desire to reawaken and radicalise both the question of Being and questioning itself, Heidegger projects the possibility of another more open development of the question '*out of itself* and *out beyond* itself' (Heidegger, 1991b: 206). Indeed, as I will argue here, it is Heidegger's radicalising of both the question and questioning that is his famous 'step back' or 'leap' out of metaphysics itself, his 'overcoming' of metaphysics. As such we need to mark the contrast Heidegger draws between the metaphysical 'treatments' of the question and what becomes his 'development' of the question – the latter exemplifying what he sees as a sustained and thoughtful 'inquiry into inquiry'[7] (1991b: 193):

> To *treat* this question as stated and posed is simply to look for an answer. To *develop* the question as it is formulated, however, is to pose the question more essentially [...] When we treat the guiding question we are transposed forthwith to a search for an answer and to everything that has to be done on behalf of that search. Developing the guiding question is something essentially different – it is a more original form of inquiry, one which does not crave an answer [...] An answer is no more than the final step of the very asking; and an answer that bids adieu to the inquiry annihilates itself as an answer. (Heidegger, 1991b: 192).

---

7   Heidegger recognises that this style of 'development', as the rethinking of the question, is fraught with possible misunderstanding, misunderstandings which he attempts to pre-empt and counter throughout his work. For instance, his thinking is inevitably, he comments, at risk of 'being accused of disdain for all sound reason' (1958: 79; cf. 1991b: 193). Furthermore, as he suggests to his students, it is also at risk of being seen merely as his own characteristic style, eccentric and excessive: 'the farfetched and one-sided Heideggerian method of exegesis, which has already become proverbial' (1987: 176). Alongside these cautions, Heidegger also takes pains to carefully outline the necessity he perceives behind his reawakening of the – his – mode of questioning from its forgottenness in metaphysics as configured by the tradition.

In other words, Heidegger strives throughout his work to develop – that is, reawaken – a thinking which refrains from grounding itself within or as any answer, a thinking which rather considers the question of Being *as* a question. He attempts to develop a mode of thinking that remains irreconcilable with metaphysical instantiations, a questioning that is concerned with opening some sort of post-metaphysical 'other side of being' (1958: 95).

As mentioned, Heidegger sees metaphysical configurations as essentially self-encompassing and delimitative. Their various instantiations are representative of a closed circularity insofar as they predetermine that which they purport to deal with.[8] For instance, as Heidegger notes, in considering fundamental metaphysical positions, our tendency is to do so 'according to the various doctrines and propositions expressed in them' (1991b: 191). However, through discussion of these metaphysical positions in the light of their major proponents and doctrines, Heidegger shows us how their conditioning grounds or origin – that which is defined as their *arche* – work to predetermine their domain.[9] He writes that, 'inasmuch as being is put in question with a view to the *arche*, being itself is already determined' (1991b: 188). Showing their circumscription within their conditions of possibility, Heidegger shows us how the various instantiations of metaphysics can be understood as 'onto-theological' and 'enframing'.

---

8   As I will discuss below, this circularity is far-removed from the positive spiralling Heidegger considers constitutive of hermeneutic investigation (see 1995b: 187).

9   Much of Heidegger's work encompasses his radical interpretations of – 'thinking conversations' with (1969: 45) – the major figures of Western philosophy as exemplifying and constituting the history of metaphysics itself. It is additionally through these conversations that Heidegger establishes the possibility of reawakening the question of Being. Joanna Hodge, for example, argues that Heidegger's readings work to 'demonstrate the contribution of these previous thinkers, then show their limitations and then seek to break elements of their work free to be used in the [his] new formation. It is the overriding importance of developing this new form of thinking which for Heidegger justifies his impositions onto the texts of Kant, of Leibniz, or indeed Aristotle' (Hodge, 1995: 149).

These categories, he tells us, are fundamentally determinant of the tradition of metaphysics. They work to configure – that is, to delimit – each domain wherein Being vouchsafes itself each time in a certain way.[10] Taken together, these determinants configure metaphysics as a 'transcendental-horizonal re-presenting' wherein everything that is, is grounded, delimited and enframed (1966: 63).

Hence, far from sustaining and developing the guiding question as question, these various inscriptions can best be described as a history of words for Being,[11] words that also exemplify the essential rigidification and preoccupation of metaphysics with grounding its domain.[12] Seen in this way, metaphysics works as a type of ordering, a calculation that makes sense of things for us but which assumes rather than questions its grounds. Overall, then, in treating the inquiry in terms of its anticipated (and given) completion, metaphysical configurations effect a closure – an emptying out – of the question as question. They forget, as Heidegger puts it, that which is 'most worthy of thought' (1969: 55).[13]

---

10   See Heidegger's *Nietzsche* Volume II (1991b: 190–192) for a discussion of the circumscriptive specificities of 'fundamental metaphysical positions' as derived from their adoption of a certain 'stance toward being as a whole [...] in conformity to the guiding question' (1991b: 190). Also note that any vouchsafing as originarily circumscribed is also always a concealing – see footnote 2 concerning the work of *Geschick*.

11   Joanna Hodge writes, 'The history of philosophy presents the history of being in the reduced form of a history of timeless metaphysical systems [...] Heidegger constructs this history of metaphysics as a history of words for being which conceals their origin in the sending or history of being. As a result of this drastic reduction of the history of metaphysics to a sequence of words for being, Heidegger reveals the obscuring of being at work in it' (Hodge, 1995: 145). For an example of this in Heidegger's work, see his *Identity and Difference*.

12   Metaphysics determines – indeed enframes – itself as both grounded and grounding, as providing both the 'ground-giving unity' for everything and the 'unity of the all that accounts for the ground' (Heidegger, 1969: 58).

13   It is in this way that Heidegger begins many of his deliberations on (re-awakening) the question of Being, situating and disclosing it as the 'emptiest' of questions and concepts (1995a: 21; 1996: 1).

It is out of this framework, then, that Heidegger develops his focus to open and develop the guiding question of metaphysics, that question concerning the meaning of Being which has hitherto been configured, indeed confined, within the various instantiations of metaphysics. Further, it is through the practice of a transformative interpretation that is to radicalise and question the thinking of the tradition, that Heidegger believes that he can not only disrupt the constitutive closure of metaphysics, but project a potential opening or overcoming of this closure. As a brief aside it is worth noting that Heidegger considers such moves as exemplary of the phenomenological project.[14] For Heidegger, after all, 'phenomenology' exemplifies not merely a stage in the tradition of philosophy, but a certain methodology, an approach that he considers to be essential to any sustained and radical interpretation with the given aim of breaking past all the rigidifications of tradition. Hence it is a phenomenological approach that consequently informs and enables not only Heidegger's interpretation of metaphysics, but his accompanying development of the guiding question.

The Methodology of Interpretation

> In the knowing awareness of thinking in the crossing, the first beginning remains decisively the *first* – and yet is overcome as beginning. For this thinking, reverence for the first beginning, which most clearly and initially discloses the uniqueness of this beginning, must coincide with the restlessness of turning away from this beginning to an other questioning and saying. (Heidegger, 1999: 5).

It is no new thing to assert here that Heidegger's conception of interpretation is inextricable from a process of destruction (*destruktion*).

---

14   See Theodore Kisiel's *The Genesis of Heidegger's Being and Time* for discussion of this point.

Phenomenological interpretation after all requires the breaking down of existing structures, and Heideggerian interpretation is no exception in its desire to free the question of Being from the rigidifications effected by its various historical and metaphysical treatments. Heidegger can, after all, only achieve this through the sustained destruction of its prevailing configurations – a destruction that is to also mark a recovery and sustaining of questioning itself. However what needs to be stressed is that unlike in our commonsense idea of destruction, Heidegger's destruction of the tradition is more an opening up of this tradition than a discarding of it. Indeed, even in considering metaphysics to be closed, and overtly indicating in several instances the need to start again with 'an other questioning and saying', Heidegger never considers this shift to entail a complete abandonment of metaphysics, something he considers impossible. As he states: 'It is hardly possible to surpass the grotesqueness of proclaiming my attempts at thinking as smashing metaphysics to bits' (1958: 93). *Destruktion*, Heidegger writes, is not to be considered as an absolute 'negation of the tradition' but rather as that 'critical process in which the traditional concepts, which at first must necessarily be employed, are de-constructed down to the sources from which they were drawn' (1982: 23). His aim, then, is not to completely extinguish the given – metaphysical conceptualisings – but rather 'to come into it in the right way' (1995a: 195; 1996: 143).[15] In other words, Heidegger stresses a necessary circularity in his approach, a circularity deemed fundamental and which must be neither avoided nor dismissed as vicious, nor 'levelled off by means of dialectic' (1995b: 187). Indeed, as a hermeneutic spiralling, this circularity contrasts with that vicious circularity indicative of clo-

---

15   As Heidegger writes, the aim of his destruction is always positive (1995a: 44; 1996: 20). Caputo also emphasises that this work of violence and destruction is necessarily linked by Heidegger, via his hermeneutic methodology, with notions of recovery and restoration: 'The recovery of the meaning of Dasein, and ultimately of Being itself, cannot be effected without deconstructive violence, even as deconstructive violence is not to be undertaken except in the service of a positive program of retrieval' (Caputo, 1987: 65).

sure that Heidegger considers to be determinant both of metaphysical constructions and of attempts to smash metaphysics to bits.

In stressing these possibilities of a positive movement of circularity and the impossibility of completely abandoning metaphysics, the Heideggerian methodology of interpretation affirms the entwined nature of notions of destruction and retrieval and repetition. As he states outright, 'Metaphysics cannot be abolished like an opinion. One can by no means leave it behind as a doctrine no longer believed and represented' (1975: 85). Now what this means is that any overcoming called for by Heidegger is far from marking out and escaping into a new domain somehow exterior to or transcendent of metaphysics. Rather in working to both awaken and free the question from the rigidified tradition and vicious circularity of metaphysics, Heidegger argues that it is the 'essential nature of metaphysics' (1969: 51), in contrast to its various fixed forms, that needs to be retrieved or rethought. However it must also be emphasised that this retrieval indicates neither an unmediated 'historical return to the earliest thinkers of Western philosophy' (1969: 52), nor any historically situated (and closed) discussion of their treatments.[16] Rather it encompasses an open reinterpretation of these various treatments – a recovery that sustains a questioning and comprises thereby a dialogue. Heidegger's rethinking is thus an operation of hermeneutic violence and repetition, a positive and sustained opening up and radicalising of metaphysics in the form of an ongoing conversation. Indeed, as Heidegger comments in 'Der Spiegel Interview': 'My whole work [...] during the past thirty years has been mainly simply an interpretation of Western philosophy' (1990b: 59).

Thus, in responding to his own calling for the overcoming of the philosophical tradition (as, that is, metaphysics), an imperative he

---

16   Heidegger states that repetition, as he understands it, 'is anything but an improved continuation with the old methods of what has been up to now'. Rather, it is indicative of a radical re-beginning inclusive of 'all the strangeness, darkness, insecurity that attend a true beginning' (1987: 39). Repetition, for Heidegger, should also be considered in terms of his delineation and appropriation of the Nietzschean idea of 'eternal recurrence'.

sees as arising within the philosophical tradition itself, Heidegger can only project his radicalising of the philosophical tradition through his understanding of metaphysics as its history. His overcoming, already stressed as necessarily non-absolute, can only take place via what he calls 'thinking conversations' with the major figures of Western philosophy – conversations which unfold as radicalising interactions and confrontational interpretations. Heidegger's mode of investigation, then, cannot be distinguished absolutely from the history of metaphysics itself: 'the overcoming of metaphysics can only be represented in terms of metaphysics itself [...] in the manner of a heightening of itself through itself' (1975: 92). As Heidegger emphasises, especially in his discussions of Nietzsche and his position within the history of metaphysics, any development of a 'counterposition' or 'countermovement' to the tradition can only be considered in terms of the tradition it sets itself as counter to:

> That in opposition to which the countermovement would set to work must itself be worthy of such work. Hence the most profound acknowledgement lies concealed in the countermovement [...] [T]he countermovement takes whatever has donned the colors [sic] of the opposition with consummate seriousness. In turn, such esteem presupposes that whatever stands in opposition has been experienced and thought through in its full power and significance [...] The countermovement must in its necessity arise from such an original experience; and it must also remain rooted in such an experience. (Heidegger, 1991b: 171–172).

Hence metaphysics as the tradition can be neither simply left behind nor uncritically repeated. Rather, it must be placed back into question. This interpretative questioning, then, constitutive of both Heidegger's hermeneutic methodology and focus,[17] exemplifies his projection of

---

17   As Heidegger stresses: 'Our reflections make it clear that in thinking the most burdensome thought *what* is thought cannot be detached from the *way in which* it is thought. The *what* is itself defined by the *how*, and, reciprocally, the *how* by the *what*' (1991b: 119). Interestingly, the way I am here talking of Heidegger's methodology of interpretation, is very similar to the way Rodolphe Gasché glosses another Heideggerian notion of relation:

an overcoming in terms not of abandonment or absolute transcendence but of repetition and incorporation. Heidegger inscribes his undertaking of overcoming a completed metaphysics within his thinking of repetition. Furthermore, his approach, in seeking a renewal of questioning, remains at best supposition. What this means of course is that any desire to develop a thinking able to distinguish itself as absolutely other than metaphysics should be seen as problematic at the very least.[18] Nonetheless, in remaining constitutively open and preparatory, Heidegger's thinking – described by him as a 'stumbling' in his *Contributions to Philosophy* – is other than the founding intentionality, the enframing, characteristic of metaphysical thinking. Paradoxically it is Heidegger's careful projection of the possibility of an overcoming as constitutively non-absolute and non-transcendental which is exemplary of that thinking which, in unfolding itself as provisional and non-absolute, thereby overcomes metaphysics. That is, it is Heidegger's thinking of a provisional overcoming that both effects and is exemplary of an overcoming of that delimitative – enframed and enframing – thinking regarded by Heidegger as characteristic of metaphysics.

In other words, Heidegger's notion of interpretation informs both his methodology and the essence of his rethinking of the question of metaphysics. That is, as he remarks apropos of Nietzsche, the 'what' and the 'how' of his thinking are necessarily reciprocally intertwined. That is to say, Heidegger unfolds his thinking of the projected overcoming of metaphysics *as* his interpretation of metaphysics. If metaphysical thinking is concerned to ground and enframe itself as a grounded or grounding onto-theology, post-metaphysical thinking *is* interpretation in a radicalised and radicalising form. It is a thinking that, as an overcoming of enframing, remains necessarily open and provisional, unable to close over or unify itself. For Heidegger, the radicalised beyond of metaphysical enframing discloses, *as* interpreta-

---

      Auseinandersetzung. See Gasché's 'Toward an ethics of *Auseinandersetzung*'.

18   It is this point that I will consider in more detail as regards the various projects aimed at thinking the 'Post' – projects which are, I consider, informed by certain of Heidegger's aims and methodology.

tion, a sustained relatedness, the open process of the in-between and of an ongoing conversation. As such, this relation cannot be circumscribed into a domain or enframed as and within any particular vouchsafing of Being.

Heidegger is furthermore careful (as is Derrida later) not to permit the terms he uses to describe this open and provisional relatedness to rigidify into and function as yet another word for or delimitation of Being. That is, his terms of relation, of interpretation, must remain open, avoiding their collapse into any metaphysical positions. They can only point towards rather than encompass the relatedness exemplified by his radical interpretation of metaphysics.[19] These terms, as quasi-substitutable and non-delimitative descriptions of the relatedness sustained by this mode of interpretation, include *Ereignis*, 'Being', and 'dif-ference' to name a few. For example, Heidegger projects *Ereignis* as describing a doubled belonging together, a reciprocal appropriation or dwelling together which is nonetheless not a collapse into unification.[20] *Ereignis* rather manifests and exemplifies the eventality of a non-unifying appropriation, the happening and sustaining of the relation between. Heidegger also signals the non-absolute nature of this thinking of the beyond of metaphysics through his use of what

---

19   Heidegger indeed consistently considers his work as only ever on the way to an answer. For instance, he concludes *Being and Time* with the statements that 'The conflict as to the Interpretation of Being cannot be allayed, *because it has not yet been enkindled*' and that his 'foregoing investigation is [itself only] *on the way*' (1995a: 487, 488). Further, he describes the various stages of his work in terms of 'way-stations' (1971a: 12) rather than as completed systems.

20   *Ereignis* has been used by Heidegger, especially in *Identity and Difference*, to depict the appropriative happening and eventality of and within relation, within the happening of relation. As translated by Joan Stambaugh in Heidegger's *Identity and Difference*, *Ereignis* becomes the 'event of appropriation'. In contrast, Albert Hofstadter translates it in his introduction to Heidegger's *Poetry, Language, Thought* as 'not just as "the *event*," "the *happening*," or "the *occurrence*," but rather as "the *disclosure of appropriation*"' (1971b: xxi). More recently David Wood has translated it as 'eventuation' in his *Thinking after Heidegger*.

Derrida terms, later, *sous rature*. This is clearly exemplified, for example, by Heidegger's effacing – moving beyond – Being while letting it still remain legible (e.g. B~~ein~~g).

Heidegger thus considers such terms as marking out relations rather than unified metaphysical concepts. Irreducible to the history of the metaphysical treatments of the question of Being, they are suggestive of another dialogic way of thinking and questioning. They exemplify a non-delimitative and provisional thinking of that which remains unrepresentable, beyond metaphysical conceptualising. They are a regioning rather than any actual bounded region. These terms thus work to sustain an aporetic openness, a relatedness or circling which collapses into neither dialectic nor any grounded and unified identity. After all, as Heidegger writes, it is 'belonging-together' that 'remains genuinely opaque and questionable' (1991c: 105). As such these terms exemplify Heidegger's non-oppositional yet radicalising relation to metaphysics – his counter position to metaphysics that is also his interpretation of metaphysics. The relation of Heidegger's thinking as an overcoming of metaphysics, to metaphysics, is thus far from simple. However, insofar as his questioning of Being remains constitutively open, his radicalised rethinking of the question of Being is essentially other than that thinking of Being configured through the delimiting frameworks of metaphysics.

Heidegger, then, in his dialogic rethinking of the question of Being, projects a potential shift beyond, and releasement from, a certain style of metaphysical conceptualising. This shift is thereby Heidegger's reawakening of the inquiry into a thinking that remains essentially unaccountable-for by metaphysics seen *as* its historical configurations. On the other hand, this development of a way as leading 'away from what has been thought so far in philosophy' (1969: 50) can necessarily only be traced in the terms of a radicalising repetition of the history of metaphysics. Heidegger's renewed questioning, his interpretation, *of* the metaphysical tradition *is* his overcoming of that tradition. However, given that this interpretation is unable to be ever completed or attained as such, Heidegger's projected overcoming must be seen as necessarily incomplete.

Picking up the Heideggerian Baton

What I want to turn to now is what I see as the picking up of the Heideggerian baton, a picking up that I see as played out in the thinking
of the 'Post'. Indeed, I suggest that the 'Post' itself should be seen as
the contemporary retrieval of certain aspects of both Heidegger's
methodology and his overriding focus. Specifically the 'Post' picks up
and asks Heidegger's question as to what might comprise a post-
metaphysics. For instance, when taken as a (necessarily problematic)
whole, the 'Post' can be seen as not only abounding with a variety of
calls to overcome metaphysics and escape its formulations, but as being itself made up of various attempts to project a style of thinking
which is to be essentially other than and outside of a prescribed metaphysics. Postmodernism, in particular, can be seen as both unfolding
and as inscribed within various discourses of crisis, critique and completion (and their consequences). Discourses concerned with depicting
what Lyotard has called the '"downfall" of metaphysics', the exhaustion or completion of philosophy and its projected and accepted death
or end,[21] and the recurring dream of beginning or instigating some sort
of 'step outside of philosophy'.[22] These discourses are thus traced

---

21   Lyotard mentions this '"downfall" of metaphysics' in his 'Presentations'
      (1983: 122). Also see Philippe Lacoue-Labarthe's essay 'The age's mod-
      esty' (1990: 1–7) for an elaboration of the acceptance of this 'exhaustion' of
      philosophy, its possibilities, and its consequences.
22   Although Derrida makes this claim in 'Structure, sign, and play' (1978b:
      284), he qualifies it immediately by remarking that the 'step "outside phi-
      losophy" is much more difficult to conceive than is generally imagined by
      those who think they made it long ago with cavalier ease'. He is, of course,
      doing something different from postmodernism. Whilst the philosophers of
      postmodernism are focused on delineating a certain outside to metaphysics,
      stepping beyond the limit of philosophy seen as metaphysics, Derrida has
      worked to critique this project itself along with a certain configuration of
      metaphysics, depicting the ambivalence and aporetic structure of any such
      thinking of the limit. See, for example, his *Aporias* on the aporetic constitu-
      tion of the notion of 'limit': 'What is at stake in the first place is [...] not the

through with demands for a 'new' thinking or logic, demands accompanied by rhetoric of 'destruction', 'deconstruction', 'clearing', 'soliciting', 'overcoming', and so forth. In other words, postmodernism may be seen as founded upon and organised around critiquing and escaping metaphysical thinking, assuming this latter project as its own (and hence integrally paradoxical) governing principle.[23] Both instigated and constituted by this perceived necessity of overcoming metaphysics – of taking a step outside of metaphysics – postmodernism (or, more generally, the philosophy of the 'Post') can thus be traced back to a certain interpretation of Heidegger and his sustained interrogation of metaphysics as a closed tradition needing to be opened and rethought. In other words, Heidegger's work should be read as the setting forth of the conditions of possibility for this first (and only) desired step of the 'Post'. Indeed Heidegger, to misappropriate Witt-

---

crossing of a[ny] given border. Rather, at stake is the *double concept of the border*' (Derrida, 1993a: 18; cf. 1982a). See Niall Lucy's *Postmodern Literary Theory* for more on this difference between Derrida's project as constitutive of a certain post-structuralism and postmodernism, a difference which is central also to my discussion of the possibility of the 'Post'.

23   As one contemporary critic puts it, 'contemporary continental philosophy dismisses, with the discourse of postmodernism, the role of origin, teleology, foundation, etc.' (Steinbock, 1997: 199). Interestingly, Anthony Steinbock goes on to argue that contemporary continental philosophy under the auspices of postmodernism is itself in crisis due to this dismissal. That is, that this dismissal which essentially equates to a naive attempt to escape Western metaphysics itself – characterised by its thinking in terms of origin, teleology etc. – results in what he terms a 'reactionary relativism' (203) and further runs the risk of totalitarianism (213). Indeed, he writes, 'In the final analysis, static origin and mere play are just two expressions of the same objectivism' (213). As such, Steinbock argues, contemporary continental philosophy needs to reclaim a dynamic understanding of origin as 'origin-originating' and hence 'generative' (202–204), enabling it to again meaningfully challenge 'essentialism, foundationalism, metaphysics of presence, etc.' (212) through its integral '*style* of approach' (201) of radical 'critique and [...] crisis thinking' (212). This latter project of course, as is the thinking it is critical of, must be seen as founded upon Heideggerian interpretation.

genstein, sets in place that ladder from which a proponent of the 'Post' can see (or indeed construct) the world 'rightly'.[24]

My aim, then, is to close this chapter with a brief discussion of some of the various attempts of contemporary continental philosophy to develop a thinking that is essentially other than metaphysical – a discussion which will preface the focus of the chapters to come. Specifically I will consider these various projections in terms of their retrieval and reinterpretation of those aspects of the Heideggerian project delineated above, in particular their common drive towards a possible post-metaphysics. For instance, as I will show, Lyotard, Deleuze (and Guattari), Levinas, and of course Derrida, all call for and expound some style of non- or post-metaphysical thinking. Other theorists, such as Lacoue-Labarthe, Nancy, Rorty, and Caputo will also bear consideration regarding their own pick-ups of and dealings with this project.

Whilst I will of course discuss these various projections of a non- or post-metaphysical thinking individually – thereby hopefully respecting their heterogeneity, their functioning *as* a multiplicity[25] – I believe that they can all be seen to base themselves (overtly or covertly) upon a Heideggerian configuration of metaphysics and upon certain of Heidegger's aims and strategies. For instance, they retrieve and sustain Heidegger's depiction of metaphysics as being essentially 'onto-theo-logical' and 'enframing' – as being, that is, a delimitative and calculative mode of thinking. The 'Post', as such, sees metaphysics as exemplary of a rigid or structuring thinking that operates as what Deleuze and Guattari have called a transcendental overcoding. It is equated to that self-affirming thinking or logic, delineated variously

---

24 Ludwig Wittgenstein, of course, in this passage from his *Tractatus Logico-Philosophicus*, also notes that this seeing of the world 'rightly' is itself the recognition that any such project is itself 'senseless' (Wittgenstein, 1995b: 189). Wittgenstein further explores this conclusion in his later work.

25 As Deleuze and Guattari stress: 'The notion of unity (*unité*) appears only when there is a power takeover in the multiplicity' (Deleuze & Guattari, 1987a: 8). They furthermore see power takeovers as characteristic moves of metaphysical thinking.

as the philosophy of presence, identity and representation, which is perceived as constructed – or, rather, given – through and by its constitutive delimitative and appropriative functioning. This thinking or logic, as simultaneously generative and hierarchising of binaries, is further seen as organising and thereby subsuming difference itself, along with the very possibility of heterogeneity. And it is this last depiction that the 'Post' uses, constructing itself as that thinking or logic which is irreducible to any metaphysical homogeneity.

Now before I begin my particular portrayals of the 'Post', it is worth looking first of all at the 'Post' in general. Basically, if we start with Heidegger's stress on the inter-relation of the 'how' and the 'what' of his thinking – whereby his methodology is inextricable from the focus or 'essence' of his thinking – metaphysics as considered from the possibility of the 'Post' encompasses far more than the consideration and answering of the question of Being. Rather it is delineated *as its consideration* of the question. That is to say, the metaphysical 'what', as Heidegger explicates it, cannot be distinguished from the way it is elaborated, from the 'how' of its thinking. For instance, as already seen in its considerations of the question of Being, metaphysics essentially works in terms of both an *arche* and *telos*, thereby instantiating its configurations as fundamentally bounded and thence delimitative. Metaphysics unfolds as an enframing, and it is this constitution that has been incorporated within – as both founding and sponsoring – the various developments of a non- or post-metaphysical thinking.

In other words, metaphysical instantiations are represented by the 'Post' as the functionings of hegemony. They are delineated *as* the functioning of regulative and teleological ideals or principles. They are, in Lyotard's terminology, 'meta-narratives'. These, both exemplary and effective of a certain closure, present themselves as able to absolutely authorise or legitimate thinking itself. So delineated, metaphysics *is* constitutively an identity politics – that is, a thinking which, as both totalising and unifying, appropriatively hierarchises, structures, and subsumes all thinking into its domain. Metaphysical thinking thus projects itself in terms of a 'transcendent compositional principle' (Deleuze & Guattari, 1987a: 266), whereby it can both oversee and encompass its domain:

> What is common to metaphysics and transcendental philosophy is, above all, this alternative which they both impose on us: *either* an undifferentiated ground, a groundlessness, formless nonbeing, or an abyss without differences and without properties, *or* a supremely individuated Being and an intensely personalized Form. Without this Being or this Form, you will have only chaos [...] In other words, metaphysics and transcendental philosophy reach an agreement to think about *those determinable singularities only which are already imprisoned inside a supreme Self or a superior I.* (Deleuze, 1990: 105–106).

Overall, then, this delineation of metaphysics, essentially common to (and instigatory of) the 'Post' in all its multiplicity, is a repetition of the Heideggerian conception of metaphysics. Metaphysics is projected by Heidegger and the 'Post', and indeed itself, as delimitative because it is transcendentally ordered. It is seen as effecting the appropriative horizoning of thinking itself.

It is thus in response to this perceived horizoning of metaphysics that projects of the 'Post' unfold themselves as both the counter-happening to and overcoming of this thinking. Metaphysical thinking as both delimited and delimitative thus, problematically, operates as the condition of possibility, the determining principle, for a thinking projecting itself as constitutively open, unenframed, and hence other. This has the paradoxical effect whereby non- or post-metaphysical thinking itself functions as an essential enframing of metaphysical thinking. Prior however to discussing this paradoxical (and very Heideggerian) relation in more detail – the consideration of which will concern later chapters – it seems pertinent to first of all briefly consider the principle that I suggest is instigatory of each and every non- or post-metaphysical project.

Now this could perhaps be best summarised as an overriding concern with difference, with the sustaining of difference and heterogeneity. It is a concern with sustaining irreducible difference and unsubsumable alterity in the face of metaphysical practices of enframing and delimitation. It is a desire for a thinking of difference that is and remains – projectively, at least – absolutely other than either the synthesising thought of dialectic, or the rigid separation of oppositional thought. Difference for the 'Post', then, is to be both respected and sustained.[26] As such, it can be seen as a certain repetition of Heidegger's ever more attentive and questioning focus on difference as difference, as what he comes to term 'dif-ference' (Heidegger, 1969: 47; 1971b). Difference *as* its sustained happening thus functions as the guiding question of the philosophy of the 'Post' – a functioning which is seen, on the one hand, as providing the conditions of possibility for a non- or post-metaphysical thinking. On the other hand, however, this functioning of difference as both question and principle – and as thereby regulative of these various possibilities of thinking – is itself exemplary of a typical metaphysical methodology. That is, (the question of) difference can perhaps be seen as representative of both the *arche* and *telos* for configurations of a non- or post-metaphysics.

These responses to – as overcomings of – metaphysics, then, should thus be seen as configurations of a thinking of difference *as* difference, of that which remains in and as difference. Difference, for non- or post-metaphysical thinking, comes to encompass and exemplify that which, differing, is unable to be subsumed, that which remains, whilst in relation, irreducible to any unity or identity or totality. The sustaining of difference *as* difference, in other words, both situates and enables projections of excess, multiplicity and heterogeneity. These, in turn, are projected as exemplifying that incommensurable other or outside to metaphysical thinking. An other which remains unsubsumable by metaphysics and thereby necessarily unrepresentable. Indeed Lyotard utters a catchcry of the 'Post' when he enjoins: 'Let us wage a war on totality; let us be witnesses to the unpresentable'.[27] Such thinking of difference is thus not only the regulating

---

26   It is due to this principle, of course, that various discourses of the 'Post' formulate themselves as a non- or post-metaphysical thinking of justice, obligation, ethics etc. This will be discussed in detail later.

27   Lyotard utters this catchcry in *The Postmodern Condition: A Report on Knowledge* (1984b: 82).

principle of the 'Post', but also its disclosure of a relation – itself irreducible – with an unrepresentable excess. The thinking of difference
thus unfolds as a thinking of excess or, rather, unfolds as the possibility of an excess which is beyond enframing. Indeed the various configurations of this thinking of difference and excess exemplify a non-
or post-metaphysics in their functioning *as other than* metaphysical
delimitation. Consequently, this functioning must itself remain *as*
other – that is, it itself must remain *as* excess and *in* difference, indeed
as necessarily unrepresentable by metaphysics.

Non- or post-metaphysical constructs must furthermore remain as singularities irreducible to any homogeneity. The sustaining
of the irreducibility of difference *as* the project of the 'Post', demands
its configuration in terms of non-totalisable and non-unifiable singularities, specificities, happenings, hecceities, and so forth, which
themselves remain incommensurable. That is, any sustaining of heterogeneity necessitates respect for singularity, and that which holds in
and as difference. To borrow from Lyotard, this way of thinking – the
'postmodern condition' – is manifested as an 'incredulity toward [any]
metanarratives' (1984b: xxiv), even towards that of the 'Post' itself.
On this basis, then, the 'Post' constitutes itself as that project for a
heterogeneity that is unable to be 'governed by pre-established rules'
(Lyotard, 1984b: 81). We might say that the 'Post' is exemplary of
Wittgensteinian language-games – constituting, that is, 'a complicated
network of similarities overlapping and criss-crossing: sometimes
overall similarities, sometimes similarities of detail' (Wittgenstein,
1995a: 32). Similarities to do with a shared Heideggerian delineation
of metaphysics, and the shared imperative of getting out of metaphysical conceptualising – that is, of situating and projecting the possibility of a non- or post-metaphysics.

As shown, then, configurations of the 'Post' are unable to be
represented as constituting a unified whole or system. In line with this
necessity, I will thus briefly show some of the main configurations of
the 'Post' as the related singularities constitutive of a heterogeneity.
Unable obviously to consider each and every configuration of non- or

post-metaphysics, I will concern myself here with the work of Lyotard, Deleuze (and Guattari), Levinas, and also with the associated projections of Derridean deconstructions. Necessarily brief, my discussion here of these various projects will be taken up in further detail in the following chapters, as will the tracing of their rather problematic relations to that mode of Heideggerian interpretation assumed as the condition for their possibilities. That is, they will be considered in terms of their respective dwellings within (and as reinterpretations of) that peculiar region opened by Heidegger via his projected 'overcoming' of metaphysics.

The 'Post' in a Slide Show

Although the technology of slide shows has of course moved on – we are more likely now to be sent a collection of digital photos or a PowerPoint presentation to browse on our desktop than gather together for an evening with a slide projector – the idea of viewing a gallery of slides seems particularly appropriate for my aims for the remainder of this chapter. Just as such a viewing gives us a bit of an insight into what should be considered important and interesting in a certain context (even if only that of someone else's holiday), these final pages will introduce and highlight particular points of the 'Post' to do with its relation with a certain notion of metaphysics. As with any slide show, however, the slides chosen for display here can in no way provide an exhaustive account of these various projects of the 'Post'.

Slide One

Our first slide shows us Lyotard's acceptance of the exhaustion and consequent crisis in metaphysical thinking. Situating his project in terms of this '"downfall" of metaphysics', Lyotard suggests opening 'another perspective [...] through which it may be possible to measure up to the crisis' (1983: 122). As such he proposes the development of a thinking that is other than metaphysics and which wages a war on the metaphysical desires for totality and unity. This thinking, then, comprises a rethinking of the functioning and configuration of difference, an imperative that Lyotard sees as arising from his initial delineation of difference as determinant and conditioning of identity politics and other totalising systems of thought. Exemplified here by what Lyotard has once termed the 'disjunctive bar' – that rigidity marking the boundaries of the 'over there the not-this, here the this' (1993: 14, 24) – difference is thus seen to operate as the founding and ordering principle of a reductive metaphysical appropriation. On this basis, any possible thinking other than through metaphysics necessitates a sort of conceptual makeover of difference, overhauling its properties so as to allow for a quite different functioning than previously thought possible.

Basically, as Lyotard sees it, when explicated in terms of metaphysical systems, difference functions as the oppositional operations structuring and legitimating its conceptualising. Thus in the overcoming of metaphysical difference, difference needs rather to be delineated and sustained *as* that which constitutively neither represents nor delimits, but holds as differing. Lyotard thus aims to deconstruct[28] the notion of difference, thinking it not as delimitative and the

---

28   Although Lyotard does, on occasion, explicitly use the term 'deconstruction' to refer to his own undertaking, it is an operation somewhat different to Derrida's own project. As David Carroll notes: 'Lyotard's use of this term is not the same as Derrida's and is derived more from the deconstructive movement in art than from philosophy. For Lyotard, it is, in a certain sense, the radical alternative to all philosophy, even critical philosophy' (Carroll, 1989: 192*n*3). That is, in contrast to Derrida's deconstruction as

condition of presentation, but rather as witness 'to the unpresentable' (1984b: 82), witness to an irreducible excess. Thought otherwise, difference is to function *as* the relation, the relation with that which remains as excess. Hence Lyotard reconfigures metaphysical difference through projecting (and affirming) its possible opening into the excess of heterogeneous multiplicity, of plurality.[29] As reconfigured, difference is thereby thought as affirmative of a certain irreconcilability or incommensurability (or, indeed, indiscernibility), which is unable to be regulated via either dualism or dialectic. This happening of difference thus opens a non-metaphysical economy that Lyotard has described in an early work as the libidinal economy of excess, desire and disorder.[30]

Now Lyotard has projected this opened possibility of difference, for instance, in this same early work, as the mad movement and production of a 'tumult of intensities' (1993: 31), and later as the uncontrollable (albeit inevitable) process of linkage (1995: 29; cf. 1993: 261). Rather than happening as appropriative operations of homogenisation, these movements depict the agonistic happening constitutive of sustained heterogeneous multiplicity. Furthermore, this happening is depicted as necessarily open via the instantiation (or irruption) of that incommensurable intensity which Lyotard comes to term the *differend*. Hence it is in working to rupture – or, perhaps, to transcend – the

---

the irrecusable movement of undecidability, Lyotard projects a thinking which de-constructs totality in order to present the unpresentable. Indeed, Lyotard states outright that deconstruction 'constitutes the only type of activity that is effective, and this is because it is functionally – the word is very bad; it would be better to say straight out ontologically – located outside the system, and by definition its function is to deconstruct everything that presents itself as an order, to show that all "order" conceals something else, something that is repressed in this order' (Lyotard, 1984a: 29, *t.m.*, cited in Carroll, 1989: 26–27).

29   The relation between Lyotard's reconfiguration of difference and his resultant projection of (and demand for) a sustained heterogeneous multiplicity will be discussed in detail in the following chapters.

30   The early work referred to here is of course that of Lyotard's *Libidinal Economy*.

appropriative fixation of difference, that Lyotard discloses the possibility of a non- or post-metaphysical thinking. This thinking is thus to function as other than metaphysics in its sustaining of difference as constitutively both open and unregulatable. Finally, it is this sustaining of difference that enables not only Lyotard's projection of a thinking of heterogeneity and plurality, but his delineation of the injustice of metaphysical homogenisation.

Slide Two

A second projection of a non- or post-metaphysics can be found within the writing of Deleuze, both with and without Guattari. This writing, despite Deleuze's own declaration that he has 'never worried about going beyond metaphysics or the death of philosophy' (Deleuze, 1995: 88), works to instantiate another possible 'beyond' of a Heideggerian-style metaphysics. Deleuze, in other words, can be seen as projecting a thinking that is to *function* otherwise than (and thereby escape from) the various delimitative processes and systems he sees as constitutive of transcendental thinking. This latter thinking he sees as resting upon what he calls systems of the One – described variously, for instance, as Oedipus and psychoanalysis, arborescence, State thinking, Royal Science, the Law, metaphysics and transcendental philosophy. He considers that such systems operate by way of appropriation and overcoding, as if inclusive of a supplementary point or dimension from which they may be configured as totalised and unified. Deleuze (and Guattari) are thus desirous of unfolding a style of thinking which is to be functionally irreconcilable with the hegemonic practices projected as inherent in and desired by such overcoded thinking.[31]

---

31   Guattari, when interviewed by Catherine Backès-Clément in 1972, describes and situates the style of thinking he and Deleuze have worked to develop: 'We set against [a] fascism of power active, positive lines of flight, because these lines open up desire, desire's machines, and the organization of a social field of desire'. It is a matter of 'allowing something to escape,

Given that they want to escape the hegemonic practices of overcoded thinking, Deleuze and Guattari instantiate a shift in focus from being concerned with the setting in place and sustaining of a transcendental viewpoint, to the opening and liberating of that which happens in (and, indeed, out from) the middle or the in-between. Thinking, with such a shift, becomes a matter not of explanation, calculation or interpretation, but rather of production, proliferation and experimentation. In Deleuzoguattarian terms this thinking from the middle should function as an unconstrained becoming, as plural becomings which are in constant escape from the 'repressive inscription or encoding of their multiple lines within a unitary development toward [...] transcendent ends or endpoints' (1995: 186*tn*8). As Deleuze and Guattari describe in *A Thousand Plateaus*, such a thinking should be a multiple-becoming and becoming-multiple, an unravelling and opening into a becoming pack or tribe.

Becoming is furthermore a matter and affirmation of movement and speed in all their unpredictability. Even God, Deleuze and Guattari write, cannot 'say in advance [...] where the line of flight will pass' (1987a: 250). Constituted as an infectious and rhizomatic burgeoning multiplicity, becoming resists any unification or delimitation. It is a thinking that breaks out of and overflows any prescriptive enframing. It is both non-ontoteleological and non-ontotheological. Overall, then, whilst Deleuze (and Guattari) might say that their interest is only in following and affirming unconstrained rhizomatic becoming – 'We weren't looking for something timeless' – on catching 'things where they were at work, in the middle' and looking 'for new things being formed' (Deleuze, 1995: 86), they nonetheless repeatedly frame this desire in terms of an escape from (and associated breaking down of) processes of overcoded thinking. In other words, their projection of unconstrained becoming exemplifies a possible beyond of

---

like bursting a pipe or a boil. Opening up flows beneath the social codes that seek to channel and block them' (Deleuze, 1995: 19).

metaphysics, a thinking that has also been described as an ethics, a ferreting out of all traces of fascism.[32]

Slide Three

In his turn Levinas also projects a possible non- or post-metaphysics. However, unlike Deleuze and Guattari, Levinas explicitly configures this possibility as *absolutely other than* delimitative philosophy. As does Lyotard, Levinas also sees metaphysical philosophy as effecting a certain suppression and appropriation of difference. Philosophy, he argues, represents a becoming Same. It is an ontological relation or event which instantiates recurring acts of synthesis, assimilation, adequation, comprehension, representation, and even alchemy. It is and effects, in other words, that takeover that brings about the 'transmutation of the other into the same' (1993: 49–50; cf. 1996b: 42). Philosophy, then, is and effects 'being's remaining-the-same in the simultaneity of its presence, in its always' (1993: 158). Philosophy for Levinas therefore results in an all-encompassing sameness or immanence. It represents the a priori deconstitution of any possibility of non-delimitable difference or transcendence, and thereby alterity. Under Levinas's conception, philosophy *is* the 'refutation of transcendence' (1991: 169) and the assimilation of alterity.

Concerned, then, with overcoming or escaping this delimitative and appropriative thinking,[33] Levinas sets forth a thinking which he posits outright as an ethics. Basically this ethics is that functioning otherwise than through the totalisations effected by metaphysical con-

---

32   See, for instance, Foucault's preface to Deleuze and Guattari's work *Anti-Oedipus* where he suggests that it might be seen as an introduction to a non-fascist life (Foucault, 1984a: xiii).

33   Levinas in fact uses Heideggerian ontology to exemplify the necessarily reductive nature of philosophy, setting his own project as a counter to it (e.g. Levinas, 1996b: 45–46). I suggest, however, that Levinas does in fact ground his project on Heideggerian-sponsored configurations of philosophy, and further fundamentally misreads Heidegger in his critique of this project.

figurations, and Levinas attempts to trace it through that irreducible relation comprising sustained difference. Levinas as such is concerned to re-establish and sustain difference in terms of transcendence and alterity – *as*, that is, the revelation of 'the very possibility of the beyond' (1993: 165), and the '*idea of the infinite*' (1996a: 19). When thought in terms of this ethics, then, difference is indicative of both a relation to a certain unmediated excess and the revelation of this excess. Disclosed in terms of a non-dialectical relation, difference consequently enables a thinking of absolute alterity determined in terms of transcendence and the infinite. Difference is thus a relatedness *in* and *as* its irreversibility. It *is* that relation of the overflowing of the circumscriptive same by an absolutely excessive and irreducible other.

In other words, Levinas postulates a non-metaphysics *as* the sustained irreducibility of difference and alterity, an irreducibility or relatedness held open *as* transcendence. Indeed, projected as a sort of primordial ethics, this non-metaphysics is unfolded *as* the 'passing over to being's *other*, otherwise than being' (1991: 3). Specifically Levinas projects this ethical relation – the sustained relation to infinity and 'the very movement of transcendence' (1996b: 39) – through such terms as 'desire' and the 'face to face', and 'the-one-for-the-other' of 'substitution'. Levinas's non-metaphysics, then, his projection of ethics, depends upon a reconfiguration of difference wherein, sustained, it operates as the extraordinary relation to – indeed, the witnessing of – the infinite. As such, holding itself open as this ethical witnessing of the infinite – the sincerity of the 'here I am' which testifies to the infinite (1996a: 105) – difference sustains and affirms the excess constitutive of transcendence. Hence it is this diachronic relation that is projected by Levinas *as* the absolute and ethical escape from totalising philosophy. Levinas's projected ethics thereby unfold as other than philosophy, a non-metaphysics. Indeed, Levinas suggests that such an ethics can only be represented as that 'voice [which] comes from the other shore. A voice [which] interrupts the saying of the already said'.[34]

Slide Four

The last slide of the 'Post' to be briefly shown here is that of Derridean deconstruction. This, notoriously, has often been glossed *as* a thinking of excess and the supplement, of fundamental and irreducible undecidability and free play.[35] Whilst again concerned with projecting the possibility of a non-delimitative functioning of difference and the impossibility (and injustice, as is emphasised in his later work) of its reduction into any economy of identity,[36] Derridean deconstruction considers difference in terms of its undecidability – for example, as 'différance'. Difference, then, *as* irreducible *is* itself deconstructed. It is opened into *its* ownmost happening *as* undecidability and excess. That is, when seen as the happening of 'différance', difference can no longer function as the marking off of limits. Rather it is (or ✗ to borrow a strategy used by both Heidegger and Derrida) the 'trace which itself can never be presented' (Derrida, 1982a: 23). Derridean deconstructions – always plural – thus rethink difference through the solicitation of the fundamental philosophical notions of limit and originary fullness, of the dream of any 'full presence which is beyond play' (1978b: 279).

---

34   Levinas makes this claim regarding ethics in *Otherwise than Being or Beyond Essence* (1991: 183).

35   John Searle, for instance, has criticised deconstruction for 'setting up a kind of "all or nothing" choice between pure realization or self-presence and complete freeplay or undecidability' (Derrida, 1995a: 114).

36   Derrida highlights the aporetic structure of any attempted reduction into an economy of identity or completion into absolute presence through tracing the undecidability manifest in and constitutive of representation: 'As corruptive principle, the representative is not the represented but only the representer of the represented; it is not the same as itself' (Derrida, 1976: 297).

Projective of an undelimitable undecidability, Derridean deconstruction functions on the one hand as absolutely other than metaphysical configuring. On the other hand, however, it deconstructs even – necessarily – its own possibility of functioning *as* such a situated other. Deconstruction indeed remains constitutively resistant to definition, unable to be totalised as a whole.[37] Re-marking the inherently aporetic functioning of notions of limit, Derrida discloses the undecidability of the in-between which in turn asks the question of the limit. Hence deconstruction discloses the play instantiated and 'permitted by the lack or absence of a[ny] center [sic] or origin' (1978b: 289), and the undecidability of any functioning limit or frame. However, *as* an instantiation of undecidability and excess,[38] deconstruction cannot be considered as the instantiation of absolute or 'complete freeplay'. After all, as Derrida writes, 'no completeness is possible for undecidability' (1995a: 115, 116). Maintaining itself, then, as open and undecidable – and further, as provisional – deconstruction only operates *as* the questioning of the functioning of delimitation. In other words, as with the Heideggerian instantiation of a 'Post' in terms of a radicalising interpretation, Derridean deconstruction comprises the entwinement of its 'what' with its 'how'. That is, it comprises no 'what', no positive formulation, which is independent of its 'how'.

Hence deconstruction can only be configured as the provisional tracing through of itself as its functioning. It is a calling into

---

37 Derrida notes on various occasions that 'deconstruction' is only one of several quasi-concepts he has used to exemplify and designate the irruptive and interruptive movement of the supplementarity of the in-between. Indeed, his project must rather remain essentially unnameable, reducible to 'neither a method nor an analysis' (Derrida, 1995c: 83, 356). As he stresses, deconstruction 'does not exist somewhere, pure, proper, self-identical' (1995a: 141).

38 Derrida configures this irreducible excess as, for example, the skidding or drifting of the play and dissemination of and in metaphor (Derrida, 1978a; cf. 1982a). He further describes this movement as resulting in a certain undecidability. In his turn, Caputo likens Derridean play to a quiet creeping over everything of a 'film of undecidability [...] so that we cannot quite make out the figures all around us' (Caputo, 1993a: 4).

question – an operation that is never completed, remaining always to come. Deconstruction, then, is a projection of difference into that irrecusable undecidability which is neither the irresponsibility of nor formula for any absolute beyond. In other words, it works to hold open and sustain itself as undecidability, and cannot be seen as projective of any positive non- or post-metaphysics. Indeed, Derrida delineates both such projects and the desire for them as exemplary of a certain hope or nostalgia for the 'myth of [...] a lost [or as yet uncreated] native country of thought' (1982a: 27). Rather, deconstruction marks the situatedness of both the within and without, tracing the porous and undecidable limit of the in-between, a task that Derrida sees as a responsibility. Indeed, as he remarks, there is nothing more responsible than deconstruction. As such, he delineates deconstruction in terms of the non-economy of responsibility, the instantiation of an opened justice: 'Justice remains, is yet, to come, *à venir*, it has an, it is *à-venir*, the very dimension of events irreducibly to come'.[39]

At this stage, then, my concern and my short slide show has simply been to suggest that the overall project of much contemporary continental philosophy – the attempted delineation of a non- or post-metaphysics – should be positioned within the Heideggerian imperative of thinking otherwise than through the metaphysical processes of delimitation. My next chapter will begin tracing in more detail the specific relatedness of these various projects of the 'Post' to this Heideggerian imperative. Specifically the following chapters will focus on fully clarifying the complex relations that exist between the Heideggerian project, those reconfigurations of it that comprise the 'Post'

---

39   Derrida makes this claim in 'Force of law' (1992a: 27). The 'to come' of
       justice has been extensively discussed not only by Caputo among others, but
       has been recently glossed by Niall Lucy throughout his *A Derrida Diction-*
       ary.

and metaphysics. Furthermore these reconfigurations will be discussed with regard to their specific (mis)readings of the Heideggerian project, readings that I will argue can perhaps be seen to institute a certain delimitation of the dreams and possibilities of the 'Post'.

2. Thinking to Excess or Getting Outside of Metaphysics

> To place thought in an immediate relation with the outside, with the forces of the outside, in short to make thought a war machine, is a strange under-taking [...] And this form of exteriority of thought is [...] a force that de-stroys both the image *and* its copies, the model *and* its reproductions, every possibility of subordinating thought to a model of the True, the Just, or the Right [...] (Deleuze & Guattari, 1987a: 376–377).

> One of the current aims of my work is to show that there is, I would not say an ontology, but a mode of relation to something which is very certain within the given, but which also transcends those very empty forms within which the given is habitually synthesized. (Lyotard, 1988: 289).

As I have suggested in the previous chapter, something like the above aim both informs and characterises much of the thinking of the 'Post'. The 'Post', after all, is organised around that set of problematic rela-tions that not only remain irreducible to any economy of the same, but mark a connection between a certain outside or otherness and that givenness the 'Post' hopes to put in question. Unable by definition to be completely disentangled, these relations are also situated within – although necessarily non-delimited by – the horizon of Heideggerian interpretation. That is, the questioning methodology of Heideggerian interpretation informs both the 'what' and 'how' of all non- or post-metaphysical thinking.[1] Hence, Heidegger inhabits and configures the

---

1   As I will demonstrate below, Derridean deconstruction is one of the clearest
     examples of that configuration of thought – explicitly stressing the essential
     entwinement of method and focus – that Heidegger opens. Following Hei-
     degger, Derrida insists that the focus of deconstruction is not only *not* sepa-
     rable or distinguishable from its method, but does not name any positive
     presentable system or formula. Deconstruction has 'never named a project,
     method, or system. Especially not a philosophical system' (Derrida, 1995c:

problematic and eventality of these projects, just as the possibility of the 'Post' inhabits (and assumes) that open regioning of thought disclosed by Heidegger. On the one hand, the desire to start again with another thinking is conditioned by Heidegger, whilst on the other the development *of* a non- or post-metaphysics is itself perhaps in excess of Heidegger's own project. It is these relations, then, that condition the possibility of all non- or post-metaphysical thinking, relations that can be neither left behind nor represented, but must be critically repeated and kept in question. Indeed the relation between Heidegger's work and the various configurations of a non- or post-metaphysics is itself a Heideggerian relation,[2] and, as the 'Post' has discovered, neither Heidegger nor metaphysics can be simply left behind or finished with.

That is, when seen as an admittedly problematic whole, the 'Post' unfolds as *in* relation to both a Heideggerian configuration of metaphysics, and Heidegger's own projections of a thinking potentially other than this metaphysics. The latter marking that thinking which, in interpreting (and thereby repeating) metaphysics, attempts to overcome it. Repeating these configurations, projects of the 'Post' present themselves as a counter-happening to metaphysics. Metaphysical thinking, *as* both delimited and delimitative, operates *as* the condition of possibility for that thinking projecting itself as constitutively open, unenframed, and hence other. Such thinking thus retraces the Heideggerian analytic in terms of both its methodology and focus. Furthermore, these various relations are best represented by Heidegger's notion of interpretation. Insofar as interpretation is the eventality of that relation that not only overflows any metaphysical economy of the same, but also remains other than that of dialectical or oppositional structuring, such relations are functionally excessive.

---

356). Rather, following on from Heidegger, deconstruction marks the doubled gesture and writing of interpretation (1982a: 329).

2   Heidegger clearly explicates the complex nature of this relation as a questioning of the structures of identity and difference in his 'conversation' with Hegel in *Identity and Difference*.

However, before beginning my exploration of these various relations, I want to first of all mark out the context and horizon of the 'Post' in a little more detail. This, I've suggested, is constituted by that Heideggerian notion of interpretation which projects itself as an overcoming of metaphysics, albeit an overcoming which is a radicalising repetition. Thus Heidegger, on the one hand, projects an end to philosophy – seen as metaphysics – and develops a thinking that 'resolutely persists in discussing the old fundamental questions in a more questioning manner' (1990a: 253). He works to develop a meditative and perhaps ethical thinking of releasement and letting-be (*Gelassenheit*)[3] that would be other than and in excess of the transcendental enframing constitutive of metaphysics. It is a thinking that is to move 'away from what has been thought so far in philosophy' (1969: 50). On the other hand, Heidegger states categorically that this projected end of metaphysics cannot result in the absolute abandonment of metaphysics. It is rather a matter of repetition, of a hermeneutic spiralling that comes back into, incorporating, the given, the beginning, the origin, indeed metaphysics, 'in the right way' (1995a: 195).[4] As such, Heidegger's projected thinking otherwise than metaphysically is itself a response to metaphysics. It is a countermovement to and questioning of metaphysics that can only remain rooted in metaphysics.

---

3   Caputo discusses Heidegger's notion of *Gelassenheit* as the possible basis for an 'ethics of dissemination, a veritable postmodern ethics' in his *Against Ethics* (1993a: 1). Such an ethics would be fundamentally and functionally irreducible to any so-called 'originary ethics', indeed being instantiated through a suspicion of all such 'fine names like Ethics and Metaphysics' (2, 6). I will be focusing on this possibility later.

4   This notion of any single proper or 'right way' is of course necessarily problematic. Whilst this notion is certainly discernible in Heidegger's thought, I argue, along with Caputo (e.g. 1993a: 227–228), for the retrieving of another Heidegger, for a thinking that constitutively cannot present itself as absolutely pure or originary or right. I suggest that it is perhaps Heidegger's proposed methodology – as also turned on his own thinking – that perhaps illustrates the 'right way'. Later I will argue that this is the way retraced by Derrida.

Hence, Heideggerian interpretation is both the condition for and horizon of non- or post-metaphysical thinking – as, indeed, is metaphysics itself. Non- or post-metaphysical thinking as such must function within this horizon whilst also exceeding it. It exemplifies that relation which is configured and interpreted as a difference that must ideally not rigidify, that must not allow takeovers, which must remain open yet effective. Thus the 'Post' is itself caught, situated, within the double bind and double writing of a ceaseless interpretation. As Lacoue-Labarthe reminds us with regards to this configuration and condition of philosophy:

> Philosophy is finished/finite (*La philosophie est finie*); its limit is uncrossable. This means we can no longer – and we can only – do philosophy, possessing as we do no other language and having not the slightest notion of what 'thinking' might mean outside of 'philosophizing'. This pure contradiction defines an impossible situation; and in actual fact the limit is, here, as far as philosophy is concerned, that of its possibility. (Lacoue-Labarthe, 1990: 4).

What this suggests, then, is that to project an outside to metaphysics – marking out or sensing the outer edge of philosophy – is simultaneously the very im/possibility of a non- or post-metaphysics, its condition and its overwhelming desire. It is the Heideggerian imperative demanding repetition, the question of interpretation as both excess and obligation – a question, that is, of difference.

Now, what this means is that the possibility of the 'Post' requires this rethinking of the concept of relation, this opening of it to that which it cannot contain – for instance, irreducible alterity and irreducible excess, infinity or indefinacy. So reconfigured, this concept of relation becomes, as it were, unthinkable.[5] Furthermore, any such

---

5   In his delineation of the 'Post' Levinas suggests that this reconfigured relation between the one and the other – a relation he describes as ethics, the-one-for-the-other – is prior to consciousness (and concepts). Necessarily non-thematisable, such a relation not only cannot, as such, be thought, but nevertheless acts as the condition for those relations which can and must – that is, those constitutive of justice.

thinking through of this relation is incredulous towards any expectations of symmetry or unity or totality or, indeed, of any projected universalising, meta-narratival legitimation or law.[6] As Lyotard tells us

> The law should always be respected with humor [sic] because it cannot be completely respected, except at the price of giving credence to the idea that it is the very mode of linking heterogeneities together, that it has the necessity of total Being. This humor aims at the heterogeneity which persists beneath and despite legitimation. (Lyotard, 1995: 144).[7]

Projections of the 'Post', then, are concerned with incredulity and with seeing the concept of relation in terms of difference. They are concerned with thinking difference *as* difference, with affirming the possibility of a thinking *as* a sustaining of difference rather than as the legitimating of identity or sameness or homogeneity. Under this formulation, the possibility of non- or post-metaphysics is the very possibility and structure of heterogeneity. It marks the heterogenesis, to borrow from Deleuze and Guattari, of potentialities that must remain non-unifiable and non-totalisable.

Concerned with escaping and disrupting metaphysical difference – its effecting of hegemonic structurings and takeovers – non- or post-metaphysical projects stress a rethinking of the relation of difference. Specifically, they repeat the complex model of difference as relation that is developed via Heidegger's notion of interpretation. Indeed it is through his reconfiguring of the relation and middleness of difference that the 'Post' aims to get beyond the rigidity of difference,

---

6   As Derrida notes, the law (or any system) is always deconstructible. He also contrasts this notion of law as system with a 'justice' that he maintains is non-deconstructible, even exemplary of deconstruction itself (1992a: 14–15).
7   Caputo tells us in his *Against Ethics* that any such thinking of heterogeneity is necessarily impious. Of course though such sustaining of questioning and difference for Heidegger stands for the 'piety of thought' (Heidegger, 1993: 341).

to break out of the all-consuming carrying on of essence.[8] Consequently, non- or post-metaphysical configurations *are* the instantiations of this rethought difference, instantiations which see difference firstly as that relation open to a certain irrepressible excess and otherness, and secondly as being itself both irrecusable and irremissible. Overall, then, it is this doubled thinking of difference, the opening *of* difference, which *is* non- or post-metaphysical – constituting both the methodology and essence of the 'Post'.

Non- or post-metaphysical thinking is thus guided by these moves. Difference, opened and rethought, is the condition for both that excess and obligation which are irreducible to the delimitative economies of metaphysical thinking. Hence, it is with tracing these various relations both in terms of their delineation *as* the possibility of the 'Post', and their instantiation *as* the situatedness of this 'Post' within Heideggerian interpretation and, further, metaphysics, that my subsequent discussion is concerned. Specifically, my aim here is to consider non- or post-metaphysical configurations as interpretations and repetitions – and perhaps misreadings – of the Heideggerian imperative to think difference (and hence metaphysics) otherwise. It is through explicating these responses to the Heideggerian imperative of thinking *at* and *of* the end of philosophy and of renewing thinking, that I am able to start my critique of such projections of the 'Post'.

I should, however, stress that in the hope of once again avoiding any too fast reductions of the differences between the various projections of a non- or post-metaphysics, I will focus my discussion on certain aspects of these delineations of the 'Post' – that is, on the rethinking of difference in terms of excess and/or obligation. These considerations will be the concern of this and the next chapter. Specifically, I will use the remainder of this chapter to consider the 'Post' as its im/possible relation with excess, and its writing of difference in terms of this excess. In the following chapter, I will focus on describ-

---

8   Levinas, for instance, formulates this desired (and ethical) breaking with
     Western thought – the conjunction, he argues, of essence and interest (1991:
     4) – as non-indifference and dis-interestedness: dis-inter-esse.

ing the 'Post' as a thinking of excessive obligation, whereby the functioning of difference is itself to be righted so as to ask and sustain questions of heterogeneity, justice, obligation and ethics. It must however be stressed again that each of these two focuses cannot be absolutely distinguished from the other. Rather excess and obligation themselves comprise an unrepresentable and excessive relation, each interpreting the other. Hence the final chapter of this section will be concerned with situating both of these configurations of difference in terms of their repetition (and perhaps misreading) of Heideggerian interpretation.

Thinking to Excess

Now, when considering a non- or post-metaphysical thinking of excess, two formulations come immediately to mind – Derridean deconstruction and the Deleuzoguattarian thinking of *délire* and *schizoanalysis*. Both of these formulations work to produce a style of thinking that breaks down, solicits, and escapes the metaphysical structure of difference. They are each seen as interested in the excess and indeterminacy of the middle and the in-between, with the overflowing of given and assumed limits and constraints:

> The middle is by no means an average; on the contrary, it is where things pick up speed. *Between* things does not designate a localizable relation going from one thing to the other and back again, but a perpendicular direction, a transversal movement that sweeps one *and* the other away, a stream without beginning or end that undermines its banks and picks up speed in the middle. (Deleuze & Guattari, 1987a: 25).

As, for instance, this affirmation of transversal movement, such thinking effects the reconfiguration of the differential structure exemplary of metaphysics. Difference is no longer the structured rigidity of dialectical or oppositional thinking, reduced to synthesis or the either/or of a binary opposition. Rather difference is broken open and made undecidable – or at least not quite decidable. It is to mark that uncontrolled proliferation or dissemination which not only makes possible multiplicity, plurality and heterogeneity, but also exemplifies that open relation with an otherness that remains necessarily unrepresentable in terms of given and legitimated difference. Throughout this chapter, then, my aim is to unfold some of these non- or post-metaphysical reconfigurations of difference *as* irreducible excess. In particular I will discuss here the projects of Deleuze (and Guattari), Levinas, Lyotard, and certain aspects of Derrida's work in some detail, touching also on Rorty's work. Finally I will contrast these non- or post-metaphysical structurings of excess, with Heidegger's own discussion of the sustained dif-fering of difference.

The Rhizomatic Difference of Deleuze and Guattari

The first rethinking of difference that opens and sustains an irreducible excess to be considered here is that instantiated as Deleuzoguattarian or Deleuzean – or as having been produced by a 'Deleuze effect'.[9] As noted in the previous chapter, Deleuze (and Guattari) propose a style of thinking which is to *function* otherwise than does metaphysical formulation. Delineating this latter as rigid, delimitative,

---

9   Deleuze focuses throughout his work on producing and depicting non-personal and non-subjective modes of individuation. For instance, in *Negotiations* he discusses proper names as effects, as belonging 'primarily to forces, events, motions and sources of movement, winds, typhoons, diseases, places and moments, rather than people' (Deleuze, 1995: 34). He stresses, for instance, that 'Félix and I, and many others like us, don't feel we're persons exactly', we are 'rather like two streams' (1995: 141). The 'Deleuze effect' is discussed by Ronald Bogue in his paper 'Deleuze's style'.

appropriative, and even fascist, Deleuze (and Guattari) project a counter-thinking which is to function instead as an open, non-teleologically and non-transcendentally organised constructivism. Constituting a non-unifying synthesising, this thinking is 'fully affirmative, nonrestrictive, inclusive'. Further, it marks a 'disjunction that remains disjunctive, and that still affirms the disjoined terms, that affirms them throughout their entire distance, *without restricting one by the other or excluding the other from the one*' (Deleuze & Guattari, 1984: 76). This mode of synthesising, in other words, both functions and legitimates itself as absolute affirmation, refraining also from overcoding or legitimating itself via any appeal to transcendence. Rather it merely functions, unfolding as that immanence that 'leaves nothing remaining to which it could be immanent'.[10] Constitutively non-delimitative, this thinking thus unfolds *as* an inventing and following of lines of escape and flight that break out of those structures and territories of identity and unity exemplary of delimitative thinking. It is a thinking that not only opens and affirms what remains in excess, but which must also itself always and already be in excess of its own delineation.[11]

Now, as Deleuze (and Guattari) see it, such thinking generates open terms or systems that affirm a certain idea of pluralism and multiplicity. It is the thinking of a non-onto-teleo-logical heterogenesis, where open systems exemplify multiplicities such as 'nomadic distributions', 'assemblages', and 'rhizomes'.[12] These, then, are character-

---

10   Deleuze and Guattari, *What is Philosophy?* (1994: 45). Overall, the Deleuzoguattarian style of synthesis as absolute affirmation cannot be situated under the aegis of any Hegelian-style transcendental or onto-teleological dialectic.

11   Deleuze elaborates this image of thought as a sort of 'leaking egg' (see Deleuze, 1995: 14). Ronald Bogue in particular draws on this expression of a 'leaking egg' in his discussion of Deleuze's style (see Bogue, 1996: 254–256).

12   Deleuze discusses 'nomadic distributions' in *The Logic of Sense* (1990: 60). Deleuze and Guattari discuss 'assemblages' and 'rhizomes' throughout *A Thousand Plateaus*.

ised by their lack (or overflow) of that overcodedness or individuation necessary for delimitative thinking ordered in terms of essence. That is, these open systems situate happenings not in terms of any postulated essences, but as states of things which are themselves 'neither unities nor totalities, but *multiplicities*':

> The essential thing [...] is the noun *multiplicity*, which designates a set of lines or dimensions which are irreducible to one another. [...] In a multiplicity what counts are not the terms or the elements, but what there is 'between', the between, a set of relations which are not separable from each other. (Deleuze & Parnet, 1987b: vii–viii).

Characterised neither by nor through any ontological *isness*, this notion of multiplicity *is* the uncontrollable stammering and flight of the *and*.[13] As open systems, multiplicities depend upon the liberation and affirmation of the *and*, of its happening as that relation which remains exterior to and independent of that which it connects. Indeed it is this liberation of the *and* that enables the Deleuzean elaboration of multiplicities as non-evolutionary and non-developmental becomings or lines of flight. As becomings, such multiplicities thus have no 'supplementary dimension' or transcendent principle that would direct or organise them.[14]

These open and nomadic distributions consequently illustrate a certain overcoming of metaphysical essentialism and delimitation. Exemplifying the unconstrained exteriority of the happening of relation, this thinking *is* the escaping and exceeding of any appeal to transcendence, of any interiorising by or subordination to the One or Law, and, consequently, *is as* a rhizomatic and creative expansion. Such thinking is thus a matter not of explanation or interpretation, but rather of experimentation and production. Indeed, it can be seen as a form of

---

13   For discussion of the substitution of the 'and' for the 'is', see *Dialogues* (Deleuze & Parnet, 1987b: 57) and *Negotiations* (Deleuze, 1995: 44).

14   See Deleuze, *Spinoza: Practical Philosophy* (1988: 128) and Deleuze and Parnet, *Dialogues* (1987b: 91–92).

empiricism.[15] Overall, then, the question guiding this thinking is not one of attaining or explaining being but of sustaining becoming – of keeping things open, of unravelling the question of being into multiple-becomings and becoming-multiple, into transversal movement and the happening of heterogenesis.

In producing itself through the functioning of that middle which is neither a unifying nor an organising relation, nor even an indication of definite distinction,[16] the Deleuzean opening of difference demonstrates the impossibility of difference functioning as a metaphysical structure for identification and legitimation. Not only does Deleuzean thinking effect the disruption of and escape from rigidified difference, but it refrains from any ontological or transcendental overcoding of this (its) happening. Difference, so reconfigured, does not come into sameness. Rather it is sustained as and through its open and excessive becoming. Hence it is via its affirmation of this functioning, that the focus of Deleuzoguattarian (or Deleuzean) thinking can be seen as absolutely other than that common to metaphysics or transcendental philosophy. *As* absolute affirmation, and thereby functionally neither delimitative nor critical, Deleuzoguattarianism marks an escape from that overcodedness which has been delineated as constitutive of metaphysics and transcendental philosophy.

Finally, it is the instantiation of this constructivism through such an opening of difference that can be seen as a repetition of the Heideggerian relation. However, whilst certainly sponsored by certain of Heidegger's emphases and strategies, this construction is imbued with the desire for an absolute escape – a desire that Heidegger of

---

15   Deleuze has himself explicitly described his (and Guattari's) thinking as an empiricism in a number of places. See, for instance, Deleuze and Parnet, *Dialogues* (1987b: vii) and Deleuze and Guattari, *What is Philosophy?* (1994: 47). Also see Patrick Hayden's 'From relations to practice in the empiricism of Gilles Deleuze', for a discussion of Deleuze's 'empiricist critique of essentialism' (1995: 301n16).

16   As Deleuze and Guattari stress, there is 'neither beginning nor end, but always a middle (*milieu*) from which it grows and which it overspills' (Deleuze & Guattari, 1987a: 21).

course considers to be impossible. That is, Deleuzoguattarianism aspires to become absolutely other or exterior, to cut itself loose from its grounds, escape its horizon, and just become without be-ing. Driven by this wish to absolutely surpass its (and any) limits, it paradoxically and consequently constitutes itself as a wish for one absolute limit or difference which would separate it from its other, the latter which *must be as if* totalised.[17] Excess, then, when constructed through the Deleuze effect, and unlike the relation opened by Heidegger, runs only one way – into becoming and exteriority. On the one hand Deleuze demands that there be 'no general prescription' and that we should 'have done with all globalizing concepts' (Deleuze & Parnet, 1987b: 144) whilst, on the other hand, this thinking is itself a prescription and exhortation for more speed, more movement, and for, indeed, more of this very style of thinking which invents rather than invests. In other words, the affirmation of excess in terms of rhizomatic growth and pure immanence is prescriptive of itself. It overcodes itself with its wish for one absolute and non-deconstructible difference.

Levinas: Difference as Ethics

A second opening of difference into irreducible excess functions as the basis of Levinas's work. Concerned with the distinction between those functions exemplary of totality as opposed to infinity, Levinas works to affirm the irreducible excess of the latter. He thus focuses on the breaking open of totality, the disruption of the reversibility of totalisable relations – their becoming-sameness – so as to account for that excess which he sees as configuring the absolute 'alterity, the radical heterogeneity of the other' (Levinas, 1996b: 36). The relation of alterity, Levinas argues – the excessive, irreversible and non-symmetrical relation binding the I to the Other (*Autrui*) – exemplifies

---

17   The ramifications of this wish will be explored in the following chapter.

the infinite. In this relation, the conjunction of the I with the Other indicates neither addition nor delimitation, but rather a certain separation and distance. Their conjunction, he tells us, is their traversing (and maintaining) of this distance. It is a relation that escapes any 're-constitution of totality' (1996b: 40), any delimitative grounding. Rather it can only be seen as a witnessing of the infinite, of the idea of infinity.

Now it is this relation that I suggest exemplifies a certain repetition of the Heideggerian relation of dif-ference, where '[b]elonging-together is precisely what remains genuinely opaque and questionable' (Heidegger, 1991c: 105). That is, although Levinas specifically situates his project (an 'other' phenomenology) as a *counter* thinking to Heideggerian ontology,[18] he nonetheless assumes and repeats certain of the possibilities opened by Heidegger. Indeed I believe that Levinasian 'conversation' repeats (although not exactly) Heideggerian interpretation.[19] For instance, conversation (elsewhere communication or saying) is, on the one hand, both conditioned by and the condition of openness and uncertainty. Further, it is exemplary of the non-totalisation of the face to face, the non-dialectical and non-

---

18   See, for instance, Levinas's *Totality and Infinity* (1996b: 45–46, 67–68). Levinas here delineates Heideggerian ontology as a philosophy of power and injustice effecting a 'reduction of the other to the same' to indeed '*being in general*' (1996b: 46, 67). Specifically he contrasts the ethical relation of the face to face with what he considers to be Heidegger's reductive inter-subjectivity.

19   Both conversation and interpretation, for instance, *as* exemplifying an open relatedness, unfold through and as the functioning of language. For Levinas, language as conversation 'accomplishes a relation such that the terms are not limitrophe within this relation, such that the other, despite the relationship with the same, remains transcendent to the same' (Levinas, 1996b: 39). Similarly for Heidegger, language as its Saying (for instance, as interpretation) is the active carrying into nearness of that it holds in, but as irreducible to, this relation (Heidegger, 1971a: 107). Heidegger further stresses that language *as* the dimension wherein such relatedness unfolds, remains other than and irreducible to either side of that in relation (Heidegger, 1971a: 107; cf. 1971b: 190–191; 1969: 38).

oppositional relation of proximity. On the other hand, it exemplifies, paradoxically, an *un*conditional relation where this proximity marks the passivity of, in Levinas's words, an 'obligation, anachronously prior to any commitment [... and ...] "older" than the a priori' (1991: 101). To quote from Levinas again, conversation illustrates that 're-sponsibility for another, an unlimited responsibility which the strict book-keeping of the free and non-free does not measure' (1991: 124). It is further a responsibility where one's subjectivity itself figures as hostage. Conversation thus escapes the delimitation exemplary of the 'ontological event' or 'adventure of being' (1991: 99). Levinas, as such, structures conversation – as the saying, the witnessing 'here I am' – as going only one way, indicative of neither conjuncture nor synchrony, but rather of transcendence. Non-reciprocative, conversa-tion happens *as* substitution, *as* one-for-the-other, and as an infinite and irrecusable responsibility.[20]

In other words, in being traversed *as* a transcendence *through* conversation and substitution, this relation remains necessarily and absolutely outside of the formally reductive orders of identity and knowledge. Rather it discloses and sustains that which remains in ex-cess of such orders: an absolute and radical alterity. Levinas aims to disclose, then, un-neutralised and unsystematised, that which *is abso-lutely other* than and in excess of the same. Consequently, it is the possibility of this excessive and irreducible relation to alterity that ex-emplifies for Levinas an escape from ontological structuration and

---

20   Levinas does of course interrupt this one-way relation with his introduction
      and consideration of the third party, through which he grounds the possibili-
      ties of community and justice (Levinas, 1991: 150, 157–161). This interrup-
      tion, although it makes the face to face problematic, does not however dis-
      turb its fundamental structure. Substitution, the one-for-the-other, remains
      prior (and fundamental) to any possibility of justice (1991: 160). This inter-
      ruption, as 'an incessant correction of the assymetry [sic] of proximity'
      (1991: 158), does however have the effect of perhaps suggesting a certain
      correspondence between Levinas here and Derrida's glosses on the Kierke-
      gaardian moment of decision (that is, the moment of judgement) as constitu-
      tively and necessarily unjustified (see, for instance, Derrida, 1992a; 1995d).

delimitation – that is, metaphysics.[21] Indeed he emphasises the excessive and non-ontological nature of his thinking of this relation, unfolding it in terms of transcendence and infinity, and delineating this transcendence as the 'passing over to being's *other*, otherwise than being. Not *to be otherwise*, but *otherwise than being*' (1991: 3).

Hence Levinas does not so much reinterpret the functioning of difference so as to allow and account for an excess, but rather reconfigures excess *as* the instantiation of infinity and the exteriority of the absolutely other. Difference is the sustaining of this excess in relation – it is transascendence and inequality, and the revelation of the 'infinite in the finite, the more in the less' (1996b: 50). Consequently Levinas's projected relation *as* revelation does not quite equate to my explication of Heideggerian interpretation as the functioning of difference. That is, Levinas attempts to show the absolute but proximate exteriority of the Other, opening difference as the rigid and one-way non-symmetry of transcendence, sustaining what must remain an impossible delineation of the exteriority and alterity of the Other. As such, the irreducibility of the ethical relation and its saying exemplifies a thinking which aspires to be *absolutely otherwise* than, in excess of and unconditioned by, ontological structuring. Indeed it exemplifies what Levinas sees as 'first philosophy'.

---

21   Although Levinas in *Totality and Infinity* projects his ethics *as* a metaphysics, in setting it as a counter-thinking to ontological philosophy, he constructs the same sort of distinction Heidegger sees between, say, meditative and calculative thinking, or open letting-be as opposed to metaphysical enframing. Further, in later work, admitting that *Totality and Infinity* is still too ontological, Levinas resorts to affirming the saying of an 'ethical language' (1991: 120), which he contrasts with the said of philosophy. Lastly, I agree with Caputo that Levinas is not configuring the 'Post' in the sense that Derrida (or Lyotard) does. However, although Caputo describes Levinas's project as a 'Neoplatonic or "hypermetaphysical" radicalizing of metaphysics' (Caputo, 1993a: 252n51), I prefer to view it as an attempted non-metaphysics, a point which will be argued in the following chapters.

Lyotard: Difference as Justice

Another thinking of excess that assumes the reconfiguration of difference can be discovered within Lyotard's work. Wanting to escape the limitations of oppositional difference, Lyotard focuses on reconfiguring difference, opening it out in order to encompass that which remains unrepresentable and unsubsumable by metaphysics and homogeneity. Now, with regards to this unrepresentable excess, Lyotard basically describes it as that irruptive happening whereby libidinal intensity or, elsewhere, the eventality of linkage, overflow that notion of difference that structures totalised and totalising identity.[22] In other words, Lyotard works to open thinking to the unconstrained exces-

---

22   This notion of the irruptive happening of the libidinal and its effects on
     delimited conceptualising can also be seen as determining Lyotard's gloss
     on (Kant's gloss on) 'enthusiasm' in *The Differend*. For example, Lyotard
     delineates Kantian 'enthusiasm' as 'blind', a '*dementia*', a 'pathological'
     outburst, a 'kind of agitation in place [...]' within the impasse of incom-
     mensurability' (Lyotard, 1995: 166, 167). Intensity, the libidinal force, in
     comparison, is described as 'panic' (1993: 12), as the indissociability of
     jouissance and pain (24), 'disorder' (30) and 'dissimulation' (52), having
     'effects but not causes' (258), and as 'cancerous' (262). Further, as intensity
     works to solicit metaphysics and difference, Lyotard projects Kantian 'en-
     thusiasm' as effecting a solicitation of the 'Idea of reason' (1995: 165), of
     rationality. Consequently, both exemplify an 'unpresentable' which remains
     undelimited and which Lyotard comes to describe as characteristic of a
     'sublime' (1995; 1985) – that which remains irreducible to processes of ap-
     propriation and differentiation, and which further constitutes a determining
     factor characteristic of Lyotard's own thinking. Lucy, for instance, argues
     that Lyotard, and postmodernism as a whole, depends on and requires a no-
     tion of the 'unpresentable' which is 'supposed to lie outside metaphysics'
     (Lucy, 1997: 120), a possibility which he further argues is, at the least,
     problematised by Derrida's elaboration of 'undecidability'. Lyotard's gloss
     on the Kantian notion of 'enthusiasm' is also considered, from a Kantian
     perspective, by Antonio Calcagno in his 'Interface: modernity and post-
     modernity: the possibility of enthusiasm according to Immanuel Kant and
     Jean-François Lyotard'.

siveness of intensity and linkage. Set out in this way, it is this possibility of accounting for excess and the unpresentable that comes to exemplify for Lyotard the whole question of justice and legitimation.[23] For example, Lyotard depicts injustice as the domination of the structure of absolute difference, a domination that he sees as imposed by homogeneity. As he puts it, the self-legitimated and complacent consensus of homogeneity 'does violence' to the possibility of heterogeneity.[24] Far from delineating the conditions for homogeneity, identity or totality – that is, injustice – Lyotard suggests that difference should rather function as the condition for justice. The matter of justice is, as such, a matter of heterogeneity, a matter that Lyotard has once described as the synchronous 'multiplicity of justices' and 'justice of multiplicity' (1994: 100). Hence, in proposing a thinking which is to *be* justice,[25] Lyotard projects a thinking of the 'Post' which strives to open the appropriative rigidity of metaphysical conceptualising into a thinking concerned to witness and affirm irreducible excess, otherness, and the unpresentable.

It is thus through his disclosure of the libidinal intensities and linkages which he considers engender heterogeneous multiplicity, that

---

23   This movement is exemplified by Lyotard's partial shift in focus from *Libidinal Economy* to *The Differend*. Indeed, he states in an interview, emphasising both their linkage and differences, that *The Differend* 'is an attempt to try and say the same things [... as *Libidinal Economy* ...] without unloading problems so important as justice' (Lyotard, 1988: 300–301).

24   The full passage here reads: 'Is legitimation to be found in consensus obtained through discussion, as Jürgen Habermas thinks? Such consensus does violence to the heterogeneity of language games. Any invention is always born of dissension. Postmodern knowledge is not simply a tool of the authorities; it refines our sensitivity to differences and reinforces our ability to tolerate the incommensurable. Its principle is not the expert's homology, but the inventor's paralogy' (1984b: xxv).

25   Derrida, as already noted, formulates justice as (the matter of) deconstruction. Caputo, running Derridean and Lyotardian deconstructive configurations of justice together to constitute what he calls a 'jewgreek' thinking of obligation in his *Against Ethics*, stresses their similarities. See Caputo's *Against Ethics* (1993a: 258*n*61) for an explication of 'jewgreek'.

Lyotard reconfigures the notion of difference, enabling it to slide non-dialectically between intensity and identity. However, this projected collapse or escape of structured difference is, Lyotard stresses, not to be considered as exemplifying a subsequent appropriation of thinking into another totalised structure of homogeneous identity. Such a shift – far from escaping the fixation of difference – would merely resituate it again as an absolute boundary, refixing its disjunction.[26] Instead Lyotard projects a thinking where difference can no longer be situated as such, where it remains indiscernible, happening as multiplicitous and disseminative. Difference is thus not so much sustained but de/dif-fused into the happenings of intensity and linkage, happenings that have 'neither programme nor project' (1993: 262). Consequently, difference (and hence thinking) becomes – and is perhaps escaped by its so becoming – this happening of intensity, which itself is an unsituatable happening of uncontrollable linkage: 'it would be one, another, and another' (1993: 261).

Productive, then, of this thinking as a de/dif-fusing of difference, linkage happens without any regulation or legitimation.[27] It is an

26 As Lyotard notes, 'it is in no way a matter of determining a new domain, another field, a *beyond representation*' (1993: 50). Indeed, to positively 'determine' a new domain would itself be an exemplary metaphysical move. Instead Lyotard projects this notion of a beyond representation as necessarily unpresentable – as a Kantian idea which possesses an '"as-if" rather than an actual existence' (Carroll, 1987: 174). Consequently, it becomes a matter of staying in the same place, but thinking it otherwise. Lyotard can be seen as such as a Kantian, something he indeed explicitly admits to on occasion. For example, among other borrowings, he traces within his own work Kant's distinction (in his Third Critique) between 'determinant' and 'reflective' reasoning/judgement (Kant, 1952: 18), privileging the latter in his own attempt to think otherwise than metaphysics – to escape what David Carroll terms 'metatheory' (Carroll, 1987: 183).

27 Lyotard does, in *The Differend,* somewhat qualify this depiction of linkage as uncontrolled. That is to say, although emphasising that linkage is a happening of excess and unregulated multiplicity, Lyotard does elaborate the (never absolute) constraints placed upon linkage by the interests (in regards to desired ends) of discrete language games or 'genres of discourse': 'A genre of discourse exerts a seduction upon a phrase universe [i.e. an event].

open and non-totalisable operation, exemplary of that unpresentable and irreducible supplementarity inherent in the Kantian 'as if', and revealing thereby an equivocalness. That is, it happens without a mandate, unauthorised except by its own happening, and is, in fact, depicted by Lyotard as the site of what he calls the 'differend'. Exemplary of those sites of incommensurable excess which overflow and rupture that which is given, destabilising both the boundaries of difference and the happening of linkage, the differend thus marks the soliciting of structures of totality, and the exposure of them to other hitherto unconsidered, unregulated and suppressed possibilities. Lyotard, in other words, depicts the differend as the intensified investment of im/possibility. It is that which remains (as yet) unactualised through – and thus necessarily incommensurable with – the given. The differend exemplifies that inevitable point of fracture within totalised structures where the possibilities for linkage are in excess of those actualisable within these structures. As Lyotard states, the differend is that 'unstable state and instant' (1995:13) indicative of excess and incommensurability, wherein something is recognised as requiring presentation which is unable to be presented within or through the given.

Hence, the differend signals the potential activation of an agonistics of im/possibility and presentation, instantiating a demand for both the sustaining of that in excess, and the investment or presentation of this excess through new unplanned happenings and linkages. In other words, the im/possibility invested within and as the differend – its called for happening – is situated within and as questions of linkage, incommensurability, and the unpresentable. In other words, the differend marks that undelimitable possibility which exemplifies that which remains at stake (and in conflict) within linkage – that is, the excess. Indeed linkage (and hence structure), Lyotard argues, 'cannot help but be the occasion for differends' (Lyotard, 1995: 140–141).

It inclines the instances presented by this phrase toward certain linkings, or at least it steers them away from other linkings which are not suitable with regard to the end pursued by this genre' (Lyotard, 1995: 84). Additionally, linkage is mediated to a certain extent by the effects of differends – the situated instantiations of intensity and unactualised possibility.

There is, as seen, no a priori or universally legitimated happening of linkage. Rather it is only regulated and held in question by the inevitable and ineradicable "'residue" of differends' (1995: 142), that unpresentable residue of excessive possibility.

In reconfiguring difference in terms of this excess, then, Lyotard develops what he has called a libidinal economy in his book of the same name. No longer seen as the fixed or structuring binary dreams of the metaphysical system, difference rather constitutes an instantiation of excess. It is held open to the potentialities of heterogeneity. So delineated, difference enables a thinking which is also open, constitutively always already opened by the differend, by that which *is* neither one side nor the other but rather an instantiation of the impossibility and incommensurability of excess. It is this affirmation of excess and incommensurability – of that which remains unpresentable within the given whilst demanding of its possible presentations – that Lyotard projects *as* a thinking which is constitutively other than metaphysics, a thinking of the 'Post'.[28]

Hence Lyotard's reconfiguration of difference *as* engendering both an irreducible excess and the 'just' thinking of multiplicity and plurality in terms of sustained heterogeneity, exemplifies another configuration of the 'Post'. In other words, Lyotard's sustaining of excess as both irreducible and incommensurable, *is* his countering of and escaping from metaphysics. Further, it is a thinking which he explicates as the possibility for justice, as will be elaborated in the following chapter. However, despite being projected as incommensurable with – although not (quite) situated as oppositional to – the metaphysical thinking of difference, Lyotard's thinking of excess in terms of a just

---

28   Niall Lucy explicates (and criticises) postmodernism's – including Lyotard's – concern with attempting to break "'free" from binary or oppositional thought' (Lucy, 1997: 148), as an attempt to project and reach the absolute other or absolute beyond of metaphysics, an attempt which, by its very nature, falls back into a metaphysical structuring of difference. As Lucy notes, Lyotard's postmodernism cannot be said to cause 'any great trouble to metaphysics' (102). These aspirations and relations will be discussed in more detail below.

and non-delimiting heterogeneity effects, paradoxically, a certain de-limitation of difference and structure. A move of a kind he has explic-itly depicted as constitutively metaphysical and unjust. So difference, whilst sustained by the differend, is also de/dif-fused by it, and Lyo-tard's reconfiguration of difference as his thinking of – and indeed his prescription for – irreducible excess, levels itself out, collapsing into a sort of 'mono-difference' (Lucy, 1997: 95).

The Derridean Deconstruction of Difference

Another formulation associated with the affirmation of excess is that of course associated with Derridean deconstruction. As noted in the previous chapter, however, *as* the tracing through of undecidability, Derridean deconstruction does not instantiate the 'Post' in quite the same way as do Deleuze (and Guattari), Levinas and Lyotard. That is, as aspiring to abandon or overcome the philosophical tradition or in-stitution in some way.[29] Nonetheless certain aspects of deconstruction can be seen as constitutive of an attempt to configure the 'Post'.[30] Specifically, as with the Deleuzoguattarian model, Derridean decon-struction sustains an excess through the use of con-stitutively open

---

29   Indeed Derrida stresses, for instance throughout 'The Villanova roundtable: a conversation with Jacques Derrida', that he loves and respects institutions and the tradition or canon (Derrida, 1997b: 8, 9–11). For example: 'I feel that, however old I am, I am on the threshold of reading Plato and Aristotle. I love them and I feel I have to start again and again and again. It is a task which is in front of me, before me' (9).
30   The complex relations existing between Derridean deconstruction and other configurations of the 'Post' – relations which also need to be considered with reference to both metaphysics and the Heideggerian project – consti-tute the focus of this book from Chapter 4 onwards.

terms or systems lacking any formalised identity in themselves.[31] However, unlike Deleuzoguattarian assemblages or rhizomes, Derrida's terms are not so much themselves exemplary of another style of thinking, but depict the instability *of* that metaphysical delimitative thinking which Deleuzoguattarian thinking tries rather to surpass. As Derrida repeatedly stresses, deconstruction does not constitute a 'philosophical system' (Derrida, 1995c: 356), counter or otherwise. Instead it merely calls the given into question, a possibility which is itself both like and unlike the functioning of the Lyotardian differend. As will be discussed later in some detail, it is through these distinctions that Derridean deconstruction demonstrates a different relation to metaphysics (and indeed to Heideggerian interpretation) than do other non- or post-metaphysical projects.

However despite these initial qualifications – qualifications that will constitute my focus later – Derridean deconstruction can still be discussed as a contextualising of excess. That is, it both provides and delineates the conditions for excess, for that which remains – as traces, cinders etc. – 'without assurance or certainty' (1995c: 360). Hence Derrida's open and empty terms, as non-originary and groundless, function as disseminative sites, marking both multiplicity and what he calls spectrality. They are, in other words, sites of disjuncture which work to disrupt the given, soliciting it in inhabiting it, infusing it with undecidability. Furthermore, these sites are exemplary of the contingency of structuration, indicating its undecidability and excessiveness. In other words, these sites effect the deconstruction of (metaphysical) totality and difference, illustrating a contamination or relation through which nothing – neither identity nor difference – remains quite clear or beyond question. In depicting and instantiating this indefinacy, these sites remain irreducible to one or other side of difference. They are not legitimated by or as difference. Rather, they

---

31   Commentators have described these open systems in a number of ways. Rodolphe Gasché, for instance, has described them as 'infrastructures' (Gasché, 1986; 1995).

are and ask the questions of difference and identity, of the conditions for difference and identity, and, further, relation.

Now, at this stage, rather than attempting to delineate (or conflate) Derrida's terms as quasi-substitutable infrastructures of excess – a focus which would work to delimit those terms – I will merely indicate some points where deconstruction reveals (and indeed instantiates) an irruption of excess and the undelimitable.[32] These points, then, are illustrative of Derrida's suspension or disabling of (metaphysical) delimitation and structural totalities, and of binary or oppositional differentiation.[33] Inhabiting yet other than that which they solicit, such points disclose the irrecusable indeterminacy of their contexts:

> [N]o context is absolutely saturable or saturating. No context can determine meaning to the point of exhaustiveness. Therefore the context neither produces nor guarantees impassable borders, thresholds that no step could pass [...] (Derrida, 1993a: 9; cf. 1995a: 152–153).

As such, every context – and hence structure and limit – is always and already open to deconstruction, no longer quite able to be fully represented. At the same time, these contexts (as structures and their limits) are not, once opened and, as such, indeterminate, to be absolutely dispensed with. Rather they must remain in question (and in memory). Regarding the context of his own work, Derrida writes:

---

32   Of course these points – singularities – are what deconstruction is all about and all that it is. As Derrida states in an interview, he has 'never had a "fundamental project"' (Derrida, 1995c: 356). His texts, as Caputo also notes, each wrestle 'anew, *de novo*, with the idiosyncrasies of ever shifting singularities' (Caputo, 1997a: 46).

33   For example, Derrida considers the deconstructive imperative of the suspension of the law in his 'Force of Law' (1992a: 23). Furthermore, in his *Against Ethics*, Caputo formulates a 'jewgreek' thinking around this necessary suspension of the law sponsored by both the Derridean and Lyotardian configurations of justice. This notion of a 'jewgreek' thinking will be discussed in detail in the latter part of the book.

I dream of a writing that would be neither philosophy nor literature, nor even contaminated by one or the other, while still keeping – I have no desire to abandon this – the memory of literature and philosophy. (Derrida, 1992c: 73).[34]

Deconstruction, then, is always and already the question of its context, that which it must simultaneously exceed and remember. However, in also asking the question of singularities which exceed and disrupt their contexts, deconstruction instantiates itself *as* these hauntological figures or points of disjuncture, these tropes of undecidability and excess. No longer seen as determined concepts belonging to the orders of knowledge and presence, these sites indicate and account for excess along various associated lines. Excess is instantiated, for instance, as those non-economies of the gift, of cinders, spectrality, the *à venir* of the promise, and as what Derrida terms a messianic structure.[35] As

---

34   Dreams, as mentioned within Derridean deconstruction, seem to function themselves as the site of doubled supplementarity and spectrality. That is, they are illustrative of an impossibility that must nevertheless remain in question and within memory. For instance, in his early discussion of Levinas, Derrida writes: 'the true name of this inclination of thought to the Other [...] is *empiricism*. [...] [This] is the *dream* of a purely *heterological* thought at its source. A *pure* thought of *pure* difference. [...] We say the *dream* because it must vanish *at daybreak*, as soon as language awakens. But perhaps one will object that it is language which is sleeping. [...] This route is quite, perhaps too, abandoned today. Among others, by Levinas' (Derrida, 1978b: 151). 'Dream', in other words, could perhaps be seen as a supplement of the structure of the promise, its im/possibility.

35   As I will show, Derrida also discusses this openness of relation as the messianic structure informing deconstruction as justice and democracy, as 'a certain experience of the emancipatory promise' (Derrida, 1994: 59). It is, he stresses, the structure of the promise, where at stake are 'responsibilities [... which ...] are heterogeneous to the formalizable order of knowledge' (1995c: 359). And, elsewhere, 'Justice and peace will have to do with this coming of the other, with the promise. [...] This universal structure of the promise, of the expectation for the future, for the coming, and the fact that this expectation of the coming has to do with justice – that is what I call the messianic structure' (1997b: 22–23; cf. 1998; 1994; 1992b). This is thus the

74

excessive, open and undecidable, these 'figures of the impossible' (1992b: 167) *are* thus other than, perhaps older than, and irreducible to either any grounds or contexts, or essence or presence – they ~~are~~.[36] And as such they all illustrate that undelimitable and non-economic relation of hauntological difference. For instance, with regards to the excessive structuration of the gift, Derrida asks:

> [I]s not the gift, if there is any, that which interrupts economy? That which, in suspending economic calculation, no longer gives rise to exchange? That which opens the circle so as to defy reciprocity or symmetry, the common measure, and so as to turn aside the return in view of the no-return? If there is gift, the *given* of the gift (*that which* one gives, *that which* is given, the gift as given thing or as act of donation) must not come back to the giving [...] It must not circulate, it must not be exchanged, it must not in any case be exhausted, as a gift, by the process of exchange [...] [T]he gift must remain *aneconomic*. (Derrida, 1992b: 166–167).

In other words, in both its instantiating of excess, and its exceeding but never escaping its metaphysical context, deconstruction *is* that excessive non-economic relation which is structured through this im/possibility of the relation of the gift. It *is* that which goes 'beyond the circle of reappropriation' and 'beyond calculation' (1997b: 18–19).[37] However, although deconstruction remains open to a certain

---

point where deconstruction in its accounting for excess opens into that question of obligation which will be the focus of the following chapter.

36   For example, in his paper 'Différance', Derrida writes regarding this excessive 'infrastructure' that as 'there is nowhere to *begin* to trace the sheaf or the graphics of *différance*' in that 'it has neither existence nor essence [... and ...] derives from no category of being, whether present or absent', then, '*différance* ~~K~~ (and I also cross out the "~~K~~ ")' (Derrida, 1982a: 6).

37   Derrida is not of course saying here that we should therefore stop calculating. Rather that although we must 'calculate as rigorously as possible [...] there is a point or limit beyond which calculation must fail' (Derrida, 1997b: 19). This he describes elsewhere as the necessity of passing decisions and judgements through that moment or ordeal of undecidability wherein the law is (and must be) suspended and reinvented each time (1992a: 23–24).

messianic structure or future, marking the im/possible situation and instantiation of excess, it *is* disclosive of a 'Post' through its disclosure of difference and the deconstruction of its rigidity. However it does not quite open into a non- or post-metaphysics insofar as it acknowledges itself as unable to absolutely escape its context in and memory of metaphysics. Overall, then, producing itself *as* the excessive and non-economic structuring *of* its relation with metaphysics, deconstruction opens difference. It solicits it, rewriting it in its undecidability.[38] Rewriting it, as such, as différance.

Rortian Pragmatism and Difference

One last attempted affirmation of excess I wish to touch on here is that set out by Rorty. Now Rorty projects throughout his work a certain revivified pragmatism that he characterises as an anti-essentialism or the recognition of contingency. Basically, this pragmatism is our accepting of the 'contingent character of starting-points' (Rorty, 1996a: 166). Further, it is the acceptance that all of our meaning making is human in origin, and that our meanings have no guarantees. They can stand only so long as we can comfortably invest in them. Seen in this way, then, the only possible supports or constraints for our meaning making are the checks and balances we meet in our everyday lives and our everyday conversations.[39] Thus it is from this perspective that Rorty argues that '[w]e should let a hundred flowers bloom, admire them while they last, and leave botanizing to the intellectual historians of the next century' (1996a: 219).

---

38   It is on this inevitability of undecidability that Derrida hangs his later arguments concerning deconstruction as the call for justice and democracy. This point will be discussed in detail in the next chapter.

39   Rorty discusses these issues in his *Consequences of Pragmatism*.

Now what this entails, then, is the belief that philosophy is only one of many kinds of writing, and is certainly not able to access or formulate any meta- or 'superconcepts' (1996a: 222). Indeed, the kind of thinking and writing that Rorty sponsors here as this rejigged philosophy is exemplified by his gloss of deconstruction: 'Derrida's point is that no one can make sense of the notion of a last commentary, a last discussion note, a good piece of writing which is more than the occasion for a better piece' (1996a: 109). In other words, under Rortian pragmatism, the thinking for what he designates a 'post-Philosophical culture'[40] would necessarily and constitutively be excessive rather than delimitative. It would be distrustful of any urge to search for superconcepts or some 'final vocabulary' (1996a: xlii). Continuing conversations and incessant reinterpretations are instead all that we can realistically hope for. Indeed, we have an obligation not to insist on hard and fast delimitation. We should resist any form of takeovers by systems promising us final grounds. For this affirmation and legitimation of excess, then, difference functions as a kind of pragmatic and contingent marker. Far from marking out identities and totalities, difference merely functions to stress the contingency and irreducibility of all of our shared 'floating, ungrounded conversations' (1996a: 174).

---

40   Rorty discusses the distinctions he makes between Philosophy, philosophy, and post-Philosophy in his 'Pragmatism and philosophy' (Rorty, 1996a: xiii–xlvii). Similar types of divisions can be found also in Lyotard's discussions of the postmodern condition (e.g. Lyotard, 1984b).

Reconfiguring Excess

As a final point, it should by now be apparent that all of these various instantiations of excess, *as* non- or post-metaphysical reconfigurations of difference, have been configured with reference to some idea of obligation and ethics. That is, having marked out metaphysics in terms of an appropriative and totalising homogeneity, the affirmation of that which is irreducible to and in excess of metaphysics is seen as an exemplary ethical move. A move in what, for instance, Foucault has once called an ethics of non-fascism.[41] In reconfiguring difference from out of its metaphysical fixation – a fixation or rigidity which functions in support of appropriative and absolute syntheses and hegemonic structurings – projects of the 'Post' are thus concerned to open difference, to think and write it differently. Reconfigured, difference is to be open to alterity and supportive of heterogeneity. It is to be ethical and thereby disclosive of an other to metaphysical formulations of the same. Consequently, as demanding the writing of difference out of its metaphysical constraints, the writing of difference differently, the guiding question of the 'Post' becomes one of righting difference.[42] In other words, I suggest that the 'Post' exemplifies a desire to configure a possible other to metaphysical delimitation – an other constituted through and exemplary of ethical strategies that are no longer dependent upon either the transcendental ideals or meta-narratives which have been seen as constitutive of metaphysics.

With reference to those projects of the 'Post' discussed above, then, each can be seen as an opening up of difference and disclosure of excess that is constitutively ethical. Now, although this reconfigura-

---

41   See, for instance, Foucault's introduction to Deleuze and Guattari's *Anti-Oedipus*.

42   Lucy discusses the conjunction – not conflation – of 'writing' and 'righting' in his explication of the political import of Derridean deconstruction (see Lucy, 1995). In terms of my discussion of the 'Post', I suggest that this conjunction illustrates the drive behind the desired reconfiguration of difference.

tion of excess in terms of ethics and obligation is to be discussed in detail in the following chapter, certain preliminary remarks need to be made. To begin with, as already mentioned, Deleuzoguattarian thinking has been described as an ethics of non-fascism. As such an ethics it thus formulates itself as the need (and responsibility) for opening things up in the face of a 'comprehensive fascism', for breaking repressive structures open and releasing those flows and lines of flight which have hitherto been constrained (Deleuze, 1995: 18–19). Levinas's project, in comparison, describes itself explicitly as an ethics where what is at stake is the sustaining of the relation of the I and the Other. Delineated in terms of the absolute height and transcendence of the Other, this relation encompasses – witnesses – the irrecusable responsibility of the I for and before this Other. In his turn, Lyotard works to reconfigure difference in the name of justice, where justice is only possible as the sustaining of multiplicity and heterogeneity. As he argues, homogeneity is injustice. Rorty also situates his projection of a 'Post' – in the form of a pragmatism that comprises a post-Philosophical culture – as a sustaining of multiplicity. Lastly, Derridean deconstruction can be seen to delineate both difference and excess in terms of undecidability in the name of justice and obligation. Indeed, as Derrida comments, he knows of 'nothing more just than what I today call deconstruction' (Derrida, 1992a: 21).

As can be seen, then, with the question of difference informing both the 'what' and 'how' of non- or post-metaphysical projections, formulations of excess cross necessarily into, and are constituted by, formulations of obligation and justice. In other words, the non- or post-metaphysical affirmation of excess enables and instantiates another side of difference – the possibility for justice and obligation, for an ethical turn to (and before) the other. It is with tracing this reconfiguration of the non- or post-metaphysical affirmation of unconditional excess into a thinking of obligation that the following chapter will be concerned.

3.   Configuring Obligation

> [F]or a while now I have the impression that it is the idea itself of an iden-
> tity or a self-interiority of every tradition (*the one* metaphysics, *the one*
> onto-theology, *the one* phenomenology, *the one* Christian revelation, *the*
> *one* history itself, *the one* history of being, *the one* epoch, *the one* tradition,
> self identity in general, the one, etc.) that finds itself contested at its root.
> (Derrida, 1995b: 71).

As we have started to see in the previous chapter, considering difference in terms of excess cannot be clearly distinguished from considering it in terms of obligation and otherness. Indeed, the sustaining of
excess as supposedly outside of and other than metaphysical totalisations of identity and unity, itself exemplifies the obligation inherent in
this reconfiguration of difference. That is, the sustaining of difference,
otherness and heterogeneity is itself the obligation of the 'Post'. Furthermore, the various affirmations of excess already discussed as possible configurations of the 'Post' themselves delineate a potential and
desired otherness to metaphysical thinking. They mark the contestation of every homogenised identity and unity. Indeed, it is perhaps
only through such contestation that an other or otherwiseness can be,
if not reached, at least discerned. Hence it is through its disruptions of
metaphysical identity and difference that excess both sets and sustains
the questions and possibilities of the other and obligation.

These various possibilities, then, are situated within the
'Post's' reconfiguration of difference in terms of excess. Such a reconfiguration thus seems to enable a possible righting of metaphysical
difference. That is, in opening it from the notions of identity and self-
interiority informing metaphysical delimitation and synthesis, these
affirmations of excess also disclose a possible otherwiseness and accompanying obligation. Excess thus seems to function as the necessary condition for a thinking of obligation and otherness. Hence it is

with tracing these various configurations of excess – otherness, obligation, and undecidability – as possible rightings of difference, that this chapter will be concerned. This time, however, I will focus primarily upon the instantiations of obligation set out by Levinas, Derrida and Lyotard, with a further consideration of their reconfiguration by Caputo.

However, before embarking on this discussion, I want to first of all mention some of the general issues that I consider are pertinent to an ethical 'Post'. To begin with, I suggest that the reconfiguration of excess in terms of obligation and otherness needs to be seen in terms of a series of non-reciprocal relations that, Heideggerian-style, remain constitutively uncanny.[1] That is, they are unable to be delimited or synthesised into any of the relations enabling totality or identity.[2] In other words, non- or post-metaphysical allowing for and tak-

---

1 Uncanniness, as Heidegger stresses it – and, as with Heidegger, my interest here is not with the specificities of the Freudian psychoanalytic reading of the uncanny – depicts a certain 'not-at-homeness' (*Unheimlichkeit*). It describes that point or moment where '[e]veryday familiarity collapses' (Heidegger, 1995a: 233). As this not-at-homeness, then, uncanniness is the disturbance of the self-interiorising and synthesising movements of identity. Uncanniness thus infuses and is the condition for every excessive relation, indeed every possibility of obligation and otherness. Inextricable from Heidegger's thinking of anxiety, which will be discussed in detail later, Heideggerian uncanniness as a not-at-homeness can be traced throughout, repeating within, the various projections of the 'Post'.

2 These non-conceptualisable relations and instantiations do, of course, run (and recognise) the constant risk of slipping back into a delimitative metaphysical conceptuality. Levinas, for example, describes this risk in *Otherwise than Being or Beyond Essence* as the tension between the (ethical) 'saying' and the (metaphysical, totalised) 'said' – a tension he further instantiates as the functioning of the 'trace' (see Levinas, 1991: 168). This risk, as Derrida describes it, is the problem of language itself. Discussing Levinas's work, he writes: 'It is not, then, simply a matter of transgression, a simple passage beyond language and its norms. It is not, then, a thought of the limit, at least not of that limit all too easily figured forth by the word *beyond* so necessary for the transaction. The passage beyond language re-

ing account of an irreducible otherness is necessarily disruptive of and otherwise than the metaphysical delimitative relations informing identity.[3] As uncanny, these relations of excess and obligation are hence informed by the irrecusability of undecidability – where relations are simply suspended, unable to work as a circular economy. Indeed, they indicate a problematic juncture in that they unfold as a 'possibility of the impossible'.[4] They exemplify those non-symmetrical and non-reciprocal relations that stand for

> the difficult or the impracticable, here the impossible, passage, the refused, denied, or prohibited passage, indeed the nonpassage, which can in fact be something else, the event of a coming or of a future advent [*événement de venue ou d'avenir*], which no longer has the form of the movement that consists in passing, traversing or transiting. It would be the 'coming to pass' of an event that would no longer have the form or the appearance of a *pas*: in sum, a coming without *pas*. (Derrida, 1993a: 8).[5]

It is the possibility of this sort of excessive and aporetic relation that enables the configuration of obligation and otherness by the 'Post'.

Within non- or post-metaphysical projects, then, this type of ethical turn to the other (even the singular other) is definitely not a turn away from or reduction of excess.[6]

Overall, then, this concern of the 'Post' with obligation and otherness must be seen as another side – perhaps even, to borrow from Derrida, a supplement – to its overcoming of metaphysical difference and delimitation. Indeed, this thinking of obligation *is* the repetition of excess itself, whereby the instantiated possibility of excess becomes the possibility for obligation. In this view, the 'Post' is that excessive thinking that desires to remain open to and responsible before otherness. Hence, when seen in these terms, non- or post-metaphysical obligation can only be configured as irreducible and even infinite, unable to be ever fulfilled or completely finished with. In other words, obligation does not function within the 'Post' as any sort of ethical overlay or delimitation of excess, as it could be argued to do so within metaphysical systems. Obligation rather, *as* a non-appropriative thinking of otherness, 'conveys the infinite' (Levinas, 1991: 12), whilst remaining constitutively undecidable. Comprised by the 'experience' of the 'plural logic of the aporia' (Derrida, 1993a: 15, 20), obligation is, by Heidegger's definition, uncanny.

Now, in a general sense, this disjunctive conjunction of excess and obligation by the 'Post' seems to suggest the possibility for a reinterpretation of ethics. Situated (and instantiated) by this reinterpretation, the experience of the aporia can consequently be considered ethical (and thereby non- or post-metaphysical) because it is constitutively non-totalising and non-totalised, irreducible to any determinate context. Such an experience is, as previously noted, perhaps best encompassed by Lyotard's famous prescription: 'Let us wage a war on total-

---

6   This ethical turn of the 'Post' must rather be seen as a (Heideggerian style) repetition of its affirmation of excess. Lyotard clearly sums up the interrelatedness of excess and ethics when he states in an interview, concerning the relation of some of his early work to later work, that *The Differend* 'is an attempt to try and say the same things' as, for instance, *Libidinal Economy*, 'without unloading problems so important as justice' (Lyotard, 1988: 300–301).

ity; let us be witnesses to the unpresentable'.[7] Similarly, in Deleuze and Guattari's terms, the ethical is to not be fascist, to not impose or constrain or delimit, but rather to allow 'something to escape, like bursting a pipe or a boil' (Deleuze, 1995: 19). As Deleuze also stresses, there should there be 'no general prescription[s]'. We should be 'done with all globalizing concepts' (Deleuze & Parnet, 1987b: 144). Seen in this way, the 'Post' asks for an ethics of non-constraint, affirmation and openness wherein the only possible ethical practice is the escape from overcodedness and delimitation. Foucault's discussion of the Deleuzoguattarian affirmation of excess in his preface to *Anti-Oedipus* clearly outlines just such a practice. Here, drawing out seven ethical principles as a guide to a 'non-fascist life', Foucault emphasises their common focus of non-restrictive affirmation. For instance, we should

> Withdraw allegiance from the old categories of the Negative (law, limit, castration, lack, lacuna), which Western thought has so long held sacred as a form of power and an access to reality. Prefer what is positive and multiple, difference over uniformity, flows over unities, mobile arrangements over systems. Believe that what is productive is not sedentary but nomadic. (Foucault, 1984a: xiii).

Such ethical possibilities are thus in no way to function as any overcoding of an already constituted (metaphysical or non-metaphysical) thinking. Rather, we need to remember that obligation, as described by the 'Post', should be seen in terms of Heidegger's delineation of meditative thinking in terms of an *'ethos'* or 'originary ethics'.

Now, for Heidegger, this notion of 'originary ethics' means a possibility of thinking that is essentially otherwise than (and, in a non-absolute sense, prior to) the constituting, and thereby delimiting, of

---

7   Lyotard calls for this 'war' in *The Postmodern Condition: A Report on Knowledge* (1984b: 82). There is, further, a suggestive trace of such a witness and witnessing in each of the main configurations of obligation to be discussed here.

thinking into 'such names as "logic," "ethics," and "physics"'.[8] Originary ethics or obligation thus cannot be seen as independent of the functioning of non- or post-metaphysical thinking. Nevertheless, and this is important, although Heidegger's projected thinking unfolds as a thinking *against* the delimitations constituting metaphysics, humanism, and values, it does not thereby 'point toward pure negation and the negative' (Heidegger, 1998: 263–65, 264). In addition, given that any ethical possibility within thinking cannot be detached from its methodological functioning, these opened possibilities constituted by the 'Post' are themselves seen as constitutive of an ethics by the 'Post'. Hence, the non- or post-metaphysical rethinking of difference with regards to the inherent problem of closure[9] is itself ethical.

This possibility could perhaps also be described as unconditional in Derrida's terms, where unconditionality is the unrepresentable and indefinite condition of non- or post-metaphysics:[10]

> Now, the very least that can be said of unconditionality [...] is that it [...] announces itself as such only in the *opening* of context. Not that it is simply present (existent) elsewhere, outside of all context; rather, it intervenes in the determination of a context from its very inception, and from an injunction, a law, a responsibility that transcends this or that determination of a given context. [...] The structure thus described supposes both that there are only contexts, that nothing *exists* outside context [...] but also that the limit of the frame or the border of the context always entails a clause of nonclosure. The outside penetrates and thus determines the inside. (Derrida, 1995a: 152–153; cf. 1976: 158).

---

8 For Heidegger's discussion of this 'originary ethics', see his 'Letter on "Humanism"' (1998: 271, 241).

9 Although I take Derrida's gloss on the impossibility of closure, which he characterises as 'posing *the question of the relations between belonging and the opening*, the *question of closure*' (Derrida, 1978b: 110), as configurative and illustrative of all non- or post-metaphysical projections, Derrida is of course here making direct reference to Levinas's work.

10 As Derrida might put it, seeing the 'Post' and its ethics in terms of unconditionality might mean that it affirms itself as a 'responsibility that transcends this or that determination of a given context' (Derrida, 1995a: 152).

To follow Derrida again, it is this unconditionality that invokes the affirmation of itself as a prescription not only for excess but obligation.[11] Considered in these terms, non- or post-metaphysics *is* the instantiation and affirmation of excess and obligation as unconditional. Consequently, as Derrida writes, with reference to Levinas's work specifically but exemplary also (albeit with certain qualifications) of all non- or post-metaphysical thinking of obligation:

> [Such] thought summons us to a dislocation of the Greek logos, to a dislocation of our identity, and perhaps of identity in general; it summons us to depart from the Greek site and perhaps from every site in general, and to move toward what is no longer a source or a site (too welcoming to the gods), but toward an *exhalation*, toward a prophetic speech already emitted not only nearer to the source than Plato or the pre-Socratics, but inside the Greek origin, close to the other of the Greek (but will the other of the Greek be the non-Greek? Above all, can it be *named* the non-Greek? [...]). (Derrida, 1978b: 82).

Now this thinking can, I believe, best be clarified through the examples of several rather problematic figures – Levinas's 'hostage', Derrida's open series of the host/guest/ghost, and Lyotard's 'the jews'.[12] These figures, then, are indicative of that uncanny excess and obligation held open via the 'Post's' im/possible and aporetic relations with alterity and exteriority. They remain irreducible not only to one or other side of the relation they depict but, further, to each other. Such configurations thus exemplify the suspension or disruption of prac-

---

11 What Derrida actually writes, in context, is: 'In the different texts I have written on (against) apartheid, I have on several occasions spoken of "unconditional" affirmation or of "unconditional" "appeal." This has also happened to me in other "contexts" and each time that I speak of the link between deconstruction and the "yes"' (1995a: 152). '[U]nconditionality also defines the injunction that prescribes deconstructing' when 'another language and other thoughts seek to make their way' and 'which are also new responsibilities' (153).

12 Levinas considers the figure of the hostage throughout his work. Derrida considers the host/guest/ghost seriasure in *Aporias* (e.g. 1993a: 60). Finally Lyotard discusses 'the jews' in his *Heidegger and 'the jews'*.

tices of identity and self-interiority. They exemplify obligation as that experience of difference that is other than that of opposition or appropriation. It is an experience that is thereby other than that of the metaphysically sponsored (and determined) condition or experience of a self-interiorising identity. It is these figures, then, that will be the focus of the remainder of this chapter.

Being Hostage: Levinas

Now to begin with, Levinas describes the unconditionality of obligation in terms of a notion of the 'hostage' and its relations with the other – relations that he describes in terms of 'substitution' and 'transcendence'.[13] Such relations, he argues, are non-conceptualisable. We cannot think them insofar as to do so requires us to lose our status as subject. Hence, the possibility of the hostage is constituted by its experience – its endurance – of difference (and alterity) as excessive and irreducible. However, the hostage is also determined by the depiction of this difference as a 'non-indifference',[14] and by the consequent thinking of an absolute and irrecusable obligation. It is this possibility, then, that *is* non-metaphysical: 'Obligation calls for a unique response not inscribed in universal thought, the unforeseeable response of the

---

13   Levinas uses a series of quasi-substitutable descriptions that do not belong to (and indeed escape) the conceptual orders of knowledge and thought with which to depict and analyse this relation. For example, in the last pages of *Otherwise than Being or Beyond Essence*, he writes: 'Signification, the-one-for-the-other, the relationship with alterity, has been analysed in the present work as proximity, proximity as responsibility for the other, and responsibility for the other as substitution. In its subjectivity, its very bearing as a separate substance, the subject was shown to be an expiation for another, the condition or unconditionality of being hostage' (Levinas, 1991: 184).

14   Levinas discusses this notion of 'non-indifference' in *Otherwise than Being or Beyond Essence*.

chosen one' (Levinas, 1991: 145). So Levinas's 'Post' is his configuration of obligation as 'the condition or unconditionality of being hostage' (184), a condition or experience that is, moreover, whilst excessive, necessarily specific rather than universal.

Now in order to best consider this instantiation of obligation, I will briefly trace its formulation within Levinas's major texts, and then discuss it with reference to certain of Derrida's engagements with Levinas. Levinas, then, begins his instantiation of the 'Post' by prescribing an escape from delimitative metaphysics, which he formulates as that thinking of totality and sameness reliant on processes of identification and appropriation.[15] These processes, he stresses, effect the subsumption of even the possibility of difference and the other. For the other to be thought and sustained *as* absolutely other requires, in contrast, a 'flight out of concepts' which does not, however, equate to 'non-thought'. More specifically Levinas depicts this flight as the possibility of a responsibility or obligation that is '"older" than the a priori' (1991: 126, 101). Obligation, he says, is thus older than and irreducible to the delimitative and dialectically oppositional structures of metaphysical thought. It is, he notes in several instances, an Abrahamic rather than Odyssean configuration.[16] In other words, it marks a

---

15   Here Levinas's argument basically repeats Heidegger's delineation of metaphysics as ontotheology in *Identity and Difference*. For Heidegger, metaphysics *is* ontotheological and thereby delimitative because it is constitutively both grounded and grounding (see Heidegger 1969: 58). In Levinas's terms: 'Essence, the being of entities, weaves between the incomparables, between me and the others, a unity, a community (if only the unity of analogy), and drags us off and assembles us on the same side' (Levinas, 1991: 182).

16   'The itinerary of philosophy [as delimitative metaphysics] remains that of Ulysses, whose adventure in the world was only a return to his native island – a complacency in the Same, an unrecognition of the Other' (Levinas, 1996a: 48). The Abrahamic flight, on the other hand, exemplifies a 'departure with no return' (49). The figure and movements of Abraham are also a focal point for Derrida and Caputo, as I will discuss in later chapters.

non-circularity and non-return which is itself an escape from the self-legitimation of the metaphysical conceptual order.[17]

In this way Levinas depicts obligation as the escape from or breaching of identity. It sustains the possibility of an irreducible otherness that remains exterior to these delimitative relations. As the remaining open to and sustaining of such alterity, obligation for Levinas cannot be discussed in terms of either identity or totality. Rather, obligation can only be illustrated as the going beyond, or transcending of being or presence. Indeed, as Levinas tells us, obligation is informed by the 'idea of the Infinite' (1996a: 55), by 'the non-present par excellence, the non-original, the an-archical, prior to or beyond essence' (1991: 10). For Levinas, before the one is (or can be) for itself – before itself and coinciding with itself – the one is always and already claimed. That is, the one is already assigned and irreplaceable. It is, as Levinas puts it, 'the-one-for-the-other'. The one is thereby always and already responsible both before the other, and for sustaining the difference between the one and the other – a difference that is not (quite) the difference between Being and beings.[18] Structured in

---

17   Although Heidegger distinguishes an open circularity – the spiralling of and in hermeneutics – from the closed and reductive circularity he sees as exemplary of fundamental metaphysical positions; Levinas contrasts this latter delimitative circularity (what he describes as an Odyssean configuration) with the irreversible Abrahamic movement of a departure without return. Hence, whilst Heidegger's aim is to come into circularity in the 'right way', Levinas's is rather to breach or escape it completely.

18   At first glance the differences between the one and the other (as Other) and between beings and Being appear similar in that for each the possibilities of the contingent term – the one and beings – are called into question by their an-archic ground in the other as Other and Being. For both Levinas and Heidegger, the one and beings are only opened to potentiality and responsibility insofar as they are disclosed within the terms of their non-synthesisable relation with the other as Other or with Being. When, that is, they are 'spoken' within this relation. However, despite these similarities, the Levinasian and Heideggerian relations do not quite coincide. Whereas Levinas traces this relation and difference in terms of the positive and transcendent infinity of the other as Other, Heidegger's notion of Being as de-

terms of the 'hither side of being' and tracing a transcendence to the 'point of substitution' (1991: 45, 146), the obligation of the one instantiates an irreversible and infinite relation which can be delineated through neither onto(theo)logical nor ontic-ontological discourse.[19]

With this in mind, then, Levinas initially describes obligation as a possible conjuncture within a sustained difference. Portrayed as the '*direct* and *full face* welcome of the other by me', it is a relation of welcome and desire,[20] where being 'face to face' means that the other is welcomed and sustained as infinitely other, as being 'outside of every order' (1996a: 53). Furthermore, in signifying a sustaining of difference and otherness, the face to face *is* non-indifference. It is the opening and exposure of the one before the other, opening the one into its 'passivity' of being 'for-another' (1991: 51). That is, it marks the Abrahamic 'adventure of the approach of the other, through the substitution for the other, by the expiation for the other' (1991: 148). It is thus the affirmation of this exposure and passivity that sustains and carries this move to the point of substitution. And it is in this experience of being laid claim to that the one (or the same) stands as hostage. Consequently, as previously stressed, this relation of proximity stands for a responsibility that is without limit or measure, and that is

---

scribed in *The Question of Being* is such that it can only be instantiated as ~~being~~, as constitutively non-positive but not as thereby negative.

19   Derrida's discussions of Levinas's work in 'Violence and metaphysics' and 'At this very moment in this work here I am' focus primarily on the projected overflowings of ontological discourse by obligation. Interestingly such a point also informs Levinas's own departure from and critique of Heidegger. Specifically he argues in 'Is ontology fundamental?' (1996a: 2–10) that our relation with the other as Other overflows the Heideggerian problematic of 'fundamental ontology' and the ontic-ontological difference.

20   Levinas makes this point in *Totality and Infinity* (1996b: 80). Further he explicates 'desire' here as a 'metaphysical desire' which *is unable to be satisfied* – metaphysics however being seen here in terms of the dimensionality of transcendence. Such desire thus 'desires beyond everything that can simply complete it [...] [T]he Desired does not fulfil it, but deepens it' (Levinas, 1996b: 34; cf. 1996a: 51–52). It is a desire for the absolutely other, the Other.

fundamentally irreducible to the delimitative and totalising movements of cognition or indeed consciousness. Indeed, for Levinas, this experience of being face to face is itself indicative of the collapse of representation and phenomenality:

> The way in which the other presents himself [sic], exceeding *the idea of the other in me*, we here name face. This *mode* does not consist in figuring as a theme under my gaze, in spreading itself forth as a set of qualities forming an image. The face of the Other at each moment destroys and overflows the plastic image it leaves me, the idea existing to my own measure and to the measure of its *ideatum* – the adequate idea. (Levinas, 1996c: 50–51; cf. 39; 1996b: 53; 1991: 88).

As the impossible thinking, or rather witnessing, of the Infinite in the face to face, obligation is thus antecedent to and disruptive of representation and philosophy. It is that 'command come as though from an immemorial past, which was never present, [and which] began in no freedom' (1991: 88). Obligation, then, is in the paradoxical situation of having already effected an interruption or disruption of identity and metaphysics, but an interruption that necessarily manifests, however, only as an imprint on or a trace within metaphysical identity. It marks that residue of infinity which signifies a beyond being. In other words, obligation exemplifies the impossibility and responsibility of thinking the infinite in the finite. Furthermore, in its preceding of metaphysical and totalised identity, this trace or residue configures the very possibility – indeed necessity – of both this very identity, and that irreversible relation constituting obligation.

Obligation, then, *is* non-metaphysics, and Levinas argues that philosophy – as consciousness, knowledge, ontology, and justice – comes later when the 'third party' interrupts and intervenes in the revelation or relation of 'the-one-for-the-other'.[21] He stresses, however, that this interruption does not actually signify either any absolute break from or delimitation of obligation. Rather, the possibility of jus-

---

21   Levinas makes this point in *Otherwise than Being or Beyond Essence* (1991: 168, 128, 160–161)

tice and philosophy is both conditional on and conditioned by the re(ve)lation of obligation: 'Responsibility for the others [...] is the adventure that bears all the discourse of science and philosophy' (1991: 160). As Levinas puts it, the 'way leads from responsibility to problems', from the ethical non-metaphysics of the 'paradox of an Infinite in relationship with the finite', to philosophy and a totalised metaphysics (1991: 161, 148). However, whilst seeing metaphysics as reliant on moves of appropriation rather than welcome, Levinas still notes a potential ambivalence in philosophy. As he writes:

> Philosophy is called upon to conceive ambivalence, to conceive it in several times. Even if it is called to thought by justice, it still synchronizes in the said the diachrony of the difference between the one and the other, and remains the servant of the saying that signifies the difference between the one and the other as the one for the other, as non-indifference to the other. Philosophy is the wisdom of love at the service of love. (Levinas, 1991: 162).

Philosophy, then, remains ambivalent insofar as it is still traced by that 'command come as though from an immemorial past' (1991: 88). Levinas further clarifies this possible ambivalence of philosophy when he considers its instantiation as scepticism. Discussed towards the end of *Otherwise than Being or Beyond Essence*, scepticism is described by him as another philosophy showing the 'rupture, failure, impotence or impossibility of disclosure' of metaphysics.[22] Depicted here, then, as the way into those problems conditioned (and opened) by an unconditional obligation, perhaps philosophy, insofar as it is still traced

---

22   See *Otherwise than Being or Beyond Essence* (1991: 168). Derrida, on the other hand, in his early engagement with Levinas entitled 'Violence and metaphysics' (published prior to Levinas's *Otherwise than Being or Beyond Essence*), presents Levinas's non-metaphysics as an empiricism: 'the true name of this inclination of thought to the Other, of this resigned acceptance of incoherent incoherence inspired by a truth more profound than the "logic" of philosophical discourse, the true name of this renunciation of the concept, of the a prioris and transcendental horizons of language, is *empiricism*'. Levinas 'totally renews empiricism, and inverses it by revealing it to itself as metaphysics' (Derrida, 1978b: 151).

with the re(ve)lations informing unconditional obligation, can disclose an instantiation of itself which is potentially irreducible to totality. After all, as Levinas asks, 'does the reason characteristic of justice, the State, thematization, synchronization, re-presentation, the logos and being *succeed in absorbing* into its coherence the intelligibility of proximity in which it unfolds?' (1991: 167, my emphasis). Now although Levinas, with his focus on the non-metaphysical instantiation of obligation, leaves this question open, he does nonetheless bear witness to it and is thereby responsible before its possibilities. In fact, it is inscribed within the relation of an ethical 'saying' with the metaphysical 'said'. On the one hand, as Levinas writes, the 'exceptional words by which the trace of the past and the extravagance of the approach are said – One, God – become terms, re-enter into the vocabulary and are put at the disposition of philologists, instead of confounding philosophical language' (1991: 169). On the other, this discourse (of philosophy itself) is always and already interrupted:

> And I still interrupt the ultimate discourse in which all the discourses are stated, in saying it to one that listens to it, and who is situated outside the said that the discourse says, outside all it includes. [...] This reference to an interlocutor permanently breaks through the text that the discourse claims to weave in thematizing and enveloping all things. (Levinas, 1991: 170).

As both assimilation and suspension, this relation exemplifies Levinas's reconfiguration of metaphysics *as* an irreducible and unconditional obligation to an absolute alterity. It is a reconfiguration of difference that *is* open. Consequently, through this instantiation of obligation, the very difference between the thinking of obligation and that of philosophy must itself unfold through the terms of non-indifference. Finally it is, of course, with regard to this notion of non-indifference as the relation between the one and the other that Derrida engages with (and intervenes in) this Levinasian picture of obligation.

Obligation Suspended: Derrida

> The work of E.L. *comprehends* an *other* manner to think obligation in the 'one must,' an *other* manner of thinking the work, and even of thinking thought. One must therefore read it otherwise, read there otherwise the 'one must,' and otherwise the otherwise. (Derrida, 1991a: 420).

> – I no longer know if you are saying what his work says. Perhaps that comes back to the same. I no longer know if you are saying the contrary, or if you have already written something wholly other. I no longer hear your voice, I have difficulty distinguishing it from mine, from any other, your fault suddenly becomes illegible to me. Interrupt me. (Derrida, 1991a: 438).

There is, as stressed in the above disclaimer, a certain 'inter(el)lacement [*entr(el)acement*]' evident between Levinas and Derrida. There is a non-indifference or non-in-difference between them, between their respective obligations and responses.[23] Specifically they meet, Levinas writes, and engage with one another in 'the heart of a chiasmus' (Levinas, 1976: 89, cited in Critchley, 1992: 13). Their work intersects, suspended and interlaced within their differences and non-indifferences. Derrida's writing on Levinas thereby takes the form of an interruption or intervention, and indeed an obligation. 'One must', Derrida tells us, 'read it otherwise' (Derrida, 1991a: 420). Following on from this imperative, Derrida is obligated to intervene within Levinas's thinking. 'He will have obligated [*Il aura obligé*]' Derrida writes at the beginning of a discussion of Levinas, a discussion that is rather *for* Levinas, for him *as* another (405). Specifically the other as Other can be neither presented nor present, and the one

---

23   Speaking about Levinas's work in 'At this very moment in this work here I am', Derrida writes: 'To say "*il aura obligé*" – in *this* work, taking into account what sets things to work within *this* seriasure – is not to designate, describe, define, show, etc., but, let us say, to *entrace [entracer]*, otherwise said to perform within the inter(el)lacement [*entr(el)acement*] of a seriasure that obligation whose "he" will not have been the present subject but for which "I" hereby respond: Here I am, (I) come' (1991a: 425–426).

must not recoil upon and into itself, into its own presence. Indeed obligation suspends both the one and the other, letting the latter 'beyond essence' (424) whilst holding the one open. Consequently Derrida, obligated, responding, and writing the otherwise otherwise, suspends Levinas: 'He is not the subject-author-signer-proprietor of the work; it is a "he" without authority' (424). That is, he continues, the work (his work), obligated and obligating, must not return to him, it must rather be suspended *as* an obligation (427).[24] Through his engagement with Levinas's thinking, Derrida is thus obligated neither to simply repeat it (that is, to send it back to him, to the origin, the same) nor appropriate it (to assimilate it into another thinking) – both moves effective of a delimitation, betraying obligation and the other.

Derrida's engagements with Levinas, then, take place in the heart of a necessary suspension, not of obligation – necessarily not of obligation – but of both one and the other. For example, Derrida argues that insofar as Levinas aims 'to inscribe or let the wholly other be inscribed within the language of being, of the present, or essence, of the same' (1991a: 412), it is an inscription therefore itself irreducible to a single signature. Furthermore, Derrida's own text is itself suspended, interrupted. For instance, one is addressed to a feminine interlocutor intervening in both Derrida's and Levinas's texts, and taking over the final pages of Derrida's text.[25] Such suspensions and interrup-

---

24   This suspension of the work is of course reminiscent of how Derrida discusses the genealogy of writing and the text, its orphaning, in *Of Grammatology*: 'if a text always gives itself a certain representation of its own roots, those roots live only by that representation, by never touching the soil, so to speak' (Derrida, 1976: 101).

25   See 'At this very moment in this work here I am' (1991a: 432–438). As Derrida remarks in an interview, his use of this strategy each time marks that moment when 'it was literally impossible for me to maintain a monologic discourse. Interlocution, the plurality of voices imposed itself in some way and I had to let it through' (Derrida, 1995c: 393). And, 'I let them, I try to let them speak' (394). This plurivocity of course always runs the risk of itself being regulated, signed. As an experience of the other it is and remains impossible. As Derrida continues, 'It is the experience itself of impossible appropriation. The most joyous and the most tragic' (395). Other

tions, functioning in response to obligation and as conditional of obligation, paradoxically illustrate both obligation itself and an otherwise than obligation.[26] As this excessive and ambivalent structuring of response and the responsibility of this response, obligation is thereby an escape from any circularity of restitution. It interrupts and remains irreducible to any circularity or economy. Indeed, it is this excess and ambivalence that constitutes for Derrida (and for Levinas) the structure and obligation informing obligation, its condition and its unconditionality. Hence, it is this structure that informs not only Derrida's response to Levinas (and the other – in 'At this moment in this work here I am' E.L. is also perhaps *elle*), but also his response to this obligation itself.

So what Derrida does to both respond to Levinas and instantiate excess in terms of this obligation, is to formulate it around this possibility or requirement of suspension. That is, he sees obligation *as* the suspension or interruption informing this same obligation. Such suspension disallows, albeit not absolutely, any (metaphysical) return to or recoil into identity and sameness. Rather it effects and sustains the openness of that relation constituted as obligation. Consequently, the Levinasian figure of the hostage is reconfigured by Derrida into the question of the host/guest/ghost,[27] where the latter depicts not so much the erasure or suspension of the one before the Other, but 'an interrupted series, a *series* of interlaced interruptions, a series of *hiatuses*', a 'seriasure' (1991a: 424).[28] For Derrida, then, in his obligated

---

texts written to indicate this 'impossibility of maintaining the mastery and control of a monologue or a dialogue' (Caputo, 1997b: 346*n*36) include 'Sauf le nom', *The Truth in Painting*, and *Cinders*.

26   Such structural ambivalence is also discernible within Levinas's conception of violence and war. On the one hand war is fixed and inherent in that 'concept of totality, which dominates Western philosophy' (Levinas, 1996b: 21). On the other, Levinas also defines war as a refusal to 'belong to a totality' (222). Derrida discusses this ambivalence in 'Violence and metaphysics'.

27   Derrida discusses the host/guest/ghost seriasure in *Adieu to Emmanuel Levinas* (1999a: 56–57, 111).

28   This work of seriasure also depicts, of course, the operations of différance and trace as configured by Derrida in, for instance, 'Différance'. Unname-

response to Levinas, both Levinas and he (and another, *elle*) are interlaced as hosts, as guests, and as ghosts.

As such the configuration of the one is interrupted not only by the approach of the other and its being as hostage, and by the entry or approach of the third party enabling identity and consciousness (as Levinas suggests), but by its (and their) own constitutive and excessive undecidability. Open and suspended, antecedent to and otherwise than any integrity or identity, Derrida's 'seriasure' – of being hostage as the one under obligation, along with the other and the relation of the one and the other – is itself an instantiation of difference and excess. Haunted and solicited by the other and its own otherness, unable to return to itself or represent itself, and unable to represent the other, Derrida's seriasure configures obligation in terms of both hospitality and responsibility, and the aporia of this relation or experience being impossible:

> To surrender to the other, and this is the impossible, would amount to giving oneself over in going toward the other, to coming toward the other but without crossing the threshold, and to respecting, to loving even the invisibility that keeps the other inaccessible. To surrendering one's weapons [*rendre les armes*]. (And *rendre* here no longer means to restore or to reconstitute an integrity, to gather up in the pact or in the symbolic.) To give oneself up [*se rendre*] and to surrender one's weapons [*rendre les armes*] without defeat, without memory or plan of war: so that this renunciation not be another ruse of seduction or an added stratagem of jealousy. (Derrida, 1995b: 74).

In tracing hospitality and responsibility in terms of the open series of the host/guest/ghost, Derrida thus reconfigures both the absolute unconditionality constituting obligation, and the absolute otherwiseness

---

able, with no 'proper essence', différance 'unceasingly dislocates itself in a chain of differing and deferring substitutions'. A chain in which it is further '*enmeshed*, carried off, reinscribed' (1982a: 26, 27). Derrida also stresses in this paper that différance cannot be thought 'on the basis of the present, or of the presence of the present' (21). Rather it 'erases itself in presenting itself' (23).

of the other. These reconfigurations can furthermore be discussed in terms of another of Derrida's 'formulas' exploring obligation and the other: 'any other is totally other [*tout autre est tout autre*]'.[29] Specifically, Derrida traces obligation through the undecidability of writing the other as wholly other, an undecidability further demonstrated by the host/guest/ghost seriasure. This instantiation, in other words, traces the suspension of any/every possible determination and delimitation. Indeed it illustrates the suspension and interruption of every possibility of identity or bounded difference. Constitutively unable to coalesce into any identity or presence (even into that of hostage), this instantiation further stresses the impossibility of legitimating any bounded or determinate experience – any definite or defined moment of relation or decision – of obligation.

Consequently, that other who/which becomes discernible in remaining indiscernible despite its unexpected and unanticipated approach, or indeed its return – think of the return of Hamlet's dad, or maybe even of Arnold Schwarzenegger in *Terminator II* – 'does not yet have a name or an identity' (1993a: 34; cf. 1995b: 74). We do not know this other. It remains, as such, always to come. The arrival of the other thus shows us the indeterminacy (or impropriety) of all notions of saturated context and identity. After all, the other never *is*. Or rather it *is* as suspended, beyond essence and/or place. It is described by Derrida as the ghost, the 'arrivant' and/or the 'revenant'.[30] It is that which (whatever, whoever), 'in arriving, does not cross a threshold separating two identifiable places, the proper and the foreign, the proper of the one and the proper of the other' (1993a: 33, 34). The

---

29   Derrida sets this formulation out in *On the Name* (1995b: 74). Caputo, in turn, in *The Prayers and Tears of Jacques Derrida: Religion without Religion*, reads *tout autre est tout autre* almost as the formula or key word of Derrida's more recent texts.

30   Derrida also explicitly discusses this deconstructive suspension of the other in terms of a 'logic of haunting', as being within not only a 'hauntology' (Derrida, 1994: 10), but within memory and mourning (cf. 1994; 1995c: 320–322; 1986b: 28–32).

other remains indiscernible, instantiating the impossible proviso of obligation *as* promise and relation: *tout autre est tout autre.*

In this way, then, Derrida sees obligation as an experience of and responsibility before the impossible. As the impossible relation with any other, that relation which is otherwise than any other relation in being the experience of the impossible, obligation can only be described as the passing through of the 'madness of the undecidable'.[31] It retraces that relation or decision that can be comfortably neither structured as a witnessing of the trace of the infinite (as in Levinasian transcendence),[32] nor affirmed by any 'theoretical assurance' (1993a: 19). Rather, it exemplifies an impossible hospitality promised before and for the indefinite, to that which remains in difference, other, and by that which remains similarly in suspension. For Derrida, the one promises hospitality before being a host, let alone a hostage:

> [T]he activating of responsibility (decision, act, *praxis*) will always take place before and beyond any theoretical or thematic determination. It will have to decide without it, independently from knowledge [...] We should therefore conclude that not only is the thematization of the concept of responsibility always inadequate but that it is always so because it must be so. (Derrida, 1995d: 26).

In his delineation of obligation, then, Derrida stresses the undecidability inscribing any and every moment of decision-making. That is, obligation marks and is marked by the aporetic moment inherent in every response, where hospitality is also always known as irresponsi-

---

31   See Derrida's *On the Name* (1995b: 59; cf. 1992a: 24). As Caputo has stressed, Derrida's explication of responsibility in terms of undecidability is informed by Kierkegaard's own delineation of the decision in terms of madness.

32   In addition, unlike Levinas's projection of obligation as instantiated through an absolute passivity (for instance, the passivity of being hostage, witnessing), Derrida configures obligation in terms of the non-passivity of the offering and giving of hospitality. See, for instance, *Aporias* and *Of Hospitality.*

bility or heresy or risk.[33] Hospitality, in other words, is unsponsored and unprotected. It prescribes a 'sense of responsibility without limits', and is necessarily 'excessive, incalculable' (1992a: 19). Hence, far from describing a contract or even a claiming, hospitality is described in terms of the structure of the promise, the *a-venir*, structures which remain open and excessive.[34] Traced by the undecidable, the decision of hospitality is transgressive of the orders of knowledge. It is spectralised:

> The undecidable remains caught, lodged, at least as a ghost – but an essential ghost – in every decision, in every event of decision. Its ghostliness deconstructs from within any assurance of presence, any certitude or any supposed criteriology that would assure us of the justice of a decision, in truth of the very event of a decision. (Derrida, 1992a: 24–25; cf. 1999a: 35).

Now what all this means, then, is that Derrida's configuration of obligation is not unconditional and irrecusable because it traces a relation with the infinite (the absolutely and infinitely other, the Other), but because it effects the deconstruction of knowledge and metaphysics. Inscribed as the promise, as the 'yes',[35] obligation is the suspension or interruption of the metaphysical economy within presence. It instantiates a spectralised economy, what Derrida also calls a weak messianic structure or future.

Derrida's aim, then, is to instantiate obligation otherwise than as either a metaphysically sponsored moral overcodedness (thereby repeating the Heidegger of *ethos* and *Gelassenheit*), or as a Levinasian transcendence. That is, in showing obligation to be both unconditional

---

33   Derrida speaks of hospitality as irresponsibility and heresy in *The Gift of Death* (1995d: 61, 26), as risk in *Adieu to Emmanuel Levinas* (1999a: 111), and as aporia and antinomy in *Of Hospitality* (2000: 77).

34   Derrida discusses the stricture of the promise in 'The Villanova roundtable: a conversation with Jacques Derrida' (1997b: 22–23; cf. 1994; 1992a). Caputo in turn comments on this structure in 'A commentary: deconstruction in a nutshell' (Caputo, 1997a: 161–162).

35   See Derrida's 'The Villanova roundtable: a conversation with Jacques Derrida' (1997b: 27).

and undecidable, placing both relations and identities in suspense, Derrida reconfigures and interrupts both the metaphysical and Levinasian relations. Indeed he is obliged to reinterpret not only the promise of the relation itself, but the being in relation of the one and the other – opening the being held in relation (for instance, as the Levinasian hostage) into the undecidability discernible within the host/guest/ghost seriasure. As such, rather than being prescriptive of limits, Derridean obligation is a working to open and unsettle limits, identities and conditions. It is a relation with the undecidable which is itself undecidable.

Derrida thus writes obligation as suspension and interruption, hospitality and responsibility – as, that is, the ethical directionality of deconstruction itself. Obligation as such both effects and illustrates deconstruction's contestation of limits: 'There is no front between responsibility and irresponsibility' (1995d: 70). Furthermore, it is as this contestation that obligation and deconstruction themselves remain in question, 'urgent and unanswered, [or] at any rate without a general and rule-governed response' (1995b: 16). Obligation is a structure of suspension and impossibility, spectralised, *à venir*. It is a passion for and before the impossible which '*necessitates* doing the impossible': 'The sole decision possible passes through the madness of the undecidable and the impossible: to go where [...] it is impossible to go' (1995b: 59; cf. 1999a: 35).

Obligation for 'the jews': Lyotard

> The question is not even [ever] that of obedience, but of obligation. The question is to know whether, when one hears something that might resemble a call, one is to be held by it. One can resist it or answer it, but it will first have to be received as a call, rather than, for instance, as a fantasy. (Lyotard, 1995: 107).

Absolute injustice would occur if the pragmatics of obligation, that is, the possibility of continuing to play the game of the just, were excluded. That is what is unjust. Not the opposite of the just, but that which prohibits that the question of the just and the unjust be, and remain, raised. [...] [M]oreover, any decision that takes away, or in which it happens that one takes away, from one's partner in a current pragmatics, the possibility of playing or replaying a pragmatics of obligation – a decision that has such an effect is necessarily unjust. (Lyotard, 1994: 66–67).

To turn now to a third configuration, obligation exists for Lyotard in correlation to the sustaining of openness and plurality. That is, Lyotard's vision of obligation is that it is both the condition for and conditioned by the interruption and suspension of homogeneity – an interruption Lyotard describes in terms of the problematic of the different. Disclosive of the unpresented and the unrepresentable, the different exemplifies both excess and what Lyotard calls 'the forgotten'.[36] Further, the differend can be seen to mark the impossible prescription of obligation towards what Lyotard comes to instantiate as 'the jews'.[37] Described as the desire for the affirmation of difference, excess, and the unrepresentable, obligation is thus the prescribing of that relation with that which remains unknowable and other – in excess of the known, forgotten. Indeed it prescribes as just that relation which, in turn, instantiates heterogeneity and plurality.

Hence, it is through his configuration of the different that Lyotard opens the question of difference into that of obligation and justice. As such, my discussion of Lyotard's thinking of obligation will be organised around these various possibilities opened by the agonistics of the different. Initially focusing on Lyotard's configuration of the different as exemplifying the unrepresentable (within lan-

---

36   Lyotard primarily talks of 'the forgotten' in his *Heidegger and 'the jews'*.

37   Using this term to illustrate the problematic of the unrepresentable in *Heidegger and 'the jews'*, Lyotard stresses that 'the jews' (always plural, lower case, and presented by and within quotation marks) are not to be confused with 'real Jews': 'it is neither a figure nor a political (Zionism), religious (Judaism), or philosophical (Jewish philosophy) subject that I put forward under this name' (1990: 3).

guage and ontological discourse) and as prescriptive of both justice and plurality, I will then turn to Lyotard's later instantiations of the differend in terms of 'the forgotten' and 'the jews'. As will become apparent, it is in terms of these instantiations that Lyotard configures thinking itself as obligation (that is, seeing it as a witnessing, a non-indifference), opening the question of obligation to that which remains other, forgotten.

To begin with, in his text entitled *The Differend: Phrases in Dispute*, Lyotard describes the differend as the unrepresentable experience within language. It is that 'unstable state and instant of language' wherein it is interrupted – and indeed suspended – by 'a feeling' (1995: 13). The differend thus marks the irruption of an uncontainable (and unrepresentable) excess or otherness within the given. It is indicative of that which is unable to be ever completely presented or assimilated. The differend shows that there is always something else at stake in, and otherwise than, the given. Something that discloses its possibility only negatively, apophatically, and which is irreducible to any homogeneity.[38] As such, the differend situates and prescribes a notion of justice which is itself not only irreducible to the processes of legitimation sustaining homogeneity, but which is constitutively disruptive of both this legitimation and homogeneity.[39]

Disclosed in this way, then, justice must constitutively *not* be 'a matter of privileging a language game [e.g. legitimation] above others' (Lyotard, 1994: 60). Consequently '[t]here is no genre whose he-

---

[38]   The differend signals that that which remains to be phrased (in language, in a homogeneity) exceeds and is otherwise than what can be (presently) phrased: 'A lot of searching must be done to find new rules for forming and linking phrases that are able to express the differend disclosed by the feeling, unless one wants this differend to be smothered right away [...] What is at stake in a literature, in a philosophy, in a politics perhaps, is to bear witness to differends by finding idioms for them' (Lyotard, 1995: 13).

[39]   The differend thus exemplifies that 'fine risk' sustained between the 'ethical saying' and the 'ontological said' that Levinas works within, and that 'possibility or condition of the impossible' within which Derrida situates and inscribes his thinking of obligation and deconstruction.

gemony over the others would be just' (1995: 158). As such, Lyotard describes justice as unable to be ever finally legitimated and made an object of cognitive representation. It cannot be defined by any actual criteria because 'the idea of criteria comes from the discourse of truth and supposes a referent or a "reality"' (1994: 98). Hence it remains necessarily unrepresentable, plural, and always to come,[40] traced by the exigency of having to 'respect as much as possible the has-it-happened-yet' (1988: 301). It thus needs to be seen in terms of plurality – or rather in terms of the *idea* of plurality.[41]

> Can there be then a plurality of justices? Or is the idea of justice the idea of a plurality? That is not the same question. I truly believe that the question we face now is that of a plurality, the idea of a justice that would at the same time be that of a plurality [...] (Lyotard, 1994: 95).

Hence, it is through his delineation of the differend as obligation before the unpresentable and as thereby prescriptive of both plurality and heterogeneity, that Lyotard is able to describe justice as supposedly different from that of metaphysical delimitation and homogenisation.[42] Justice thus functions as the minimal guiding principle – the 'guiding thread' (1995: 134) as he put it – of plurality. However as obligation

---

40   This characteristic of Lyotard's depiction of justice as being always a matter of the future, never given or finished with and always in question, is also similar to Derrida's explication of such terms as 'justice' and 'democracy' in recent works. For example, in 'Force of law', he writes: 'Justice remains, is yet, to come, *à venir*, it has an, it is *à-venir*, the very dimension of events irreducibly to come' (Derrida, 1992a: 27).

41   As was noted in the previous chapter, Lyotard makes some of the moves of a Kantian-style 'critical watchman'. Delineated by him in the mode of a Kantian Idea – as the 'as if' (Lyotard, 1994: 77–78), the maximization of a concept, where 'one follows the concept beyond what reality can give it as sensible to subsume' (58) – the ideas of justice and plurality are thereby irreducible to any hypothetical imperative or verisimilitude which, *as such*, would belong to experience, able to be described and derived, given (46).

42   Lyotard depicts 'injustice' as the domination of absolute difference imposed by homogeneity, whereby its required and self-legitimated consensus 'does violence' to heterogeneity (Lyotard, 1984b: xxv).

before the unrepresentable, justice paradoxically prescribes and further regulates plurality, requiring it to be sustained *as* just and heterogeneous. That is, as exemplary of a Kantian regulatory idea, justice functions *as if* able to ground and regulate the plurality it prescribes. In other words, as Honi Fern Haber has described it, justice comes to function as if it is a 'transcendent standard', a 'universalistic principle of constraint'.[43]

However this suggests that this configuration of justice, although formulated to take account of the unrepresentable, nonetheless functions to delimit and regulate the plurality it prescribes. Although Lyotard registers this paradox or circularity – 'What are we doing here other than navigating between islands in order paradoxically to declare that their regimens or genres are incommensurable?' (1995: 135) – his projection of obligation remains constitutively caught within it. However, far from simply denying this paradox, Lyotard sees it as constitutive of the 'Post' itself. It is thereby exemplary of his suspension or interruption of any so-called 'universal tribunal or last judgment' (134). Consequently justice, although functioning *as if* a universally regulative (that is, metaphysical) idiom, remains only an idea held in question by the differend. There is, he writes, 'not "language" and "Being,"' but simply 'occurrences' before which one can and must 'bear witness' (181).

At this point, however, Lyotard rephrases his discussion of justice. For instance, in *Heidegger and 'the jews'*, Lyotard reconfigures the differend itself, instantiating it here in terms of 'the forgotten'

---

43   See Honi Fern Haber's 'Lyotard and the problem of pagan politics' (1995: 146, 147). William Rasch argues much the same point in his discussion of the 'self-referential' paradoxes inherent in (and constitutive of) postmodernism (Rasch, 1994: 55). For example, discussing Lyotard's image of the archipelago in *The Differend* (Lyotard, 1995: 130–131) – his analogy regarding the operation of judgement and justice – Rasch notes that Lyotard there, despite his avowed aims, 'depicts the special status enjoyed by the one discourse which claims that no discourse has a special status' (64).

and as 'the jews'.[44] Like Levinasian obligation, the Lyotardian differend must remain an-archical and immemorial. Although it is outside of and unrepresentable through time and memory, it also signifies an impossible, albeit necessary and interminable, anamnesis. As he writes, 'The Forgotten is not to be remembered for what it has been and what it is, because it has not been anything and is nothing, but must be remembered as something that never ceases to be forgotten' (1990: 3). Thinking, as such, is that obligation towards the differend, that obligation to remember that 'one never stops forgetting what must not be forgotten, and that one is not quit either just because one does not forget the debt' (84). Lyotard configures such thinking as testimony and anamnesis, as a writing that, although not a philosophy, cannot forget philosophy.[45]

Lyotard thus depicts with this the movement of a non-Hegelian dialectic, wherein thought (reconfigured *as* obligation) is the minimal act of remaining sensitive to the forgotten and the unrepresentable. The working through of this dialectic thus does not lead to any culmination either on the one hand as synthesis and assimilation within memory or, on the other, as extermination, excision, or exorcism out of memory. Rather, insofar as 'the elimination of the forgotten must [itself] be forgotten in order to be accomplished' and as this forgetting 'testifies to the fact that the forgotten is always there', the play within forgetting and anamnesis remains in movement, obligated and unsynthesisable. Obligation is therefore no longer delineated in terms of the disclosure through the differend of the opened possibility and responsibility for instituting and sustaining plurality and justice. Rather – even more simply – it marks a call for forms of thinking or writing that do not quite forget the fact that 'the jews' (not real jews, as Lyotard stresses) are, always already, forgotten and/or subsumed. It is, in other words, an obligation for otherness that does not instantiate

---

44   Lyotard also signifies the unrepresentable as the question of 'Auschwitz'. On this point see *The Differend* and *Heidegger and 'the jews'*.

45   Interestingly Lyotard also associates this obligation of thinking with deconstruction (see Lyotard, 1990: 59, 71).

itself *as in* any relation *with* this otherness. It is, Lyotard writes, a thought concerned with that which 'cannot be interiorized, represented, and memorized', which does not 'mix things', and which is necessarily only ever a 'bad witness' (1990: 29, 59, 81). Instantiated not *as* a relation as such *with* an other or otherness, but as the impossibility *of* this relation, such obligation remains unable to directly and unproblematically present either itself or that otherness it is responsible before:

> This writing preserves the forgotten that one has tried to forget by killing it; it advances in the direction of the immemorial through the destruction of its representations and of its witnesses, 'the jews'. (Lyotard, 1990: 43; cf. 26).

Exemplifying the doubled impossibility and necessity of attesting to the unrepresentable, Lyotard thus keeps obligation open as that irrecusable question or sensitivity which does not formulate or prescribe any particular response. After all, as he remarks, 'there is no good way of being a hostage' (1990: 23). Prescriptive only of a sensitivity towards the question – the disaster or abyss – of the unrepresentable, obligation is constitutively open and irreducible in its instantiation.[46]

---

46 This is the point upon which Lyotard's critique of Heidegger's 'fault' with regard to his involvement with 'the greatest horror' of Nazism (Lyotard, 1990: 57) is based. That is, that in Heidegger's thought – which comes very close to that of 'the jews' (79) – the strength and integrity of his questioning nonetheless fails: 'If there is a "fault" [...] it is due to this weakness, this deficiency in accomplishing the "it is necessary to deconstruct and rewrite"'. There is then 'a region that it does not open, that will remain closed, fallen, abject, outside its project' (64).

The Flesh of Obligation

So what we can see, then, is that obligation for the 'Post' traces what must remain an impossible relation with and response to an otherness that is constitutively unpresentable within metaphysics. *As* this impossible relation and response, obligation is thus described as being open and irrecusable and, further, undelimitable. Indeed, it functions as the imperative behind all attempts to think difference differently, to think it specifically in terms of non-indifference. What this means, then, is that obligation is itself the exemplary project or problem of the 'Post'. Indeed, the tracing of obligation not only underlines the question and problem of the other within the metaphysical economy of the same, but also, on the other hand, brings into question the unconditional affirmation of excess associated with non- or post-metaphysical projects, whilst paradoxically instantiating itself as this excess.

It is thus at this point of suspension between excess and obligation that I want to briefly introduce what I see as another instantiation of the 'Post' and obligation. This is the work by Caputo who wants to further instantiate – and respond responsibly before – the relatedness of excess and obligation. After all, as he sees it, we are always and already 'in the midst of multiple obligations, in the plural and the lower case' (Caputo, 1993a: 6). Delineating obligation as excessive, irreducible and non-negotiable – it happens, it is the fact of 'our factical life' (25, 7) – Caputo, however, does not focus on any sustaining and witnessing of otherness *as* otherness (as absolute alterity or exteriority). Rather he is concerned with the imperative of response, on responding even though we may never 'know the origin of obligation' (7). Arguing that much of the discussion of obligation and ethics by the 'Post' is still too pious, still too interested in legitimating itself in terms of its pursuing or authorising of an other *as* other, and in situating both itself and this other *as* other than and therefore irreducible to the same or metaphysics, Caputo stresses rather the impiety of response. In particular, he sets out a minimalism where response is the only moment or experience of obligation that should be pursued and instantiated. It is *responding to* rather than *legitimating* the other as absolutely other which is his priority. Now this means that he instantiates obligation neither in the terms of any overarching theory of metaphysical or originary Ethics, nor as any kind of legitimisable ethical relation, nor even through any instantiated 'Post'. Obligation is rather described as a sort of pragmatics. It is instantiated in terms (and in the middle) of 'disasters' and 'flesh'. It is, he stresses, very fragile and necessarily earthbound.[47] In other words, he inscribes the relation with the other within 'flesh', within its disasters and its contingency. As he puts it, 'the needs of flesh are all you need for obligation' (237).

Hence, for Caputo, obligation is to be seen in terms of response to – rather than any substantiated relation with – any/every other. 'Flesh' subtends the question of obligation, disclosing it as a need for response where both this need and response have no need of further legitimation. Configured under the law of flesh – the 'relation of flesh to flesh' (217) that can only be instantiated through flesh – obligations cannot be organised under or by any *arche* or even *telos*. Rather, obligations simply happen 'because they happen' and only happen 'for the while that they happen' (247). As seen, then, although Caputo configures obligation in terms of an excessiveness, he situates it within 'the irreducible realm of that facticity which [...] does not submit to neutralization' (25). Although excessive, obligation for Caputo is not the *affirmation* of any unconditional excess, of that which remains absolutely irreducible to metaphysics. It is not the affirmation of an infinite or infinitely different otherness. Instead, configured in terms of flesh, obligations (perhaps) supplement and suspend such affirmations so that they merely call for and mark a response to specific disasters and proper names (28, 69, 237). Hence, far from affirming either itself or unconditional excess in terms of any irreducible or infinite otherness – a move that Caputo calls simply a

---

47   Although Caputo stresses the factic 'earthiness' of both obligation and response, I am sure he would see these relations of obligation extending should we ever come into contact with non-terrestrial life.

'fabulous story' (79) – Caputo's minimalist instantiation of obligation is tied to the immediacy and undecidability of facticity:

> Obligations do not derive from some central source of power. Obligations are strictly local events, sublunary affairs, between us. They are matters of flesh and blood, without cosmic import or support. (Caputo, 1993a: 227).

Obligations, then, for Caputo *are* factically instantiated. They happen in response to the excesses and disasters of factical life. They mark an impious happening and response, a happening that happens 'with or without sacred names, with or without the Infinite' (237). Excessive, indeed overwhelming, such obligations neither instantiate nor prescribe any impossible relation which is to sustain any absolute (or even indefinite) other – not, even, their own configuration. Rather they instantiate a response to flesh where the 'why' sinks into the 'because' and does not really matter. In other words, Caputo's earthbound obligations interrupt and suspend all those pious configurations of the 'Post' desirous of affirming unconditional excess or otherness. They happen not in the name of an absolute other, or even of any other other, but under the factic names of flesh. Caputo, then, through this instantiation of obligation within flesh, effects a reinterpretation of the problem or project of the 'Post'. Perhaps, as he suggests, the possibility of the 'Post' does not lie in instantiating any absolutely incommensurable other to metaphysics, but rather in simply resituating, reinterpreting and responding to the problem.

Now, it is thus this suggested resituating and reinterpreting – this supplementing – of those configurations of the 'Post' concerned to explicate obligation (and excess) in terms of a relation with an absolute alterity, which I believe needs to be considered further. Such a reinterpretation might not only show us that those attempts of configuring excess or obligation as absolute or unconditional are still far too pious, but might perhaps also open some other way along which the 'Post' might be instantiated. Consequently, it is the possibility of this other way that still needs to be unpacked, a discussion that also needs to consider what the idea of the 'Post' actually entails. For example, *how* does the 'Post' as a non- or post-metaphysics stand in relation to that metaphysics which it is aspiring to overcome? Furthermore, how does this possibility of another way for the 'Post', as prefaced by Caputo, relate to the configurations of excess and obligation that I have outlined above? It is with such questions that I begin the following chapter.

4.   The Question of the Frame

> But what has produced and manipulated the frame puts everything to work
> in order to efface the frame effect, most often by naturalizing it to infinity
> [...] (Derrida, 1987: 73).

As we have seen so far, then, the aim of escaping or rewriting metaphysics and metaphysical difference is the focus not only of Heidegger's work but of much of the 'Post'. And we've also seen that as far
as the 'Post' goes, this rewriting has been accomplished through affirming irreducible excess and/or obligation. Now although I have discussed these affirmations separately in the previous two chapters, they
do not of course form an opposition. Far from it. Rather, given that
they are both configured in terms of unconditionality and undecidability, they work in relation with each other. Their relationship does,
however, point to another distinction – that between what I see as non-
metaphysical and post-metaphysical constructions. Now this distinction has so far gone unflagged in my discussion, as if it is self-evident
and not requiring explication. However, once flagged, it will provide
me with a framework for problematising not only the various instantiations of excess and obligation I have considered so far, but their
relations to both Heidegger's project and metaphysics itself. Hence I
intend, after an initial consideration of this distinction and its implications, to return again to the presumption of an exhaustion within philosophy. An exhaustion that I suggest is inextricable from both metaphysics and the very affirmations of excess and obligation that have
set themselves up as the possible beyond of this metaphysics.

To begin with, we need to look more closely at the terms
'non-metaphysics' and 'post-metaphysics'. Although they were both
initially used to simply mark a distinction or distance from metaphysics – that is, to indicate a style of thinking that was apparently beyond
or otherwise than that characteristic of metaphysics – they are identi-

cal in neither their form, focus, nor function. However, while this distinction has been neither overtly underlined nor developed so far, nor even instantiated *as* a difference as such, it has been briefly mentioned as perhaps informing the mode and degree of the 'Post's' disruption of metaphysics.[1] Nevertheless, the site of this distinction remains problematic in that both non- and post-metaphysical projects hold the aim of problematising metaphysical projections of difference. Despite this, and although this distinction is perhaps only of degree, it is instrumental to my discussion of the viability of the 'Post' and its attempts to think beyond or otherwise than metaphysics.

The question remains though as to why we should only now look at this distinction. Certainly, given my earlier focus on delineating some of the attempts made to overcome or escape metaphysics, establishing a distinction between non- and post-metaphysical attempts has been of less importance than outlining their common aim of tracing a thinking that is outside of or other than metaphysics. And, indeed, the importance of developing or maintaining a distinction between non- and post-metaphysics appears debatable. Surely it is enough, having shown metaphysics to be a fixed regulatory system that culminates in and circulates a homogeneity, to trace the positivity of a style of thinking that would affirm (and indeed prescribe) heterogeneity, pluralism, and difference. Surely, to insist upon a distinction within this latter affirmation is once again to make yet another exemplary metaphysical move of delimitation and hierarchism. However, although it must be emphasised that I am in no way formulating a fixed distinction or hierarchy, non- and post-metaphysical projects are nonetheless not conflatable. They not only seem to function differently, but they are situated differently with regard to metaphysics – *if,* that is, metaphysics itself *can* be considered as identifiable and delimited. It is perhaps in terms of a response to this last point that a distinction between non- and post-metaphysics can be most clearly argued for.

---

1   See my footnote 3 in the previous chapter.

What I am suggesting here, then, is that a distinction between non- and post-metaphysical projects can perhaps be determined by looking at their relations with metaphysics. That is, it can perhaps be ascertained at the level of each project's determination of itself in relation to metaphysics. Now although both non- and post-metaphysics situate themselves with regard to some notion of an outer edge to metaphysics – that is, metaphysics as an exhausted and closed system or tradition[2] – they determine and indeed use this edge somewhat differently. However, before exploring these differences in detail, I should start by briefly reiterating their common usages of this edge.

First of all, they both use it to situate their respective suspensions or interruptions of metaphysical processes. In other words, it is via this edge that non- and post-metaphysical projects are able to situate and distinguish both themselves and a notion of metaphysics. Secondly, they both use this outer edge of metaphysics to determine their own unconditionality – their apparent independence from 'every determinate context' as Derrida has put it (1995a: 152). For instance, both non- and post-metaphysical configurations are able to put forward the possibility of their unconditionality – instantiated, for instance, as a supposedly unconditional excess or obligation – because they see themselves *as* being somehow different to metaphysics. Specifically, they see themselves as having escaped or overcome processes of delimitation and representation – processes that they see as enabling metaphysical transactions of identity. Seen therefore as part of the edge holding between metaphysical systems and non- and post-metaphysical projections, this notion of unconditionality can, however, also function to mark a distinction between non- and post-metaphysical projects.

For instance, non-metaphysical projects characteristically aim to develop a thinking that is absolutely independent of metaphysics.

---

2   See, for instance, Philippe Lacoue-Labarthe's description of philosophy in *Heidegger, Art and Politics: The Fiction of the Political*. Here he states, for instance, that 'if the thing still exists, it does so now only as a tradition; and a tradition that is now closed', and that 'Philosophy is finished/finite [...] its limit is uncrossable' (1990: 1, 4).

They strive for that thinking which is not possible or permitted within metaphysical transactions, and which affirms their absolute (albeit impossible) unconditionality. They therefore tend to describe metaphysics as if it is completely closed or exhausted, and their focus is on what might be possible outside of metaphysical conceptualisation, contextualisation and construction. Having determined metaphysics as delimiting in its interest in essences and the ontological 'is', non-metaphysics constructs itself as absolutely and even infinitely open. Such a thinking thus tries to mark itself off clearly from metaphysics. It *is* (or should be) constitutively different. Now such thinking is of course best exemplified on the one hand by the Deleuzoguattarian affirmation of the 'and', and on the other by the Levinasian idea of an infinite ethical transcendence. Overall, then, non-metaphysical projections not only present themselves as counter to and other than metaphysics, but through this work to enframe metaphysics. Metaphysical delimitation and closure is the condition for their own non-delimitation and absolute openness.

Post-metaphysical constructions have, on the other hand, a considerably more nuanced relation with metaphysics. That is, rather than aiming for a space or thinking that is supposedly independent from that of metaphysics, post-metaphysical projects are concerned with the question and possibility of the limit itself. The *question* of difference is thus their major focus. As such, whilst still situated within the problematic of a certain closure or exhaustion of metaphysics, I suggest that post-metaphysical projects see themselves as still in a relationship with metaphysics. A relationship that is other than that of the postulated absolute difference required by non-metaphysics. Indeed, in questioning the possibility of any absolute difference, post-metaphysical projects destabilise the closure of metaphysics. They remain in dialogue with metaphysics. In other words, for post-metaphysics, metaphysics itself may become a question. Hence, far from desiring to be somehow exterior to metaphysics, post-metaphysical configurations still inhabit metaphysics, interpreting and deconstructing[3] it in a way that is, I think, made possible by Heidegger. They become that questioning which, functionally ambivalent, 'must think metaphysically and at the same time think out of the ground of metaphysics, i.e., in a manner that is no longer metaphysical' (Heidegger, 1998: 232). As Derrida puts it:

> There is no sense in doing without the concepts of metaphysics in order to shake metaphysics. We have no language – no syntax and no lexicon – which is foreign to this history; we can pronounce not a single deconstructive proposition which has not already had to slip into the form, the logic, and the implicit postulations of precisely what it seeks to contest. (Derrida, 1978b: 280–281; 1976: 24).

On this basis, post-metaphysical projects emphasise the inevitability of undecidability, contamination, relation, and what Lyotard has termed the differend – points or borders where difference can only be considered with reference to the indefinite rather than any infinite.

Hence, although both non- and post-metaphysics determine themselves in terms of unconditionality, they see this unconditionality quite differently. On one hand, non-metaphysical projects construct themselves *as* the thinking of an unconditional excess and/or obligation that is to be absolutely exterior to – unconditioned by – any metaphysical space or system. On the other, post-metaphysical projects affirm excess and obligation in terms of an irrecusable and unconditional undecidability, the latter a move that also disrupts so-called metaphysical decidability and delimitation.

Metaphysics, then, *as* disrupted, is posited either as absolutely overcome, or else as remaining in question. It is either delimitable and the question concerns its outside, or the question is to do with the very

---

3   I must stress that I am not here simply equating the post-metaphysical project with Derridean deconstruction. Although I argue that deconstruction is indeed a post-metaphysical project, I will attempt to show that it can also be distinguished from other post-metaphysical projects. This distinction will be made with reference to the relations holding between post-metaphysical projects (including that of deconstruction), metaphysics and the Heideggerian project.

possibility and process of delimitation. As such, although non- and post-metaphysics both assume the exhaustion or suspension of metaphysics as their condition of possibility, they are simply not conflatable. At the same time, however, we need to realise that the site of their distinction also cannot be grounded as such. Given that post-metaphysics cannot, by its own determination, be definitely distinguished from non- metaphysics or even metaphysics, this distinction must itself remain undecidable and in question. Hence it remains a question as to whether non- or post-metaphysics *can* counter the thinking of metaphysics. Whether, that is, they *can* offer any coherent alternative to metaphysics. Now this question has of course remained open since Heidegger's recognition of both the importance of overcoming metaphysics and instantiating another thinking, and the impossibility of actually leaving metaphysics behind.[4] And it is this question that now needs to be addressed with reference both to Heidegger's work and the 'Post'.

The Impasse of Metaphysics

To reiterate, then, insofar as metaphysics has been set out as an appropriative, totalising and homogenising system, any and every possibility of generating a counter-thinking to it seems to depend on the prerequisite of its exhaustion or completion. That is, metaphysics must be delineated *as if* a closed system in order for there to be the supposedly open thinking of non- or post-metaphysics. It is only through the instantiation of some definite boundary that metaphysics is able to be determined as firstly closed and secondly exhausted, and as thereby at an impasse and giving rise to the question both calling for and enabling non- and post-metaphysical configurations. What this shows us,

---

4   See, for instance, Heidegger's *The End of Philosophy* (1975: 85) or his 'Introduction to "What is metaphysics?"' (1998: 278–279).

then, is that the closure of metaphysics is itself only made possible through processes of delimitation and homogenisation – processes which, supposedly metaphysical, nevertheless also paradoxically enable the open processes of non- and post-metaphysics. Instantiated therefore by both and by neither of the sides it serves to determine, this boundary or frame serves several purposes. It determines metaphysics as having reached an impasse, it affirms the possibility of metaphysics being exceeded or overcome, and, as I will show, it serves to distinguish non- from post-metaphysical projects.

So, to tackle the first of these, we need to keep in mind that it is via Heidegger that metaphysics is described as a closed system.[5] As Heidegger puts it, metaphysics has closed down into a sequence of words for Being, or 'fundamental metaphysical positions', both of which delimit the open possibilities and question of Being (1991b: 190–191). Further rigidified as history or tradition, this sequence, in Heidegger's words, closes off 'any possibilities for essential inquiry'. It forgets and exteriorises that which is 'most worthy of thought' (1991b: 205; 1969: 55). In other words, in its representing of Being, such a sequence marks a circularity that is both delimitative and interiorising, lacking the potentiality which informs Heidegger's counter notion of a radicalising repetition and thinking. In fact, as Heidegger sees it, metaphysics completes its sequence – that is, exhausts its possibilities – with the 'calculative thinking' (1966: 46) of the 'will to will' (1975: 92–93), thinking which is indicative of a certain configuration of *techne* as technology.[6]

---

5   An instantiation that is, of course, influenced by his readings and interpretation of Nietzsche (see Heidegger's *Nietzsche* Volumes I–IV).

6   'The basic form of appearance in which the will to will arranges and calculates itself in the unhistorical element of the world of completed metaphysics can be stringently called "technology." [...] The name "technology" is understood here in such an essential way that its meaning coincides with the term "completed metaphysics"' (Heidegger, 1975: 93). This, however, is not quite to say, as has been previously suggested in other considerations of Heidegger's relation with technology (e.g. W.B. Macomber, 1967: 198–208), that technology *only* exemplifies this completion of metaphysics and

Nonetheless, although Heidegger depicts metaphysics as if it is both closed and exhausted, his projection of a counter-thinking does not assume the abandonment of metaphysics.[7] Far from simply being abandoned, metaphysics is to be radicalised and, by this, placed in question and under interpretation. As a non-negative and non-vicious spiralling, this hermeneutic process thus exemplifies a possible non-delimitative and non-enframing mode of thinking or questioning. It is a thinking that, *as* interpretation, *as* constitutively open and non-enframing, disrupts the very processes of enframing, and traces the possibility of a certain open relatedness. Discussed by Heidegger via, for example, such terms as *Gelassenheit* and *Ereignis*, this relatedness collapses into neither dialectic nor any grounded or delimited identity or fundamental metaphysical position. Instead it traces an in-betweenness, the relation, for instance, held open by Heidegger as dif-ference.[8] Specifically, then, it depicts that uncanny belonging together which not only does not become a unity or sameness, but also does not comprise a simply oppositional relationship of otherness. In other words, whilst Heidegger sees his counter-thinking to metaphysics as certainly other than and different to metaphysics, it is not absolutely beyond or cut off from metaphysics.

---

the end of thinking; or that technology itself represents the delimitation of the open possibilities of *techne* (possibilities considered by Heidegger in 'The origin of the work of art'). Or, further, that the domain of technology precludes *any* possibility of 'essential thinking'. On the contrary, it is only one mode of Dasein's relation with technology that manifests as an enfram-ing 'calculative thinking'. Heidegger indicates that there is another relation or comportment to technology that discloses technology in another way – a possibility that he delineates through such terms as *Gelassenheit* (1966: 54–55) and *Ereignis* (1969; 1971). This possibility of reading Heidegger as suggesting another open relation with technology is, for instance, also pur-sued by Simon Cooper in his 'Beyond enframing'.

7   Heidegger elaborates on these points in *The End of Philosophy* (1975: 85) and *The Question of Being* (1958: 93).

8   Heidegger unpacks this relation of 'dif-ference' in 'Language' (1971b: 202–203).

Nevertheless, although Heidegger's counter-metaphysics in no way assumes or demands the abandonment of metaphysics, it does still assume that metaphysics itself, uninterpreted, is exhausted and at an end.[9] After all, as Heidegger sees it, when metaphysics is gathered into its history, *as* its tradition of onto-theology, it is no longer able to question its grounds, conditions or situatedness. It is concerned with conceptualising its own circularity and closure[10] rather than with questioning these very concepts and processes. Under this framework, then, although metaphysics cannot be abandoned, its possibilities are fundamentally exhausted. Hence it is on this basis that subsequent non- and post-metaphysical configurations need to be understood.

However, before I continue, I need to stress again that non- and post-metaphysical projects, although constructed as other than metaphysics, do not themselves comprise any identity or unity. This is exemplified by what appears to be a merely functional distinction between non- and post-metaphysical configurations – a distinction that constitutively must not be identifiable as either grounded or given or natural. After all, as Derrida reminds us, it is the very possibility of the idea of any identity or self-interiority that needs to be 'contested at its root' (Derrida, 1995b: 71). Nevertheless, as I've shown, non- and post-metaphysical configurations do work from a distinction that situates on one side the circular discourse of metaphysics, whilst situating themselves on the other. Furthermore, although all non- and post-metaphysical instantiations remain in some relation with metaphysics, whether oppositional or interpretative, they do nonetheless determine themselves as somehow other than – perhaps even untouched by – both the constitutive exhaustion of metaphysics and the automated functions of homogenisation that sustain it as onto-theology (for Heidegger) and fascism (for Deleuze and Guattari). This distinction, then,

---

9   See, for instance, Heidegger's 'The end of philosophy and the task of thinking' (1993: 432–433).

10   Heidegger sees this as the task of Nietzsche in particular. Indeed he argues that Nietzsche is the last metaphysician of the West, and that his philosophy represents the culmination, the gathering, of all the metaphysical tradition (see his *Nietzsche* Volumes I–IV).

along with the 'Post's' assumption and requirement of the closure of metaphysics suggests a boundary which functions delimitatively only one way, in one direction, from one standpoint.

For instance, the first stage is the depiction of metaphysics as having reached an impasse, as being absolutely closed and exhausted. This exhaustion, secondly, is itself presented as if delimited by the very boundary which both instantiates it and is made possible by it. Thirdly, with only metaphysics *as such* exhausted and deadlocked, only its counter-possibilities – as opened within and generated by this same boundary – are absolutely non-delimitable and free. This differentiation thus depends on the boundary itself operating as if it is rigid and impermeable, indeed absolute – a requirement which is at the very least problematic given that both non- and post-metaphysical instantiations place the rigidity of difference in question, with this questioning itself comprising post-metaphysical projects.

Posited only by non- and post-metaphysics,[11] and thereby functioning as what Derrida calls a 'difference without presence' (1981: 210), this boundary instantiates the paradox not only of an interpretative relation generated by and open on only one side, but also of a difference or distinction which is itself both marked and undecidable, effaced in being traced. Put crudely, under the framework delineated by non- and post-metaphysics: if difference is rigid and naturalised, both controlled and controlling, it is a metaphysical structure; if, on the other hand, difference is delineated as contingent and flexible, uncontrollable and unpredictable, it both escapes and disrupts metaphysical processes and structures. As such, the description of the difference between metaphysical structures and non- and post-metaphysical projections as if it is determining and rigid, is itself a move that potentially sets back in place a metaphysical difference. This difference would then, by definition, homogenise metaphysics

---

11   By its definition by non- and post-metaphysical projections, metaphysics instantiates itself as if it can have or allow no outside or other. Consequently, from its own perspective, it has no boundary or outer edge as such.

and non- and post-metaphysics by setting them up in terms of either a synthesisable dialectic or a hierarchising opposition.

If, on the other hand, the difference between metaphysics and non- and post-metaphysics is not to function as a metaphysical distinction, it is instantiated in terms of undecidability and the resultant possibility of uncontrollable contamination and dissemination, of rhizomatic proliferation or production. In other words, any difference between metaphysics and the 'Post' would itself become unstable. Resulting in the possible breakdown of the functioning of this difference or boundary, this paradox perhaps ultimately effects an affirmation of undecidability, thereby further problematising the initially assumed closure of metaphysics. Hence, this boundary remains problematic in that its functions and effects vary with the standpoint taken.[12]

Thus it is only through a suspension of this undecidability that this boundary is able to operate in positing metaphysics as both exhausted and closed. Also problematic is the fact that metaphysics is interpreted as closed through a discourse which, even though by definition is non-totalisable and open to heterogeneity, disallows the affirmation of the other *if* that other *is* metaphysics.[13] Indeed, if the only open possibilities are those independent of metaphysical structures,

---

12   The problematic boundary or distinction I am here tracing perhaps functions in a similar way to Derrida's notions of 'hymen' in *Dissemination* and 'frame' in *The Truth in Painting*, both of which exemplify the 'double mark' of the between (1981: 193).

13   This is specifically the problem criticised with reference to Lyotard's (and also to a certain reading of Derrida's) work. (See, for instance, Honi Fern Haber's, William Rasch's, and Samuel Weber's work on Lyotard). For example, on the one hand either Lyotard's libidinal economy must be all-inclusive, unable to differentiate or judge between just and unjust discourses. Or, on the other hand, it can judge between and prescribe positions and discourses, permitting some whilst excluding others. If the latter, however, it thereby functions as if it was the very metaphysical economy it tries to escape. Or, again, maybe the very stating of this problem in terms of an opposition is making yet another metaphysical move. This impasse will be discussed in detail in the following section.

metaphysics *can* be neither open nor generative of possibilities. Requiring a more detailed consideration, it is this impasse concerning the possibility of both a boundary or difference and that thinking which escapes metaphysics that will be the focus of the following sections.

Now to best consider the various possibilities and implications informing this impasse and boundary, I want to return again to those instantiations of non- and post-metaphysics outlined earlier. Those instantiations to be discussed include what I see as the non-metaphysical configurations of Deleuze (and Guattari) and Levinas, along with the supposedly post-metaphysical possibilities projected by Lyotard, Rorty, Caputo, and Derrida. Described earlier as counter-responses to an assumed metaphysical delimitation and exhaustion, these responses were then defined as resisting and escaping the homogenising structures and processes of metaphysics. However, these same instantiations now need to be considered with regard to *how* exactly they situate themselves as other than and outside of metaphysics. That is, it is now imperative to consider whether and how each resists or escapes the impasse constituted and disclosed by metaphysics.

Non-Metaphysics or Metaphysics Returned

As we know, then, non-metaphysical projections present themselves as if they are absolutely independent from and other than metaphysical systems. Deleuze (and Guattari), for instance, set forth a thinking that they see as a liberation and affirmation of excess and becoming. This sort of thinking becomes possible, they say, when we reconfigure the notion and function of middleness. This done, thinking can become rhizomatic, where rhizomatic thinking is plural, made up of becomings which are multiple, heterogeneous and unpredictable. Such thinking is 'constantly breaking out of [...] repressive inscription or encoding', and constitutively exceeds any 'unitary development toward [...] transcendent ends or endpoints' (Deleuze, 1995: 186*tn*8). Hence

Deleuze (and Guattari) base the difference between the metaphysical and rhizomatic modes of thinking on the supposedly absolute distinction between the 'is' and the 'and'.[14] And it is with the formalising of this distinction that metaphysical and rhizomatic configurations can be seen as functionally distinct and independent from each other – as constituting a non-synthesisable opposition.

It is on this basis, then, that Deleuzoguattarian rhizomatics constructs itself as inherently non-prescriptive and non-totalising (metaphysics of course being both of these things). However, in its otherness to metaphysics, Deleuzoguattarianism affirms only itself. Any move out of this production from the middle is seen to entail the invocation of something outside or transcendent that, in turn, effects the arresting of movement and the stilling of becoming. So, in prescribing and affirming only *its* own movement, this thinking emphasises and indeed rigidifies its difference from metaphysics. It stands for 'a force that destroys [...] every possibility of subordinating thought to a model of the True, the Just, or the Right' (Deleuze & Guattari, 1987a: 377). Furthermore, along with being constructed as if absolute and irreducible, this difference between metaphysics and Deleuzoguattarian rhizomatics also suggests as an ethical prescriptive exhorting still more speed and movement. After all, as Deleuze notes, 'What's so shameful is that we've no sure way of maintaining becomings, or still more of arousing them'.[15]

It is thus these various moves and their implications that need to be considered with regard to the delineation of metaphysical thinking as impasse. First of all, we can note that the Deleuzoguattarian distinction between metaphysics and their non-metaphysical projections describes the latter in terms of an exteriority that is paradoxically enabled by this distinction, whilst also producing the distinction. That is, this distinction is both grounded by and the grounds of their ethical

---

14   This distinction is discussed by Deleuze in *Negotiations* (1995: 44), and
      Deleuze and Parnet in *Dialogues* (1987b: 57).
15   Deleuze makes this claim in *Negotiations* (1995: 173). Deleuze also talks of
      rhizomatic practice as ethical elsewhere in *Negotiations* (e.g. 1995: 133–
      134, 141).

practice which remains irreducible to the homogenising practices of metaphysics. As such, through the instantiation of this distinction, Deleuzoguattarian non-metaphysics makes a number of apparently metaphysical moves. These include the rigidifying of the difference between itself and metaphysics, a rigidifying which assumes that that which is held in difference *can* be absolutely differentiated, and that they can be determined *as such*. As rigid, this difference delimits that which is held in difference. For instance, as the other of non-metaphysics, metaphysics is delineated as both closed and as the absolute boundary of non-metaphysics. Furthermore, affirming only itself, Deleuzoguattarian non-metaphysics overcodes itself in its prescribing (and desiring) only its type of speed, movement and becoming. Hence, in relying on these moves to distinguish itself from metaphysics, Deleuzoguattarian non-metaphysics remains tied to metaphysics. Whilst affirming itself *as* absolutely other than metaphysics, and insofar as this very affirmation is itself metaphysical, Deleuzoguattarian non-metaphysical rhizomatics remains unable to escape the impasse of metaphysics.

The second non-metaphysical configuration I will discuss here is Levinasian ethics. As shown previously, this also instantiates itself as fundamentally other and exterior – and, in this case, prior – to the delimitative processes of metaphysics. Processes that, as Levinas describes them, generate and formalise only the Same. Concerned with the possibility of experiencing the other as absolutely Other, Levinas puts forward a non-metaphysical thinking of unconditional obligation. As such, Levinasian non-metaphysics is a bearing witness to the other as Other, to its being infinitely other. It shows us the irreducible excess and exteriority of that supposedly held in (and known through) relation. Described by Levinas as generating the possibility of an ethics rather than that of metaphysics as knowledge – the former being concerned with the other as Other, whilst the latter traces the domain of the Same – such an ethics affirms a 'transcendence, an exteriority, more exterior, more other than any exteriority of being' (1991: 156).

Consequently, structured with regard to the paradox of the Infinite,[16] the ethical re(ve)lation is not only incommensurable with the formalising relations tied up with language and knowledge, but constitutively unrepresentable.[17] Indeed, Levinas's non-metaphysical ethics *is* both the revelation of and relation to the unrepresentable. It firstly *reveals* the absolute exteriority of the non-metaphysical through an ethics structured in terms of the re(ve)lation of an unconditional obligation, and secondly *reveals* this re(ve)lation itself through the structure of the trace.

Obligation, then, is set out by Levinas as an-archic. Unrepresentable either in terms of synthesis or difference, obligation *can only be* absolutely exterior to the formalised, delimitative and comprehensible orders of the Same. In this way, ethics and metaphysics *are* incommensurable. Indeed, as Levinas goes on to show, metaphysical thinking (as knowledge or even justice) becomes possible only after the interruption of the ethical relation. However, as was noted in the preceding chapter, this interruption both does and does not mark the boundary between ethics and metaphysics. That is, although constitutively unrepresentable, the ethical re(ve)lation does mark metaphysical thinking, instantiating a 'trace of a diachrony that does not enter into

---

16   For Levinas the idea of the infinite is paradoxical insofar as it 'consists in thinking more than what is thought and maintaining what is thought in this very excess relative to thought – in entering into a relationship with the ungraspable while guaranteeing its status of being ungraspable' (1996a: 55).

17   Levinas outlines this incommensurability in terms of a distinction between the 'saying' and the 'said' in his *Otherwise than Being, and Beyond Essence*. Here he explicates the 'saying' and the 'said' as different, arguing that the 'said' establishes ontological and self-identical being, whilst 'saying' exemplifies the 'beyond being and non-being, beyond essence' of the ethical 'one-for-the-other involved in responsibility (or more exactly in substitution)' (Levinas, 1991: 45). However, although he sets out their necessary difference, Levinas also argues that there is a irreducible tension between the 'saying' and the 'said'. That the 'saying' as a 'trace' which has 'never been present' and which 'does not belong to the assembling of essence' (168), is nevertheless 'present' within the 'said' without being subsumed by it.

the present, that refuses simultaneity' (1991: 170). Unrepresentable, this trace paradoxically exemplifies and repeats both the boundary and a certain ambivalence or complicity between ethical re(ve)lation and metaphysical thinking. Absolutely irreconcilable and different, ethics and metaphysics are nonetheless in a relation of non-indifference.[18] It is thus with regards to this problematic that Levinasian ethics needs to be considered as to whether it escapes the impasse of metaphysics.

Now, as a fairly obvious starting point, this move of affirming the other as absolute exteriority is guided by the assumption that this exteriority *as* both absolute and unrepresentable *can* be so traced and instantiated. As we saw with Deleuzoguattarian rhizomatics, the affirmation of absolute exteriority assumes that it *can* be distinguished – indeed, known – *as* absolute exteriority. Further, it is fundamental for Levinas not only that this absolute exteriority can be distinguished, but that the distinction between the exteriority 'known' through ethics as obligation and the interiority of the Same 'known' by metaphysics be instantiated only as an *ethical* – thereby non-metaphysical – relation. In other words, as the prerequisite for the very possibility of such an ethics, this distinction must be sustained only through ethics, as only in that way *can* the absolute exteriority affirmed by ethics remain as such. Hence, this relation *as* ethical is constitutively asymmetrical. It is open only the one way and affirms only non-metaphysics or ethics itself.

A circularity can be discerned, therefore, in this production of a non-metaphysics. A pure unconditioned exteriority can, after all, only be affirmed as itself (that is, as 'pure' and absolute) by the instantiation of a rigid distinction or boundary that is both the condition of the possibility of such exteriority and prescribed by it. Through such a boundary, non-metaphysics assumes and effects the closure of metaphysics whilst enabling its own open styles of thinking. In other words, this difference functions within a circular logic of affirmation. This difference affirms and instantiates the possibility of a non-

---

18   And for Levinas, of course, non-indifference exemplifies the ethical relation of obligation itself.

metaphysics that, in turn, affirms and instantiates this difference, and metaphysics is seen to be closed through the affirmation of either this difference or non-metaphysics. This in itself seems to lead us to an impasse. Although the production of such a difference is fundamental to the possibility of a non-metaphysics, such a move is by definition proscribed by non-metaphysics as being delimitative and thereby metaphysical. The non-metaphysical affirmation of exteriority is as such functionally delimitative, and thereby remains within the domain and impasse of metaphysical thinking.

Another trace of the metaphysical impasse infusing non-metaphysics can be ascertained with regards to the latter's vision of itself as a reconfigured empiricism. Now by this I mean not so much the structuring of thought and knowledge only through sensuous experience where 'everything in the understanding comes from the senses' (Deleuze & Parnet, 1987b: 54), but rather that thinking which is by definition resistant to the conceptual (a.k.a. metaphysical) structuring of knowledge. Such a thinking would be an empiricism in its projection of a domain not structured in terms of universal (or universalisable) principles or processes of conceptual abstraction. It would be an empiricism in its affirmation of that unrepresentability or exteriority *unable as such* to be instantiated through metaphysical structures. Indeed, with regard to the non-metaphysical instantiations I have considered, Deleuze describes his own work as a 'radical empiricism',[19] and Levinas is so described by Derrida in 'Violence and Metaphysics' for his affirmation of absolute exteriority or alterity in *Totality and Infinity*. To borrow from Derrida, then, the work of both Deleuze (and Guattari) and Levinas can be described as empiricism because of their shared affirmations of a practice of exteriority as a style of thinking. It is a practice that must renounce the delimitative strategies of metaphysics and conceptual regulation for a thinking

---

19   See, for instance, Deleuze and Guattari's *What is Philosophy?* (1994: 47). Deleuze's work is also discussed as an empiricism by, for example, Bruce Baugh in 'Transcendental empiricism' and Patrick Hayden in 'From relations to practice in the empiricism of Gilles Deleuze'.

based on a desired unrestricted affirmation of the 'and' (Deleuze) or the Other (Levinas).

Overall, then, both Deleuze (and Guattari) and Levinas see non-metaphysics as the *practice* of difference as an unsynthesised *relation*. The possibility of such practices, however, has been brought into question by Derrida in 'Violence and Metaphysics'. Here he argues, with reference to Levinas's work, that such empiricism is 'the *dream* of a purely *heterological* thought at its source. A *pure* thought of *pure* difference' which 'must vanish *at daybreak*, as soon as language awakens' (Derrida, 1978b: 151). That is, the thought or experience of a 'pure' exteriority or difference can only be either absolutely unrepresentable and therefore unable to be traced or instantiated in terms of *any* logic – even through a logic affirming only difference and relation – or it is always and necessarily informed by that metaphysical logic it works to counter. Either way, I suggest that the non-metaphysical thinking of exteriority and relation requires the maintenance of an absolute or pure difference and must thereby be seen as still caught in the impasse of the metaphysical thinking of difference.

Post-Metaphysics: On the In-between

> Why is it necessary to *obliterate* this notion of exteriority without erasing it, without making it illegible, by stating that its truth is its untruth, that *true* exteriority is not spatial, that is, is not exteriority? That it is necessary to state infinity's *excess* over totality *in* the language of totality; that it is necessary to state the other in the language of the Same; that it is necessary to think *true* exteriority as non-*exteriority*, that is, still by means of the Inside-Outside structure and by spatial metaphor; and that it is necessary still to inhabit the metaphor in ruins, to dress oneself in tradition's shreds and the devil's patches – all this means, perhaps, that there is no philosophical logos which must not *first* let itself be expatriated into the structure Inside-Outside. (Derrida, 1978b: 112).

As was pointed out earlier in this chapter, what I call post-meta-physical projects hold a more nuanced relation with metaphysics than do non-metaphysical projections. That is, I suggest that they unfold as a Heideggerian-style interpretation of metaphysics rather than as any configuration supposedly independent from metaphysics. Focused on exploring some of the questions and functions of difference and iden-tity rather than on generating any supposedly absolute or pure exteri-ority, post-metaphysical instantiations show us the irrecusability of undecidability. Indeed it is with regard to their focus on undecidability that post-metaphysical configurations can be questioned as to whether they actually illustrate a possible escape from the impasse of meta-physics. It is to discuss this issue that I now turn to the projects of Lyotard, Rorty, Caputo and, lastly, Derrida.

To begin with, although parts of Lyotard's work could ini-tially be seen as productive of a non-metaphysics in the form of a thinking of intensity – what Lyotard called in his book of the same name a 'libidinal economy' – which is instantiated otherwise than through any 'so-called labour of the concept' (Lyotard, 1993: 256), his later concerns mark his work as more in line with a post-metaphysics. Indeed, even when proposing intensity as the basis for a purely libidi-nal economy, Lyotard stresses that 'it is in no way a matter of deter-mining a new domain, another field, a *beyond representation*' (50). Rather, he is concerned to show how metaphysical difference is al-ways disrupted by an excessive and irrecusable undecidability. Spe-cifically, he discusses this undecidability with reference to the effects of the unpresentable, which he has traced, for instance, via such fig-ures as 'the differend', 'the forgotten' and 'the jews'.[20]

Now these figures all situate and exemplify that which re-mains unpresentable within metaphysical 'grand' or meta-narratives. They instantiate the very possibility of disruption or dispute – signal-ling not only the activation of an agonistics in presentation, but the

---

20   Lyotard discusses 'the differend' in his book of the same name, *The Differ-end: Phrases in Dispute*, and the figures of 'the forgotten' and 'the jews' in his *Heidegger and 'the jews'*.

consequent possibility of heterogeneity itself. In other words, through their disruption of the homogenising structures and systems of metaphysics, and as situating an irrecusable undecidability, these figures open a post-metaphysical thinking. I should also note that for Lyotard (and for the other post-metaphysical projects I am concerned with here), such disruption is itself a thinking of justice, where justice is the recognising of the agonistics at work in processes of presentation and judgement. For instance, as Lyotard sees it, thinking must not only respect the exigency of the 'has-it-happened-yet' (1988: 301), but account and allow for that which has not as yet happened or has perhaps been silenced.

In other words, it is in the name of a potential justice of multiplicity that Lyotard works to keep structures and difference open.[21] The figures of the differend, the forgotten and 'the jews', themselves constitutively undecidable, thus configure Lyotard's post-metaphysical thinking as a thinking of obligation and justice. That is, such thinking operates through the principles that not only are all systems and structures (described by Lyotard in terms of linkages and differences) both contingent and unjust in that every such structure or possible structure 'cannot help but be the occasion for differends', but there can be no structure 'whose hegemony over the others would be just' (1995: 140–141, 158). Lyotard's post-metaphysical thinking, then, not only holds metaphysical meta-narratives and structures in question, but remains itself in question. By definition it can (or, rather, should) *only* be instantiated as an obligation for both the possibility of justice and the unpresentable.

It is in these terms, then, that Lyotard's post-metaphysics needs to be considered as to whether and how it has avoided the impasse of metaphysics. Firstly, although Lyotard's focus has been to disrupt metaphysical narratives through tracing their possible exposure to a certain situated unpresentable – rather than the non-meta-

---

21   Lyotard discusses the justice of multiplicity (and the multiplicity of justices) in his and Jean-Loup Thébaud's *Just Gaming*. I considered some of Lyotard's concern with these notions in the previous chapter.

physical attempts of escaping metaphysics by instantiating and affirming this unpresentable itself – he has nonetheless set out this questioning as itself instantiating (and requiring) a difference between itself and metaphysics. Such a difference, whilst perhaps not situating Lyotard's post-metaphysics as absolutely beyond or outside of metaphysics (as a non-metaphysics), does however situate it as other. That is, the thinking that Lyotard projects as counter to metaphysical homogeneity is, by definition, other in its constitutive openness before an unpresentable. In this way, Lyotard requires just as rigid a difference or boundary between metaphysics and his post-metaphysics as non-metaphysics needs to instantiate its possibilities as absolutely independent of metaphysics. Distinguishing totalising and homogenising metaphysical meta-narratives from the proliferating and heterogeneous micro-narratives, this boundary further works as the prescription for the latter possibility – and positivity – of heterogeneity. In other words, as with the non-metaphysical projections considered earlier, Lyotard's post-metaphysical thinking instantiates a circularity by which metaphysics is both delimited and abandoned.

A further point to consider here concerns Lyotard's emphasis on a mode of difference that is to function as otherwise than metaphysical difference. Basically, rather than setting in motion functions of homogeneity, difference must instead set heterogeneity in motion. It must both disclose and legitimate heterogeneity. Hence the function of difference – overtly one of opening up heterogeneity – becomes the legitimation and regulation of its functioning as the principle of justice. Levelled out, difference collapses into what Niall Lucy has called a 'mono-difference'.[22] That is, difference as the principle of both justice and heterogeneity is collapsed into that demand exemplified by the differend: the demand for 'just' regulation of both presentation and possibility. Difference as such once again functions to regulate the possibilities it both enables and produces, and is thereby functionally metaphysical. Further, as both prescriptive and protective of particular kinds of incommensurability – for instance, the incommensurability

---

22   Lucy makes this point in *Postmodern Literary Theory* (1997: 95).

between genres – Lyotard's post-metaphysical difference functions once again as delimitative.

Lyotard's reconfiguration of difference, then, is through and through metaphysical. It is caught in the impasse of its instantiation of and reliance on difference being functionally metaphysical. Although Lyotard reconfigures difference with regard to the unpresentable, he nonetheless fails to disrupt or interrupt its functioning as a mode of legitimation. Further, the focus of this practice of legitimation has, if anything, been extended through Lyotard's reconfiguration of difference. That is, from the legitimating of homogeneity by metaphysics, Lyotard's post-metaphysical thinking *as* a reconfiguration of difference, is the legitimation not only of a delineation of metaphysics *as* homogeneity but of its own instantiation of itself as making possible both heterogeneity and justice. Hence, as a practice of legitimation, Lyotard's post-metaphysics cannot be seen as either exemplifying or instantiating a thinking that functions as other than metaphysical thinking. Indeed, when structured in terms of an obligation towards the unpresentable – an obligation to bear witness to the unpresentable, with an additional focus on disclosing or generating an idiom or genre through which the unpresentable might be either firstly presented or, better, secondly not forgotten – Lyotard's post-metaphysics can again be seen to function as a metaphysics.

That is, although Lyotard, especially in *Heidegger and 'the jews'*, is extremely careful not to let his thinking of obligation fall into the metaphysical trap of prescribing or legitimating any particular response to the unpresentable, nevertheless the very desire and exigency of somehow acknowledging the unpresentable even as unpresentable (for instance, as through the differend, the forgotten and 'the jews') must be seen as caught up in the metaphysical work of conceptualisation and comprehension. In instantiating itself as the *desire* (and ability) to present the unpresentable, even through such non-positive modes as testimony and anamnesis, Lyotard's post-metaphysics *is* constitutively metaphysical.

The next post-metaphysical configurations I intend to discuss are those put forward by Rorty and Caputo respectively. Taking the breakdown of philosophy's (metaphysical) meta-narratives – what Rorty describes as 'Platonism', and Caputo describes as philosophy's 'fine names'[23] – as their starting points, both Rorty and Caputo propose minimalist styles of thinking through which they hope to cope with the contingencies and disasters of an already assumed undecidability and plurality. Rorty, for example, aims to introduce a pragmatism able to deal effectively with the relativist, contingent and plural positions and conversations of our 'post-Philosophical culture'.[24] On the other hand, Caputo proposes a thinking of 'proper names', 'disasters' and 'obligations' – all of which are always plural and in lower case – which would focus on the happening of our factical life, dealing with the facticity and contingency of 'flesh'.[25] Overall, neither Rorty's nor Caputo's minimalism seem to be overly concerned with generating any actual alternative to either metaphysical method or thinking, or relativism – unlike the aims of both non-metaphysical projects and Lyotard's post-metaphysics. Rather, they focus on finding a way of dealing with *what is*, *if* the collapse of the 'fine names' is assumed. However, although Rorty and Caputo are both concerned with the questions and problems consequent on such a collapse, their respective instantiations of a post-metaphysical thinking are not conflatable.

Concerned with questions of utility rather than truth, Rorty portrays a post-metaphysics that is in no special or necessary interpretative relation with metaphysics. That is, rather than highlighting the question of the end of metaphysics, Rorty tells us that we should simply be content to 'let a hundred flowers bloom'.[26] Far from holding

---

23   Rorty talks about 'Platonism' in *Debating the State of Philosophy* (1996c: 33), and Caputo discusses philosophy's 'fine names' in *Against Ethics* (1993a: 6).

24   Rorty discusses Western society and culture as 'post-Philosophical' in *Consequences of Pragmatism* (e.g. 1996a: xl).

25   Caputo's first detailed exposition of these issues is to be found in *Against Ethics*.

26   Rorty's suggested botanising can be found in his 'Philosophy in America today' in *Consequences of Pragmatism* (1996a: 219).

some special status, then, metaphysics and the end of metaphysics are just different kinds of writing. Metaphysics, however, is in particular a kind of writing that is not very useful for generating or dealing with the 'pragmatic, short-term reforms and compromises' needful for the factical or public domain of 'competing interests' (Rorty, 1996d: 17; cf. 1996e: 69). He believes that to ask philosophy – or, rather, Philosophy – to intervene in these areas is to ask too much of it. So, Rorty's pragmatism simply presents and legitimates itself in terms of utility. Indeed, the pragmatist thinks

> that in the process of playing vocabularies and cultures off against each other, we produce new and better ways of talking and acting – not better by reference to a previously known standard, but just better in the sense that they come to *seem* clearly better than their predecessors. (Rorty, 1996a: xxxvii).

On this basis, then, vocabularies, conversations and cultures can only be considered as to whether they can be useful in the production of 'new and better ways of talking and acting'. However, it is also clear that Rorty is quite certain about just what these better ways of talking and acting should look like. Specifically, they should bring about the furthering of a democratic – that is, American[27] – liberal pluralism. Far from letting every flower bloom, then, Rorty comes down on the side of particular ones. He prefers, for instance, democratic liberal pluralism (in the guise of pragmatic, short-term reforms and compromises) over philosophy (as Philosophy, Platonism or metaphysics).

For Rorty, then, with the stress of his pragmatism being on furthering the aims of a liberalist and pluralist society, aims for which

---

27   Rorty expounds democracy as American in his *Achieving Our Country* where he follows Whitman in seeing 'the words America and democracy as convertible terms' (Rorty, 1998: 17). Caputo critiques this conflation – and accompanying complacency – in his *More Radical Hermeneutics* (Caputo, 2000: 116–124). Rorty's conflation of his 'ideal' thinking with his country, would also need to be considered with reference to Heidegger's delineation of open thinking as necessarily Greek or German (see Heidegger, 1990b: 63).

it remains apparently irrelevant as to whether they possess any meta-physical or transcendental grounding or authority, pragmatism has no intrinsic relation with metaphysics. Delineated along a sort of utilitarian line, Rortian pragmatism is effectively dissociated from and avoids metaphysics in any state. Furthermore, Rorty's pragmatism marks a breakdown of the 'distinction between philosophy and the rest of culture' (1996c: 35). Not only, he argues, is his post-metaphysical pragmatic thinking unrelated to metaphysical thinking but it cannot even be seen as the practice of a distinguishable philosophy. By definition, then, Rortian pragmatism not only does not constitute an alternative to metaphysical philosophy but under its framework the very making of any such alternatives or distinctions is no longer of any real interest or use.[28]

Nevertheless, via its desire for new and better ways of talking and acting, we can see that Rorty's pragmatism is construed around the liberal pluralist aim of consensus and conversation. And this is an aim that he has additionally described as the building of 'utopian social hope'.[29] This hope, then, sustains Rortian pragmatism, enabling its

---

[28] Rorty criticises what he terms 'post-Nietzschean European philosophy' (as distinguished from the pragmatic tradition of 'post-Darwinian American philosophy') for wishing to formulate a 'new philosophical method or strategy' (e.g. 1996c: 34–36). As such he values a 'philosopher' such as Derrida in terms of private rather than public uses: 'I think of the Nietzsche-Heidegger-Derrida assault on metaphysics as producing private satisfactions to people who are deeply involved with philosophy (and therefore, necessarily, with metaphysics) but not as politically consequential, except in a very indirect and long-term way' (1996d: 16; cf. 1996f: 46).

[29] See Rorty's *Debating the State of Philosophy* (1996a: 49) and of course his *Philosophy and Social Hope*. As part of this conversation with Habermas and Kolakowski, Rorty is further described as a 'philosopher of the "American Dream"' (Niznik & Sanders, 1996: 118) – a description that he moreover accepts (123; cf. 1998). However with his pragmatism being described here as a dream which affirms a certain hierarchy of values (e.g. the 'thesis about the priority of democracy to philosophy' (117)), it can no longer be ascertained to be of general use. That is, its potential utility depends upon certain preconditions being met (e.g. 117). Indeed, as Rorty admits at this debate: 'It seems to me that there is not much use for my brand of futuristic

desired practice of short-term reforms and compromises able to deal with relativism and contingency. However, this hope also assumes not only that certain kinds of consensus or conversation are of more use than others in building this ideal, but further that consensus or conversation is itself not only always possible but desirable. In other words, in being organised around the ideal it both assumes and desires, Rortian pragmatism instantiates itself in a similar way to one of Heidegger's fundamental metaphysical positions. That is, it sees itself as providing an answer – or the only reasonable answer – to an already assumed post-metaphysical relativism. This is thus a move that assumes the complete comprehension of both metaphysics itself and its succeeding post-metaphysical relativism. Indeed, it's a move which closely resembles those which Heidegger situates as constitutively metaphysical. Furthermore, as assuming – and answering – a post-metaphysical relativism, this move can be seen to covertly repeat the ploy of Lyotard's post-metaphysics and Deleuzoguattarian and Levinasian non-metaphysics whereby metaphysics is already dismissed as both closed and finished.

Caputo, on the other hand, although he too assumes a certain post-metaphysical relativism, does not seem to delimit his own post-metaphysical focus in quite the same way. First unfolding his 'contributions to' a minimalist 'poetics of obligation' in *Against Ethics*, Caputo sets out a post-metaphysical thinking of obligation that operates in the absence of the 'fine names' and 'capital letters' of the stories of both metaphysics and non-metaphysics:

> Obligation happens.
> That is where I must start, not because it is my *fundamentum inconcussum*, but because I do not know where else to begin. I begin wherever I am, in the

---

romanticism until you have established the standard institutions of constitutional democracy' (124). These 'standard institutions', however, themselves remain unquestioned (see Caputo, 2000: 84–124). Rorty's conception of hope is also critiqued by Ramón Santos in 'Richard Rorty's philosophy of social hope'.

midst of multiple obligations, in the plural and the lowercase, nothing capitalized or from on high. (Caputo, 1993a: 6).

However, although describing his thinking of obligation as a minimalism and thus other than metaphysics, Caputo is not concerned to legitimate this thinking *as* other than metaphysics. Stressing the double bind of most non- and post-metaphysical undertakings, he argues that '[w]e cannot just avoid or simply step outside metaphysics [...] That would be a hypermetaphysical undertaking'. Further, that the 'time has come to overcome the "overcoming of metaphysics," or to make it plain that the point of overcoming metaphysics is to "not-be-overcome-by-metaphysics"' (Caputo, 1993a: 220, 221; cf. 93). Far from aiming to be somehow independent from metaphysics, such a thinking perhaps instead simply supplements the stories of both metaphysics and the 'Post'. Caputo's minimalism, then, can only be a partial response.

So, while Lyotard's post-metaphysical aim was, for instance, to reconfigure the question of difference as relation – opening it towards justice and the unpresentable – Caputo's is simply to respond to the effects of difference. Rather than requiring any ideals of unconditional affirmation that are themselves paradoxically dependent on a move of totalising negation, Caputo situates his thinking of the possible effects of and responses to difference within a thinking of flesh and proper names. Flesh, itself irreducible, contingent and subject to disaster, thus marks the site of what can only be localised factical obligations and responses. Not so much prescribing but inscribed with obligations, the consideration of flesh in no way entails a reliance on any absolutes. Hence it is with this focus on flesh that Caputo perhaps resituates the project of the 'Post', insofar as minimalism and flesh can supplement the fabulous stories of *both* metaphysics and non- and post-metaphysical affirmations of absolute otherness or unrepresentability.

Overall, then, although starting with a similar affirmation of both relativism and its consequent minimalism to Rorty, Caputo's post-metaphysical thinking remains distinct from Rorty's. Rather than attempting to *answer* the problem of relativism, as does Rortian pragmatism, Caputo instead opens post-metaphysics as the possible functioning of the supplement. In other words, Caputo's focus on the supplement and on flesh *is* his reinterpretation of the problem and possibility of the 'Post'. After all, as delineated by Derrida, neither the supplement – being both surplus and substitute[30] – nor its functioning can be delimited or act to delimit. As Derrida puts it, the 'supplement is always the supplement of a supplement' (1976: 304). Hence, in being both exorbitant and parasitic, the supplement marks a necessarily open process. It exemplifies that notion of play (to borrow again from Derrida) that is unable to ground or configure itself with regard to any notions of origin or the proper.

Configured with reference to Derridean deconstruction, Caputo's minimalism unfolds not *as* any one fabulous story, but in response to all such stories. His post-metaphysics is constitutively unable to be configured in terms of either any desired ideal or organising principle, or any teleological or utopian hope, desire or dream. Constitutively localised and partial, a supplementary response, Caputo's thinking is not so much *of* but situated *within* difference. Inextricable thereby from the 'there is', and consequently inscribed only in terms of localised obligations and response, it remains 'without "why"' (1993a: 223). As such, rather than closing the 'Post' down, Caputo's aim is to keep it open – not via reference to any absolute, but as the functioning of a supplement. Aiming neither to answer nor overcome metaphysics in any of its guises, and also to avoid the violence that results from attempts by so-called fabulous stories to 'stop the slippage, to erase the ambiguity' (222), Caputo's minimalism reopens the project and possibility of a post-metaphysics.

Finally, the last post-metaphysical project I wish to consider here is of course that of Derridean deconstruction. Although often de-

---

30   Derrida describes the supplement as surplus and substitute in *Of Grammatology* (1976: 144–145).

scribed as a thinking of absolute excess and freeplay,[31] Derridean deconstruction must be considered rather as an exemplary thinking of the question of the in-between, the supplement and undecidability. Disclosed as both a plurality and indefinacy – and constituting neither a distinguishable system nor even quite a method[32] – Derrida is concerned to depict the instability and openness within all systems and methods presenting themselves as distinguishable and therefore delimited. As such deconstruction simply works to open limits and boundaries to contestation, disrupting both their operation and desired effects. It thus traces not only the effects of undecidability, but situates the ordeal of undecidability *as* the possibility – and promise – of justice and obligation.

It is consequently through this focus on undecidability that Derridean deconstruction can disrupt the type of affirmations typical of both metaphysical systems and much of the 'Post'. Specifically, as deconstruction demonstrates, many of these affirmations of identity and the Same, or of difference, excess or the other, are traced with a dream or desire for an absolute or ideal of some kind. Hence, in considering these systems, deconstruction stresses their undecidability and that of their presupposed boundaries and limits. However, in so doing, deconstruction functions not from any defined position exterior to these systems or structures, but from within. That is, it too functions through the logic of supplementarity, as both surplus and substitute. It is as supplement, then, that deconstruction questions all processes of delimitation and differentiation – including those by which deconstruction itself may be distinguished. More specifically Derrida con-

---

31   Derrida, despite the frequent misreading of him by his critics, is consistently careful to dissociate the 'undecidability' opened by deconstruction from 'indeterminacy' and 'free play', and to refute any suggestion that his deconstruction is an instantiation of absolute 'free play' or 'nihilism' (cf. Derrida, 1995a: 148–149; 1986a: 124; 1991c: 107–108).

32   As Derrida states in an interview: 'I have never had a "fundamental project." And "deconstructions," which I prefer to say in the plural, has doubtless never named a project, method, or system. Especially not a philosophical system' (1995c: 356).

figures deconstruction itself in terms of the structure of the *à venir* – it must remain always to come, instantiated only as a promise.[33]

Hence, it is through its disclosure and affirmation – as well as inhabitation – of undecidability that deconstruction opens a post-metaphysics that radicalises rather than simply repeats metaphysics. Insofar as deconstruction remains functionally open, a supplement of undecidability, it instantiates the possibility of an open way for not only the 'Post' but metaphysics. In these terms, metaphysical systems and structures have not so much been abandoned or overcome by deconstruction but reopened and brought back into question. In other words, deconstruction does not so much work to legitimate an escape from the perceived impasse of metaphysics, but resituates it – and by resituating it, it brings the very delineation of metaphysics *as* an impasse back into question. That is, if through deconstruction Derrida demonstrates that the closedness of metaphysics – its being at an impasse – is dependent upon a certain suppression (perhaps forgetting) of undecidability, then his affirmation or instantiation of such an undecidability *as deconstruction* entails the questioning of this so-called closure and impasse of metaphysics. Once undecidability and supplementarity are so instantiated, then *every* delimitation comes back into question, including that of metaphysics.

Sustaining its openness without desire for or recourse to strategies that would be metaphysical – in the delimitative (and delimited) sense designated earlier – Derridean deconstruction (along with Caputo's projection of minimalism) exemplifies a thinking that seems

---

33 This configuration of deconstruction through the structure of the promise – as always to come – initially seems to bear some resemblance to Lyotard's explication of the postmodern in terms of 'the paradox of the future (*post*) anterior (*modo*)' (Lyotard, 1984b: 81). However, although this Lyotardian future is disclosed as something absolutely new and other to the already given, it is nonetheless possible. The postmodern artist or writer is 'working without rules in order to formulate the rules of what *will have been done*' (81). The Derridean promise, on the other hand, is necessarily a structure of the impossible. This latter condition will be discussed in detail in subsequent chapters.

to be of an open post-metaphysics. They thus suggest the possibility of another way for the 'Post', where post-metaphysics is that questioning which instantiates itself as both a style of thinking informed by undecidability – rather than as or through affirmations of any absolute excess or obligation – and a response. As such, both of these projects bring the processes of delimitation and legitimation back into question, thereby questioning the very definition of metaphysics that has sponsored the very possibility of the 'Post'.

It is thus through these projects that are situated within whilst also instantiating undecidability, that we realise that post-metaphysical projects cannot *as such* be situated *beyond* metaphysics. However, although all the post-metaphysical projects discussed here display an interest in undecidability, it is via their instantiations of this undecidability that we can ascertain whether they sustain their relation with (non-) metaphysics as open or closed, undecidable or decidable. For example, in instantiating undecidability through the affirmation of the absolutely unpresentable, Lyotard's post-metaphysical thinking remains caught within the horizon of metaphysics. So too does Rorty's instantiation of pragmatism as an answer able to account for and legitimate a certain useful (and controllable) undecidability. Indeed, not only is undecidability effectively delimited through being *legitimated* as the condition for post-metaphysical thinking, but such legitimation further closes down the potentially open relation between the 'Post' and metaphysics. Caputo and Derrida, on the other hand, seem to work to sustain both undecidability and the open paradox of their relations with metaphysics. Through their situating of their own work neither simply beyond the workings of delimitation nor within the workings of excess or relativism, but rather within the very possibility of such a distinction, Derrida and Caputo question the designated, indeed prerequisite, closure of metaphysics. Further, this post-metaphysical thinking leaves open the issue of its relation to not only metaphysics, but to that questioning interpretation delineated by Heidegger as a counter-metaphysical thinking.

Consequently, it is this post-metaphysical sustaining of open-ness and undecidability that now needs to be reconsidered with regards to the bases of this work – the consideration of which will lead us once again back to Heidegger's projection of a counter-metaphysics. Hopefully further exploration of the relation sustained between Heidegger's counter-metaphysical thinking and the post-metaphysics delineated, for example, by Derrida and Caputo, will clarify the potential openness – and way – of a post-metaphysical ethical thinking perhaps able to escape the impasse of metaphysics. If so, we will need to look at this thinking again with regards to its instantiation of itself in the names of justice and obligation. In other words, we will need to ask whether this thinking is, in fact, the basis for an effective post-metaphysical ethics. It is this path, then, that now needs to come into question, and will be the focus of the chapters of the next section.

Part II

Thinking Post-Metaphysics and Ethics

5. The Guiding Question of Post-metaphysics

> It is certainly true that [...] questioning, in contrast to all scientific investigation, can never be accommodated within a determinate domain or activated within such an enclosed sphere. This questioning *must first form its own interrogative space* in the act of questioning, and only in the act of questioning is it capable of *keeping* this interrogative space *open*. (Heidegger, 1995b: 174).

As the previous section has shown, the driving force of my discussion of non- and post-metaphysics has been to consider several related factors – their ground, certain of their instantiations and a question. The ground is of course Heidegger's project of overcoming metaphysics along with metaphysics itself, and the question can perhaps be written as follows: 'What is post-metaphysics?' These two factors, even at this stage in my discussion, can be seen as indissociably related. They necessarily entail and involve each other. Until now, however, my discussion of the question of the 'Post' has primarily taken the form of tracing several of its instantiations. I have, in other words, focused on exploring possible answers to the 'What is?' Furthermore, as I have argued earlier (under other terminology), these suggested answers to the question 'What is post-metaphysics?' have fallen into two possible categories: unconditional excess and/or obligation.

Up to now, then, I have discussed these various instantiations with the aid of a series of complex distinctions and/or relations – between excess and obligation, between non- and post-metaphysical configurations and a certain metaphysics, and between non- and post-metaphysical projections themselves. This latter one also opens an even more problematic distinction between those functions affirming unconditionality over undecidability. However, what I want to suggest now is that each of these instantiations – when delineated in terms of their major proponents and propositions – effectively constructs what

Heidegger has called a 'fundamental position' with regard to the 'Post'. That is, they treat the question of the 'Post' by suggesting a possible answer to it. However, as Heidegger tells us, this actually has the effect of stifling the question as a question. Instead of the question being important, what takes over is the delineation of a response to it. For example, if the question 'What is post-metaphysics?' is seen as productive of an answer of 'unconditional excess', then the focus turns to delineating this 'excess' as unconditional. Now for Heidegger this is as interesting as carefully colouring between the lines in a colouring book. It might show how painstaking you are in not going over the edges, but that's about all. So, in contrast to this work, Heidegger also suggests the possibility of actually 'developing' the guiding question, of reawakening it as a question. And it is this possibility that he describes as the basis for a *counter*-metaphysics.[1] With this possibility as our starting point, then, the issue becomes whether any of these instantiations of the 'Post' does this work of developing and reawakening the question of the 'Post'.

Before, however, I engage with this possibility in any detail, I need to unpack these issues a little further. For instance, the idea that there is actually a similarity between many of the non- and post-metaphysical projects and what Heidegger describes as the fundamental positions of metaphysics needs much more clarification. Now where I think the similarity holds up is in the fact that both can be more concerned with generating an answer to the instigatory question than with thinking the question itself through. This similarity is not, of course, a new idea. I have already suggested that the major problem faced by and framing the 'Post' is its paradoxical relation with metaphysics. After all, as was argued in the previous chapter, instantiations of the 'Post' that dogmatically assert their difference from metaphysics rely on processes of differentiation through which their difference to metaphysics is overtly affirmed whilst being functionally negated or undermined. Their assertion of incommensurability is only made

---

1   For Heidegger's discussion of the possibility and condition of a counter movement in philosophy, see his *Nietzsche* Volume II (1991b: 171–172).

possible by moves that bring about a sort of totalising negation of metaphysics. Indeed, to make completely sure, they portray metaphysics as doubly closed. It is described both as a delimitative process, and an exhausted product.

In working from this description, much of the 'Post' thus seems to take as its guiding principle the idea that the overcoming of metaphysics must entail its abandonment. Hence much of the 'Post' seems to be informed by an ideal of instantiating another style of thinking which is somehow irreconcilable with and beyond metaphysics.[2] Such an ideal thus depends on this paradoxical affirmation of closure. However, as I have shown, such an affirmation itself remains irreconcilable with the directive around which the 'Post' seems to be structured, a directive that demands the affirmation only of openness. So the 'Post' is situated in an impasse. Its instantiation as an affirmation of openness and plurality depends upon its setting in place a delimitative boundary – a move that is itself constitutively metaphysical. In effect, metaphysics is the inescapable ground and horizon of those non- and post-metaphysical configurations that aim to instantiate a 'beyond' of metaphysics.

Now what I think all of this means is that, despite propaganda to the contrary, there *can* be no absolute boundary separating metaphysics from non- and post-metaphysics. Rather metaphysics and the question of the 'Post' configure and inform each other. Non- or post-metaphysical instantiations cannot be absolutely decontaminated of metaphysics, and, further, any desire for such purity is itself meta-

---

2 Caputo, of course, stresses the impossibility of this ideal when he discusses both Derrida's and his own thinking: 'For after all, we do not make the mistake of thinking *the* impossible is real, nor do we make the Kantian move of treating it as a foreseeable regulative ideal. The gift of which deconstruction dreams and by which it is impassioned will not be the object of a simple Kantian faith in a non-empirical ideal which exceeds the limits of experience and science, no future-present which establishes an ideal horizon of expectation that we simply seek after' (Caputo, 1997b: 170). Caputo also notes that 'Derrida's point is not to find a spot of simple exteriority to the circle [...] The point is not to escape the circle' (172).

physical. Metaphysics thus repeats its moves throughout non- and post-metaphysical instantiations, haunting them. Metaphysics, as Heidegger, Derrida and Caputo stress, can be neither absolutely renounced nor shaken off. 'We cannot just avoid or simply step outside metaphysics' (Caputo, 1993a: 220). Any such move is simply impossible.

Under Heidegger's logic, then, insofar as much of the 'Post' treats the question of its own possibility by repeating (rather than questioning) this impossible move, they effectively stifle this same possibility. They set out versions of what a 'Post' that is beyond metaphysics might look like. They assume their own situatedness 'beyond' as given and thereby pre-determine their possible configurations. This, as Heidegger emphasises, effectively stakes out the field of the 'Post'[3] or, to revisit my earlier analogy, sets out the lines within which instantiations of the 'Post' can colour. This focus thus leaves unquestioned the very conditions of possibility – the lines – required by such configurations. So, on this basis, it can be seen that my earlier attempt to explicate the 'Post' by delineating some of its concrete instantiations does not in fact enable me to actually consider the question of post-metaphysics *as such*. That is, *as* a question and *as* an effective possibility.

---

3   Heidegger's focus on developing the question (of 'being', of 'metaphysics') is grounded by his critique of the fundamental positions of metaphysics – that they are '*preoccupied with the answer*' (Heidegger, 1991b: 190). Such conditioning, he also says here, is manifested by an a priori 'staking out of the field and [...] establishment of the [desired] goal' (194).

Beginning Again with Heidegger

If, then, I can go no further for the moment in unfolding the 'Post' via outlining its various instantiations, the time has come to open another approach to our question of 'What is post-metaphysics?' Now one such possibility is, of course, that which Heidegger uses to counter the rigidity set in place by the fundamental positions of metaphysics. Specifically, he argues for the 'development' of the question '*out of* itself and *out beyond* itself', a move that entails the 'unfolding of a more original inquiry' (1991b: 206). Heidegger puts forward, then, this development as that questioning which 'does not crave an answer' (1991b: 192), and which rather sustains the openness of the question. Such an approach thus exemplifies a resistance to closure, and might thereby indicate a way to reopen both the conditions and possibilities of the 'Post' as questions. Going back to Heidegger might, in fact, indicate a way for the 'Post' out of its impasse.

Another reason for going back to Heidegger is that the question of the 'Post' (along with its various instantiations), as I've previously noted, must be seen as both grounded and activated by Heidegger's project of overcoming metaphysics and starting over again with thinking. In turn this suggests that the impasse reached by particular instantiations of the 'Post' may perhaps be the result of a too hasty reading of Heidegger's work. Hence, with these points in mind, it is time to look again at the overall trajectory of Heidegger's work. Certain of his disclosures might not only show us a way of developing the question and possibility of the 'Post', but also indicate a way of further explicating the point touched on earlier. That is, that the distinction between functions disclosing absolute unconditionality and undecidability might differentiate a potentially open post-metaphysical thinking from other closed instantiations of the 'Post'.

In other words, an interpretative repetition of Heidegger's project might show us a way of rethinking the 'Post' as a question. Once again, however, as was made manifest earlier, this is not to be attained through any systematic exegetic unfolding of Heidegger's project. Rather, my spiralling back to Heidegger's work will be undertaken solely with the aim of exploring his projected methods for reawakening questioning: his reformatting of interpretation and repetition.[4] As such, in interpreting Heidegger, I will primarily be focusing on the ways in which Heidegger argues that the processes of interpretation and repetition not only work to radicalise, but might themselves be opened and radicalised. Under this model the development of my guiding question 'What is post-metaphysics?' will entail a process of radicalised repetition and interpretation. Keeping in mind the necessary circularity of the hermeneutic process – where, as Heidegger stresses, the aim is not to still or dismiss this circularity but to 'come into it in the right way' (Heidegger, 1995a: 195) – such an approach thus demands the retrieval and reinterpretation of the grounds of the guiding question. Hence, my development of the question will mean a reconsideration of the first factor driving my initial engagement with the question. That is, the relation with metaphysics that informs Heidegger's project of overcoming metaphysics.

Now at this stage we already know that Heidegger's aim is not simply to rethink the Western philosophical tradition, but to project this thinking itself as a radicalising interpretation.[5] And we also know that Heidegger achieves these aims by linking the process of interpretation with the possibilities of *destruktion* and originary repetition. In this way, he describes it as that strategy of questioning and *destruktive* repetition which neither exemplifies nor entails any return to a 'point of departure' (1995b: 187), and which culminates in neither transcen-

---

4   We need to remember here that for Heidegger this or any methodology cannot be separated out from its focus: 'The *what* is itself defined by the *how*, and, reciprocally, the *how* by the *what*' (Heidegger, 1991b: 119).

5   This double project also grounds the aims of non- and post-metaphysical projects. However, as I have shown, most of these projects have ended up resembling the metaphysics they attempt to replace, Derrida's and Caputo's work perhaps being the exceptions. These latter projections, as potentially exemplifying an escape from the impasse of metaphysics, will be discussed in more detail below.

dence nor synthesis. In other words, it represents a positive circularity able to release those hitherto hidden counter-possibilities that had been stifled and closed over. Marking a non-absolute overcoming, Heidegger's interpretation is thus the radicalising of that which it repeats, the releasing through repetition all of the 'strangeness, darkness, [and] insecurity' (1987: 39) of non-originary beginnings.[6] Indeed, it is the uncanniness of the 'belonging-together' effected by that interpretation as repetition that 'remains genuinely opaque and questionable' (1991c: 105).

It is this description, then, of interpretation as a strange repetition and relatedness – the point where I left off my earlier engagement with Heidegger – that now needs further consideration. In seeing interpretation as that positive circularity and open questioning through which metaphysics can be overcome – or, better, *destruktively* repeated – Heidegger requires that interpretation itself remains a process which is constitutively open and genuinely questionable. Questioning that which it repeats, it must also question *its* own development as this openness. Indeed it is through its questioning of its own disclosures that interpretation exemplifies the development of the question and, thereby, Heidegger's counter-metaphysical thinking. With Heidegger's projection of the constitutive *dis*-closure of interpretation *being* his overcoming of metaphysics – note the inseparability of the 'what'

---

6   This 'strangeness' and 'insecurity' is exemplified by the ambiguity of those terms used by Heidegger to delineate interpretation. For instance, *Ereignis*, '~~Being~~', 'dif-ference', 'the mystery'. None of these terms can be presented or delimited into concepts as such. Rather, they perhaps function as what Heidegger glosses in his early work as 'formal indications'. 'Formal indication' is an anticipatory pre-figuring of a phenomenon, a 'methodological moment' which Heidegger argues – as clarified by Theodore Kisiel – 'stays clear of all arranging and clarifying', leaving 'everything undecided' (Kisiel, 1995: 170). Configured under this methodology, philosophising unfolds as 'a never-ending "way"' which is 'charged with the skepticism of radical questioning' (Kisiel, 1995: 235, 233; cf. Caputo, 1997b: 139–140). Although, as Kisiel notes, Heidegger was to drop this terminology, the methodology opened as 'formal indication' informs his radicalised and radicalising hermeneutics.

and the 'how' of his thinking here – these open processes of interpretation indicate an approach that might do several things. Firstly it might work to develop and sustain post-metaphysics as a question. Secondly it might suggest a way out of the impasse which enframes many of the contemporary instantiations of the 'Post'. And, thirdly, it might better explicate that open potentiality I see enabled through Derrida and Caputo's work.

Dis-closing Interpretation

So, projected as the combination of *destruktion*, originary repetition and questioning, interpretation is constitutively open. And, in releasing strangeness, darkness, and insecurity, it remains in question. As Heidegger suggests, it discloses – and is constituted as – an uncanny and sustained non-dialectical relatedness which 'renounces all claim to an[y] ultimate understanding' (Kisiel, 1995: 173). Now it is on this basis, then, that I suggest that we can perhaps see interpretation as informed by what I will call a 'logic of anxiety'. I should however stress here that by 'logic' I do not mean that logic which Heidegger associates with the methodological strategies and structures of onto-theological metaphysics.[7] Rather I mean a sort of non-ontotheologic and non-logocentric logic, a logic that operates as – and, indeed, constitutes – a minimal strategic formulation. And I want to suggest that in its affirmation of openness and insecurity rather than closure, such a logic is informed by what Heidegger portrays as the uncanny structure of anxiety.

So I want to suggest that it is this 'logic of anxiety' that sustains interpretation as both a questioning and the uncanny relation it

---

7   See, for example, Heidegger's consideration of logic in his 'Letter on "Humanism"'.

sets in place.[8] Now although the notion of anxiety was initially intro-duced by Heidegger to explicate the authentic potentiality of what he called the 'Being-in-the-world' of 'Da-sein',[9] the use of anxiety as a structure of open possibility is also present throughout Heidegger's later work, albeit alternatively described as *Ereignis, Gelassenheit* or dif-ference. Indeed I would go so far as to suggest that the structure I'm describing here as the 'logic of anxiety' actually enables Heidegger's overall counter-metaphysical project. So on this note I will use this section to trace the functioning and effects of this notion of anxiety firstly from its informing (and opening) of human *ek-sistence*, to its substantiation of interpretation as that open questioning which marks an uncanny relatedness. Indeed, as I will show, it is actually only from its opening of human existence into its potentiality, that anxiety can refigure interpretation as a non-coincidence and sustained holding in relation. Anxiety thus opens the possibility of sustained difference, of dif-ference, and, as I will demonstrate, it is in terms of this possibility that post-metaphysics itself may be developed and sustained *as* a question, and thereby perhaps escape the impasse of its instantiation by metaphysics.

Now, although my repeating of this logic of anxiety from a phenomenon informing human existence to a structure configuring Heidegger's actual counter-metaphysical project may seem arbitrary and unjustified, it is in fact a repetition of Heidegger's own procedure. Indeed, as far as Heidegger sees it, it is only through an 'analytic of

---

8   As structuring the possibility of an uncanny relation, the 'logic of anxiety' works to bring the 'unobtrusive "is"' (Heidegger, 1998: 362) of metaphysical essentialism into question. Heidegger further describes this relation and work with such terms as *Ereignis, Gelassenheit* and dif-ference. The possibility of a minimal 'logic' is also used by Derrida to explicate the im/possible thinking and uncanny relations described, for instance, in terms of undecidability, supplementarity, and différance.

9   I here follow Joan Stambaugh's translation of *Being and Time* (Heidegger, 1996). In her preface she notes that '[i]t was Heidegger's express wish that in future translations the word Da-sein should be hyphenated [...] a practice he himself instigated' (1996: xiv).

the Dasein' (1995a: 37) that the problematic of philosophical questioning *can* be reopened as a question. The possibility of interpretation is, in other words, profoundly phenomenological.[10] After all, as Heidegger stresses, philosophical questioning only has meaning for us as a 'human activity' (1995b: 19). Hence the horizon of the problematic of philosophical questioning *is* Da-sein itself *as* itself. We can recapitulate Heidegger's logic here as follows. First of all, recognising that the 'old established habits of thinking in the sense of metaphysical conceptions' have closed over the problematic of philosophical questioning, Heidegger sets out to reawaken that which has been stifled and forgotten, along with that which has 'always remained unasked' (1958: 79; 1969: 50). Secondly, arguing the need to develop this problematic '*still more* radically', to come into it in the right way, Heidegger suggests that the most fruitful ground for letting these 'ancient fundamental questions spring forth anew' is that of human existence itself.[11] Consequently, just as, for Heidegger, the phenomenological exploration – indeed, interpretation – of the question of human existence provides the grounds and tools for his rethinking of the Western philosophical tradition, so too this methodological strategy informs my argument that the logic of anxiety structures not only Da-sein but Heidegger's notion of a radicalised interpretation as a counter-metaphysics.

So, to follow Heidegger in this way, it seems that an explication of human existence might indeed exemplify a possible approach to the question of post-metaphysics. So far so good. However, what we now need to look at is how Heidegger actually reinterprets Da-sein

10   Or, as Heidegger also puts it, 'The phenomenology of Dasein is a *hermeneutic* in the primordial signification of this word, where it designates this business of interpreting' (1995a: 62).

11   See *The Fundamental Concepts of Metaphysics* (1995b: 359, 350). This is, of course, also the path followed by Levinas. Pursuing a related phenomenological path, Levinas also suggests that it is only through an analytic of human existence (as an inter-relatedness, Being-with) that thinking and being can be released from the restrictive framework of that ontological thinking which he delineates as a philosophy of the Same.

and philosophy through the structure of anxiety. How exactly does the logic of anxiety open Da-sein and philosophy to their inherent strangeness and insecurity? How, in other words, might it enable a post-metaphysics? To answer this we need to look again at Heidegger's early works – for instance, *Being and Time*, *The Fundamental Concepts of Metaphysics* and *The Basic Problems of Phenomenology* – where anxiety radicalises the 'being-thereness' of human existence.[12] It is only through the advent of states of mind like anxiety that Da-sein is able to conduct itself into its 'there' and grasp its beingness as its 'current factical potentiality-for-Being' (1995a: 355). Mediating Da-sein's existential possibilities and informing Da-sein's ways of being (its being-in-the-world and being-there), anxiety discloses Da-sein to itself.

Now what this actually means is that anxiety opens Da-sein to its undelimitable potentiality. Basically, as Heidegger stresses, it is 'essential to the basic constitution of Dasein that there is *constantly something still to be settled*' (1995a: 279). Specifically, anxiety marks the 'call of care' (actualised into 'conscience') through which Da-sein is brought into an uncanny and non-coincident relation with itself, or, better, with its ownmost potentiality. It mediates Da-sein's coming into relation with itself, its 'repetition' of itself *as* the being-thereness of its potentiality. Conditioned by anxiety, existing *as* the – its – disclosure of its own 'ecstatic'[13] non-coincidence, Da-sein is sustained as

---

12   Although I here take the possibilities of Da-sein's 'fundamental attunement' to be instantiated in terms of anxiety, Heidegger also considers 'profound boredom' to have a similar function in *The Fundamental Concepts of Metaphysics*. He also notes in *Being and Time* that other states of mind can have a similar function.

13   'The term "ecstatic" has nothing to do with ecstatic states of mind and the like. The common Greek expression ekstatikon means stepping-outside-self. It is affiliated with the term "existence." It is with this ecstatic character that we interpret existence' (Heidegger, 1982: 267). Heidegger also designates this ecstatic stepping-beyond as the non-absolute 'transcendence' constitutive of Da-sein's existence as Da-sein: 'the being that we ourselves in each case are, the Dasein, is the *transcendent*' (1982: 298; cf. 1998: 108). Further, stressing the open potentiality affirmed by Da-sein's ecstatic stepping-

a non-totalisable relation of non-synthesisable proximity with itself. And it is on this basis that anxiety also takes on a more familiar role: it traces Da-sein's fundamental unease in the face of its openness and non-coincidence.

Hence, in being attuned and structured through anxiety, Da-sein is constitutively open. It is unable to attain wholeness or sameness in or as itself.[14] Now what this means is that, as structured within the frame of Da-sein's being-in-the-world whilst also disclosive of this frame, anxiety shows Da-sein's being-thereness to be a strategic and uncanny relatedness that cannot be represented through the various onto-theologic stances of metaphysics.[15] That is, anxiety effects a making-strange. It lets resonate an uncanniness that cannot be made to settle into metaphysical delimitation. And, as such, it does not itself

---

beyond, Heidegger suggests in his 'Letter on "Humanism"' that Da-sein, in this mode, *ek-sists*.

14 Heidegger argues in *Being and Time* that, although Da-sein as instantiated through anxiety is constitutively open, Da-sein usually works to delimit this openness and close over its ownmost being as potentiality, to thus dim anxiety. This dimming down allows Da-sein to maintain itself in 'tranquillised familiarity', in a comfortable 'everyday lostness in the "they"' (Heidegger, 1995a: 234). In this way, Da-sein pretends to a reassuring, although inauthentic, wholeness.

15 This is not to say, however, that such (uncanny) structures or relations which cannot be delineated within those processes constituting metaphysical delimitation – processes which, for instance, instantiate such concepts as *logos* only in terms of the problem of the copula (see Heidegger, 1995b: 323; 1998: 362) – remain beyond interpretation. As Heidegger puts it, 'something can very well be inconceivable and never primarily disclosable through reason without thereby excluding a conceptual grasp of itself. On the contrary: if its inconceivability as such is indeed to be disclosed properly, it can only be by way of the appropriate conceptual interpretation – and that means pushing such interpretation to its very limits' (1998: 50). This pushing of interpretation to its 'very limits' exemplifies Heidegger's project of overcoming metaphysics. Further, the relation of radicalised interpretation to rational conceptualisation remains the focus of contemporary projects of non- and post-metaphysics. The relation that Heidegger here projects has however been, I suggest, rigidified into an absolute difference by many of these projects.

function as any ordering or regulatory principle. Rather it itself remains in question. After all, as Heidegger stresses, '[t]hat in the face of which one has anxiety is characterized by the fact that what threatens is *nowhere.*' The 'threat itself is indefinite' (1995a: 231, 232). So, once opened and non-coinciding, Da-sein can be neither delimited nor enframed. And this, as I've outlined earlier, has repercussions not only for any projection of Da-sein, but also affects the instantiations of philosophy.

That is, if, as Heidegger argues, the fundamental questions of philosophy can only be rethought through an explorative rethinking of Da-sein's being, then the disclosure of Da-sein effected by anxiety also opens the fundamental questions of philosophy. In other words, with Da-sein being the effective 'ground' of philosophical questioning, Da-sein's constitutive lack of totality also stresses the partiality and lack of closure of philosophical instantiations. And this is, of course, despite all the efforts of philosophical instantiations to substantiate their own all-encompassing completion. The logic of anxiety holds Da-sein, philosophy and interpretation open, preventing them from rigidifying back into any metaphysical frames. So it is in this way that interpretation, when seen as *destruktive* repetition, effects a releasement. On the one hand, it *is* the releasing and letting be of what Heidegger calls 'the nothing' and 'the mystery' – disclosures that, although not the same, indicate that which (both as relation *and* 'content') cannot be enframed metaphysically.[16] On the other hand, in enabling what Heidegger sees as an overcoming of metaphysics,

---

16   Heidegger talks about 'the nothing' in 'What is metaphysics?' (Heidegger, 1998: 89), and 'the mystery' in *Discourse on Thinking.* Overall he is careful not to explicate either 'the nothing' or 'the mystery' in the same way as he sees metaphysics delineating beings or events (see Heidegger, 1998: 89–90). Indeed explication itself – in terms of being a metaphysical process of re-presentation – is replaced by the processes constituting Heidegger's radicalised interpretation: 'if heretofore the reigning essence of thinking has been that transcendental-horizonal re-presenting from which releasement [...] releases itself; then thinking changes in [this] releasement from such re-presenting to waiting upon that-which-regions' (1966: 74).

interpretation marks a releasement into another way of thinking. And this is a way that remains constitutively open, unfolding as the questioning development of that which grounds it. Now although I have here distinguished these two possibilities of dis-closure and releasement, they are indissociably linked. For instance, they both start with a kind of 'failure' of metaphysics. First of all, 'all utterance of the "is" falls silent in the face of the nothing' (1998: 89; cf. 1966: 67–68). That is, 'the nothing' and 'the mystery' are only able to be instantiated through Heidegger's radicalised interpretation: as, that is, a non-representing thinking.[17] Secondly, it is these interpretative processes that enable a 'releasement towards things and [an] openness to the mystery', and thereby perhaps exemplify a 'path that will lead to a new ground and foundation' (1966: 56–57).

Hence the notion of interpretation that is enabled by this logic of anxiety itself brings about an overcoming or opening of metaphysical thinking. It is the figure of anxiety itself which grounds and configures Heidegger's projected interpretation of metaphysics as his overcoming of metaphysics. And it is also this configuration through anxiety that ensures that this overcoming is never absolute. It neither represents nor instantiates any absolute abandonment or rejection of metaphysics. Not only does Heidegger (and later Derrida and Caputo) reject any such supposition as grotesque, but this structure of interpretation simply does not allow it. Interpretation *is itself* a relation unfolding neither synthesis nor absolute difference. As Heidegger stresses, it is a relation that must remain (and *is*, through anxiety, *held*) open, reaching closure in neither Da-sein nor metaphysics, nor collapsing one into the other.[18] After all, if held solely in Da-sein, inter-

---

17   Heidegger discusses such thinking as a 'waiting' which 'lets re-presenting entirely alone'. Such thinking, he continues, can have 'no object' as such, it must rather remain open, an 'openness' (Heidegger, 1966: 68). He also here distinguishes between a 'calculative' thinking as representational and metaphysical, and what he terms 'meditative' thinking as a 'letting be'.

18   Silvia Benso has discussed this open relation as configuring an 'ontological ethics' which, she argues, is 'inspired – though never developed – by Heidegger' (Benso, 1994: 177). Although I disagree with Benso here, believing

pretation would collapse into humanism and/or anthropology whilst, if held in metaphysics, it would collapse into nihilism. As these two fundamental positions are of course two of the stances against which Heidegger projects his work, interpretation must be construed in terms of neither of them. Rather, as the opened dif-fering and belonging together sustained through the logic of anxiety, interpretation escapes the impasse of metaphysics. It neither effects nor requires the delimitation or closure of metaphysics, let alone the instantiation of an absolutely different language and thinking. It is instead simply the way through which Heidegger aims to 'reawaken an understanding for the meaning of this question' (1995a: 1).

Developing the Question out of its Impasse

> Here something else takes place than a mere restoration of metaphysics. Besides, there is no restoration which could merely accept something handed down to it, as someone gathers the apples which have fallen from the tree. Every restoration is an interpretation of metaphysics. Whoever believes that he [sic] can penetrate and follow metaphysical questions more clearly today in the entirety of their nature and history, should, since he likes to feel so superior as he moves in clear regions, consider one day

that Heidegger on the contrary does, to some extent, develop this relation, I agree with the point that in this relation the existence of the human being (its be-ing) cannot be absolutely differentiated from the question of metaphysics (as the question of Being): 'In the ontological ethics the human being and Being come close to each other in the communality of a same destiny, in such a way that in each, the other is at stake, and properly, there can be neither human being without Being nor Being without human being. But this can be said only in the reciprocity and cor-respondence of the relationship, and any absolutization on only one side – only the human being or only Being – proves to be meaningless' (Benso, 1994: 179–180). I will pick up Benso's own development of this relation as an 'ethics' later, suggesting that thought in such a way, Heidegger's project has important implications for the potentially open post-metaphysical work of Derrida and Caputo.

whence he has taken the light to enable him to see more clearly. It is hardly possible to surpass the grotesqueness of proclaiming my attempts at think-ing as smashing metaphysics to bits and of sojourning at the same time, with the help of those attempts, on paths of thinking and in conceptions which have been derived – I do not say, to which one is indebted – from that alleged demolition. (Heidegger, 1958: 91, 93).

So we can see that for Heidegger every attempt at directly overcoming or abandoning metaphysics – at trying to cross the line one way or another – will circle back into metaphysics, reaching an impasse in its attempts. Indeed, he asks us to consider our options if 'even the lan-guage of metaphysics and metaphysics itself [...] *as* metaphysics, formed that barrier which forbids a crossing over of the line'.[19] Given then that any direct attempt of 'smashing metaphysics to bits' merely brings about a replacement of metaphysics, Heidegger argues that it is only by way of a method of radical repetition and interpretation that metaphysics *can* be opened and overcome.

Heidegger's notion of interpretation, then, enables and unfolds *as* this questioning of metaphysics – a questioning which, making no attempt to absolutely escape metaphysics, opens it to its dif-ference and potentiality. Interpretation thus works to reawaken metaphysics from its 'hardened tradition' (Heidegger, 1995a: 44). It aims to bring metaphysics 'into the open, and out of the framework and boundary posts of contrived disciplines' and its various fundamental positions (1995b: 359). However, I repeat here again that interpretation effects this transformation not by instigating any absolutely new beginning but, rather, by affirming the 'circular character of philosophical thought' (1995b: 187). Even when Heidegger does seem to be calling for another style of thinking,[20] this other thinking is disclosed through a 'leap' or 'step' that can only ever be prepared for.

---

19   Heidegger makes this claim in *The Question of Being* (1958: 71). More specifically, he directs this question to Ernst Jünger, to whom the text *The Question of Being* is addressed.

20   Although Heidegger argues the impossibility of getting absolutely outside or beyond metaphysics and metaphysical language – the point I am here stressing – he does suggest and prepare for the possibility of another style of

So it is on this basis that Heidegger's projection of anxiety would seem to provide a possible point of entry to the questions of both metaphysics and the 'Post'. Traced from the analytic of Da-sein, but not reducible to Da-sein, anxiety thus informs the relation of difference that Heidegger sees as operating between Da-sein and metaphysics – a relation which, in turn, reopens (post-) metaphysics *as* a question. That is, the logic of anxiety shows Heidegger's project of interpretation to be an *originary* repetition. Far from a simple repetition of what has been 'handed down' (Heidegger, 1958: 91; cf. 1995a: 437–438), this interpretation has its 'roots [...] essentially in the future' (1995a: 438). Interpretation thus repeats and thereby develops metaphysics, bringing it into (its) question and its potentiality. Under Heidegger's phenomenological framework, the constrained potentiality of metaphysics – that potentiality which has been hitherto delimitatively configured in terms of various fundamental metaphysical positions, and then further closed off via certain instantiations of non- and post-metaphysical thinking – *can* be opened. Further, as remarked earlier, Heidegger only ever projects his work as *being on the way* towards opening a system of thinking which is constitutively counter-metaphysical:

> But above all, the thinking in question remains unassuming, because its task is only of a preparatory, not of a founding character. It is content with awakening a readiness in man [sic] for a possibility whose contour remains obscure, whose coming remains uncertain. (Heidegger, 1993: 436).

---

thinking. Such thinking, he suggests, is best prepared for through a 'meditative' 'listening', 'waiting' and a certain 'silence' (e.g. Heidegger, 1966; 1971a; cf. 1995a: 207–208). This thinking, however, as previously noted, although differentiated from a certain metaphysical thinking, does not entail an absolute rejection of metaphysics. Rather, it is prepared by an open re-interpretation or development of the grounds of metaphysics. It repeats the grounds of metaphysics dif-ferently: 'The countermovement must in its necessity arise from such an original experience, and it must also remain rooted in such an experience' (1991b: 172; cf. 1975: 92).

Instantiated thereby as both an opened potentiality and the opening of this potentiality, I thus argue that Heidegger's radicalising of interpretation develops the question of metaphysics '*out of* itself and *out beyond* itself' (1991b: 206) and into, in fact, the potentiality of post-metaphysics.

Considered in this way, then, Heidegger's development of a post-metaphysics in no way resembles those contemporary instantiations that simply 'treat' the question 'What is post-metaphysics?' Such configurations – inclusive of Deleuze (and Guattari)'s, Levinas's, Foucault's, Lyotard's and Rorty's work – in their acceptance of the strategic delimitation or totalising negation of metaphysics, end in the vicious circling of an impasse. The possibility for the development of the question as delineated by Heidegger, on the other hand, is configured as the opened potentiality and process of that interpretation which remains in and as a question. So developed, the question of post-metaphysics remains a question of undecidability. It is here, then, within this region of sustained dif-ference disclosed by Heidegger as potentiality and undecidability, that I suggest that the work of Derrida and Caputo is situated. That is, both Derrida and Caputo focus on repeating not the impasse of metaphysics but rather that process of disclosure which Heidegger delineates as (and through) an anxiety informed interpretation. Derrida and Caputo, basing their work upon this Heideggerian possibility, in effect repeat Heidegger.

Developing Post-metaphysics: Derrida and Caputo

> [T]he most rigorous deconstructions have never claimed to be [...] possible. And I would say that deconstruction loses nothing from admitting that it is impossible [...] For a deconstructive operation *possibility* would rather be the danger, the danger of becoming an available set of rule-governed procedures, methods, accessible approaches. The interest of deconstruction, of such force and desire as it may have, is a certain experience of the impossible. (Derrida, 1989c: 36).

As previously shown, many of the contemporary instantiations of a non- or post-metaphysics, rest upon that delimitation of their other – that is, metaphysics – which results from a too hasty interpretation and closure of both Heidegger's project and metaphysics itself. That is to say, although they tend to base their affirmations of a movement beyond metaphysics in that Heideggerian rhetoric concerning the end and overcoming of metaphysics, they seem to forget that Heidegger's projected overcoming of metaphysics in no way entails (or, indeed, can entail) its absolute abandonment. Consequently, many of these instantiations focused on delineating a non- or post-metaphysics *as such*, circle back into metaphysics. And, as such, they exemplify both Heidegger's argument concerning the circular character of philosophy, and his stress on the impossibility of ever escaping this circularity. That is, their very constitution and functioning as a desired non- or post-metaphysical thinking which nonetheless instantiates metaphysics, substantiates Heidegger's argument that it is impossible to get outside of metaphysical thinking and language.

However, whilst metaphysics seems to inescapably condition all non- and post-metaphysical thinking – both haunting it and bringing it to an impasse – the work of both Derrida and Caputo assumes a different relation to this metaphysics than tends to be found structuring other configurations of the 'Post'. Specifically, Derrida and Caputo outline a post-metaphysical thinking that is constitutively open, working to develop rather than actually answer the question 'What is post-metaphysics?' Consequently, both Derrida and Caputo 'repeat' (in Heidegger's radicalised sense) certain of Heidegger's interpretative disclosures, and thereby escape the metaphysical impasse that I have argued repeats in other non- and post-metaphysical instantiations. This 'repetition', then, suggests the presence of an open relation between Heidegger's projection of a counter-metaphysical thinking and this subsequent work by Derrida and Caputo. Indeed, Derrida's and Caputo's delineations of a post-metaphysical potentiality *are* an 'interpretative repetition' of Heidegger's project. As I have already stressed, in my discussion of the similar relation that I suggest holds between Heidegger's project and metaphysics, within the conditions of such a relation neither Derrida nor Caputo are interested in simply repeating Heidegger (or metaphysics). They are not aiming to simply take up what has been handed down.[21] Rather, their focus could perhaps be seen as a wanting to sustain that open potentiality which Heidegger discloses. In this way, Derrida and Caputo (along with Heidegger) set out their thinking as the sustained questioning of that which they 'repeat'. Such thinking, then, rather than instantiating or repeating any sort of fundamental position, functions through – and indeed instantiates – a logic of supplementarity and undecidability, of anxiety.

At this point, then, we can see Derrida's and Caputo's post-metaphysical thinking as the development of the question 'What is post-metaphysics?' I now intend to pick up my discussion of Derrida's and Caputo's projections both where it was left off at the finish of the previous chapter – that is, as instantiating a logic of supplementarity and undecidability – and as the radical repetition and interpretation of certain of Heidegger's projected disclosures. I also want to suggest that it is from this ground that Derrida and Caputo can both perhaps be seen to project a path out of the impasse of metaphysics.[22] However these paths, as with Heidegger's, must remain potentiality only, *à venir*. Indeed if, as I argue, these paths are enabled by a logic of anxiety, they can effect neither any actual delineation nor affirmation of a path out of metaphysics. Rather they can only exemplify a bringing into question of all paths, a disclosure of their supplementarity and unde-

---

21   Indeed, as Caputo so aptly puts it, he (along with Derrida) is interested in thinking and reading Heidegger against himself, in configuring another Heidegger. For instance, the Heidegger Caputo works to portray is a Heidegger who has Derrida whispering in his ear (Caputo, 1987: 5), a 'demythologized' Heidegger (Caputo, 1993b: 7; cf. 1993a: 227).

22   I must stress that although I suggest that the work of both Derrida and Caputo escapes the impasse of metaphysics, their projected paths are not of course fully conflatable. They neither follow nor project the same path. Once again this is a repetition of Heidegger, who argues that his work traced a series of non-progressive and non-conflatable paths or ways.

cidability. As such, supplementing the fabulous stories of *both* metaphysics and the 'Post' and, further, of the Heideggerian project, these paths focus on keeping these stories (and any others) as loose and free as possible. In Caputo's terms, these paths mark 'an operation aimed at appreciating that tenuous and delicate situation of judgment which is addressed by the name "undecidability"' (Caputo, 1993a: 3).

What I want to suggest here, then, is that unlike other instantiations of the 'Post', Derrida and Caputo write out of – and, indeed, repeat – that space, potentiality and logic which I have argued is opened by Heidegger. That is to say, both Derrida and Caputo work from within the horizon of the Heideggerian problematic, repeating the Heideggerian 'logic of anxiety', and it is via this logic that they seem able to keep a certain thinking of post-metaphysics open and loose.[23] Used by Heidegger to radicalise ideas of relation and interpretation, this logic of anxiety, when repeated by Derrida and Caputo, basically structures what Derrida terms in recent work the 'ordeal of the undecidable' (Derrida, 1992a: 24). That is, the logic of anxiety unfolds that ordeal wherein the same is unable to remain as and in itself to the exclusion of an/y other, and wherein any delineation of ab-

---

23   As is Heidegger, Derrida is concerned to try and not let the concepts he uses stabilise into fundamental metaphysical positions. Along with arguing that deconstruction itself can only be a sustained questioning of method – 'a complicated discourse on the concept of method' (Derrida, 1995c: 187) – Derrida instantiates his terms as the invoking of a certain in-betweenness and undecidability, a space which exceeds any dialectical opposition or synthesis. Furthermore, his terms themselves are constitutively unable to be either positively defined or presented. Each one is 'an aconceptual concept or another kind of concept, heterogeneous to the philosophical concept of the concept, a "concept" that marks both the possibility and the limit of all idealization and hence of all conceptualization' (Derrida, 1995a: 118; cf. 1982b). Caputo also works with terms that escape all but a minimal conceptual delimitation. For instance, as he makes clear in his *Against Ethics*, the undecidability of 'flesh' cannot be instantiated through the representative discourse of metaphysics – although, of course, it also cannot be instantiated absolutely outside of it. 'Flesh', rather, can only be instantiated (and respected) through a discourse that attains to neither closure nor absolute transcendence nor synthesis.

solute self-coincidence is seen to be only a metaphysical dream or desire. This logic of anxiety thus traces the opening of the same, showing it to be always and already contaminated by the other. Such a logic thus results not in any essentialist decidability, but in an irrecusable undecidability.

As the instantiation – or instantiated effect – of this logic of anxiety, undecidability restructures (or deconstructs) the notions and functions of delimitation and enframing. Informed by the non-coincidence of the same and its openness to an/y other, undecidability keeps boundaries open and porous both ways. That is, although a rupture of the same, undecidability nonetheless also refrains from deciding *for* the other – a move which would, in effect, itself affirm the other as decidable, *as Other*, and thereby constrain undecidability. Hence, as distinct from any Levinasian formulation, Derrida – having stressed the irrecusable openness of the same – also stresses the constitutive undecidability of the other. As he writes in 'Sauf le nom', *'tout autre est tout autre'*.[24] Exemplary of the functioning of this 'logic of anxiety', this phrase marks the structure of an impasse: 'the ordeal of the undecidable [...] is never past or passed, it is not a surmounted or sublated (*aufgehoben*) moment'.[25] However, unlike that impasse which is repeated in other non- and post-metaphysical configurations – that is, that vicious circling set in motion by a strategy of totalising negation, of looking for that 'spot of simple exteriority to the circle' (Caputo, 1997b: 172), and which simply marks the inescapability of metaphysics – the impasse of undecidability impassions deconstruction. It instantiates 'a passion for the impossible' (1997b: xix).

---

24   For Derrida's discussion of this phrase, see *On the Name* (1995b: 76). As previously mentioned, this formula also becomes one of the mainstays of Caputo's discussions of Derridean deconstruction and, further, grounds the orientation of much of Caputo's own most recent work. He has extensively discussed this phrase in *The Prayers and Tears of Jacques Derrida*.

25   See Derrida's 'Force of law' (1992a: 24). This is also Caputo's interest in the undecidable. Indeed regarding Derridean deconstruction, Caputo delineates it as 'a passion and a prayer for the impossible' (Caputo, 1997b: xx).

For Derrida and Caputo, then, far from indicating any collapse, this impasse traces the very im/possibility of the 'Post'. Far from closing everything down, it opens a post-metaphysical thinking of opened potentiality. Far from trying to find a way of breaking the impasse, then, of getting beyond or outside of it, both Derrida and Caputo stress the necessity of remaining informed by it. Hence, rather than configuring this impasse through the delimitative logic of metaphysics, Derrida and Caputo instantiate it through the Heideggerian logic of anxiety and, further, as a call for justice.[26] That is, both Derrida and Caputo see this sustained undecidability as an irrecusable call for justice – for what they further stress can only be a miscegenated and anxious 'jewgreek' justice.[27] Now, very briefly, this is an aporetic, undecidable and im/possible justice. It can never become complacent or beyond question. Indeed, as I've mentioned already, both Derrida and Caputo stress as essential its structural eventality as 'ordeal' and as 'impossible'.

It is under this logic, then, that the undecidability instantiated by Derrida and Caputo needs to be seen as a deconstructive repetition of the Heideggerian projection of interpretation. Indeed, for both Derrida and Caputo, projections of a post-metaphysical potentiality can only be instantiated in terms of the relations of anxiety, non-coincidence and undecidability that Heidegger opens. Indeed, as never completely over, this 'ordeal of the undecidable' unfolds deconstruction *as* the potentiality and question of post-metaphysics. Hence it is this possibility that will be the focus of the following chapter. However, it must be stressed again that although Derrida's and Caputo's

---

26   As Derrida writes, 'the condition of possibility of deconstruction is a call for justice' (Derrida, 1997b: 16).
27   Derrida uses this term in his discussion of Levinas's project in 'Violence and metaphysics' (Derrida, 1978b: 153), and a similar one – 'Judaeo-Greek' – in his 'Force of Law' (1992a: 56). Caputo, in his turn, uses it throughout his work as enabling and characterising the possibility of a minimally metaphysical justice. 'Jewgreek' justice, as Caputo glosses it, is the possibility of a miscegenated and non-originary justice that encompasses both the aporetic tension of the im/possible, and the facticity of 'flesh'.

instantiations – or, rather, interpretations – of Heidegger's counter metaphysical thinking as the possibility of jewgreek justice and unde-cidability, are both configured and held open through a certain repeti-tion of this 'logic of anxiety', they nonetheless remain non-conflatable, non-coinciding, in relations of difference. In other words, it is *as such* that these instantiations need now to be mapped – that is, in difference and in dialogue. And it is *as such* that we need to have a look at what exactly they might be able to do as a post-metaphysics.

6.   Repetitions

In accordance with what is only ostensibly a paradox, *this particular* unde-cidable opens the field of decision or of decidability. It calls for decision in the order of ethical-political responsibility. It is even its necessary condi-tion. A decision can only come into being in a space that exceeds the calcu-lable program that would destroy all responsibility by transforming it into a programmable effect of determinate causes. There can be no moral or po-litical responsibility without this trial and this passage by way of the unde-cidable. Even if a decision seems to take only a second and not to be pre-ceded by any deliberation, it is structured by this *experience and experiment of the undecidable.* (Derrida, 1995a: 116).

Let us review where we are so far. I have argued that Derrida's and Caputo's post-metaphysical thinking is an open reading or repetition of Heidegger's counter-metaphysical project. Also that, when viewed through the lens of Heidegger's 'logic of anxiety', the 'Post' forms a pattern where a post-metaphysics might be seen as a workable possi-bility. Certainly it would seem evident that when viewed through this lens, such a 'Post' can only mark a question – or a questioning – with no determinate answer, whereas other versions examined have been seen to founder in paradox by trying to assert or justify an actual an-swer to the question 'What is post-metaphysics?' So the 'Post', then, might benefit from remaining undecidable. To put this another way, perhaps the '*experience and experiment*' of undecidability marks the potentiality for a post-metaphysics that is neither constrained nor col-lapsed by the inescapability of metaphysics. And in this case, unde-cidability could be seen as both an interpretation of a certain Heideg-gerian thinking and methodology – his 'logic of anxiety' – and the potential opening of a post-metaphysics that might not give in to para-dox.

At this stage, however, we still need to flesh out these claims. Specifically I need to clarify just how this work of Derrida and Caputo exemplifies a development – in the sense that Heidegger applauds – of the question of post-metaphysics, and thereby exemplifies an escape from the impasse reached by other configurations of the 'Post'. Finally I will look at some of the differences between Derrida's and Caputo's work. Far from being the same, their respective instantiations should be seen as inter-relating but non-coinciding ways aimed at opening and developing the potentiality of a post-metaphysics.

Now to best situate this discussion, perhaps a brief recap is in order. Basically, as discussed in the previous chapter, the 'logic of anxiety' that I see as enabling Heidegger's projected radicalising of interpretation, is that logic which both projects and informs what I've described as an essential non-coincidence. This non-coincidence, in turn, exemplifies a relation that is neither a synthesis nor an appropriation. Rather, it is a relation of difference through which is sustained all of the strangeness and uncanniness of a lack of coincidence. The 'logic of anxiety' is thus a logic of difference – not of difference as absolute separation, but as that uncanny non-coincidence which is nonetheless a sustained holding in relation. Further we know that it is this uncanny holding in relation that Heidegger uses *as* the basis for his radicalised thinking and methodology. Interpretation, in other words, marks a repetition that radicalises that which is repeated, where the repetition and what is being repeated do not coincide.

So it is via this logic that Heidegger is able to rethink the processes constitutive of metaphysical (that is, onto-theological) systems. Specifically, it is this logic that grounds and enables, in the first instance, all of Heidegger's controversial work regarding his own *destruktive* repetitions of the history of metaphysics.[1] For example, his

---

1   For examples of Heidegger's readings of the history of metaphysics, see his various discussions of Nietzsche and Hegel. Much of this work by Heidegger, as Joanna Hodge explicates, exemplifies fairly violent re-readings of those philosophers and their fundamental positions which Heidegger considers to constitute the closed history and tradition of onto-theology: 'His readings demonstrate the contribution of these previous thinkers, then show their limitations and then seek to break elements of their work free to be used in the [his] new formation' (Hodge, 1995: 149). David Wood also dis-

interpretations of this history actually repeat it differently, opening it up to what he sees as its unthought. Secondly, I believe that this logic and method makes possible another way of reading Heideggerian interpretation. Specifically, we can see it as instantiating either the possibility for a post-metaphysical ethics or ethical strategy, or at least as indicating a certain ethical commitment towards openness and difference. This latter possibility suggested by such terms as dif-ference and *Gelassenheit*.[2]

My next step is clear. I will argue that it is just this notion of interpretation as perhaps suggestive of an ethics that has been taken up and repeated by Derrida and Caputo. I also believe that it is this Heideggerian notion of interpretation which, when retrieved and repeated through the work of Derrida and Caputo, can actually configure post-metaphysics as an ethics. However, before I move on to explore this in detail, I do need to further spell out certain aspects of the relations that I have suggested hold firstly between Heidegger and Derrida and Caputo, and secondly between Heidegger and the other configurations of the 'Post' I have discussed. More specifically, given that these relations do take the form of repetitions, we need to look again at Heidegger's distinction between two types of repetition. I should also note

---

cusses Heidegger's notion and use of repetition in his *Thinking after Heidegger*.

2   Caputo recognises this possible Heideggerian ethical commitment when he states at the beginning of his *Against Ethics* that he has 'always made it my business to defend ethics, a more originary ethics, an ethics of *Gelassenheit* and letting be, an ethics of dissemination, a veritable postmodern ethics' (Caputo, 1993a: 1). This statement prefaces his sustained attempt to resist any instantiation of 'originary ethics' and to rather disseminate and affirm a minimalist deconstructive ethical possibility that he characterises as a 'poetics of obligation'. Some other considerations of the ethical possibilities of Heidegger's thought include Lawrence Hatab's 'Ethics and finitude: Heideggerian contributions to moral philosophy', Krzysztof Ziarek's 'The ethos of everydayness: Heidegger on poetry and language', Charles Scott's *The Question of Ethics: Nietzsche, Foucault, Heidegger*, and John McCumber's *Metaphysics and Oppression: Heidegger's Challenge to Western Philosophy*.

that not only is this a distinction which Heidegger himself uses, but it is that by which I have differentiated between the post-metaphysics projected by Derrida and Caputo and those other non- and post-metaphysical configurations. To summarise: for Heidegger in *Being and Time* repetition has two aspects or possibilities – as, of course, do history and tradition,[3] and Da-sein itself. On the one hand, just as it is understood in everyday usage, repetition is simply the taking up or reinstating of that which has been passed down, without question. However, on the other hand, and more radically, it can also be seen as a process of *destruktive* interpretation, a retrieval that for Heidegger is also necessarily a questioning. It is, of course, with the possibilities opened by this latter notion of repetition that I am primarily concerned, as indeed are Derrida and Caputo.

So Derrida and Caputo repeat Heidegger in this second sense. It is thus a repetition that, although certainly taking up certain of his disclosures, also submits them to ongoing critical interrogation.[4] On the other hand, although I have suggested earlier that other non- and post-metaphysical configurations of the 'Post' also repeat Heidegger's thoughts of a projected 'end' to and 'overcoming' of metaphysics,

---

3   This doubledness of history is considered with reference to Derrida's (and Heidegger's and Husserl's) work by, for instance, Claire Colebrook in 'The future-to-come: Derrida and the ethics of historicity'. Here Colebrook explains how history is instantiated not only as a closed (and capitalised) 'History', but as an 'errant historicity' (1998: 358). Colebrook then suggests not only that 'the contamination of philosophy's closed History by this errant historicity might [...] lead us beyond the putative closure of Western metaphysics', but that 'an attempt to move beyond the [closed] historical motif might provide quite new ethical horizons' (358, 359).

4   Both Derrida's and Caputo's interrogations of Heidegger are ongoing processes as can be evidenced in their changing of their interpretations. See, for example, Caputo's brief discussion of his changing of focus and interpretation with regard to Heidegger's work (Caputo, 1993b: 1–2). For Derrida, Heidegger's work not only cannot be passed over, but remains a source of open questions (Derrida, 1989b: 7). The inescapability of Heidegger is also acknowledged by Edith Wyschogrod in her essay 'Without why, without whom: thinking otherwise with John D. Caputo' in *A Passion for the Impossible: John D. Caputo in Focus* (2003: 301–302).

they repeat this possibility in the former – closed – sense. In fact, as I have argued, these other configurations seem to simply accept this 'end' as their starting point and aim to describe some other region or form of thinking which is to be somehow independent of metaphysics. As a result such configurations seem unable to escape that paradox or impasse which arises when it becomes clear that metaphysics is itself inescapable. To describe these points another way, I suggest that these latter configurations rest upon a reading of Heidegger that is focused solely upon repeating the 'what' of his work, excluding the 'how'. Now this is a strategy of delimitation that Heidegger sees as not only exemplary of the tradition of metaphysics as a system or process aiming for some closure, but a grave mistake.[5] Derrida and Caputo work to repeat, on the contrary, Heidegger's strategic entwining of the 'what' and the 'how'.

Overall, then, in their questioning repetition of that methodology which Heidegger instantiates, Derrida and Caputo aim to keep this methodology (and indeed Heidegger) open. And it is this strategy that I believe enables their development of that ethical potentiality which, although I argue is opened, is perhaps never fully developed by Heidegger. One quick aside with regards to this point. Joanna Hodge suggests that this lack of development might be due to Heidegger's focus on two not quite equivalent projects. Of these, as she clarifies, one is his explication of the history of metaphysics as a closed tradition, whilst the other is his attempt to develop a 'new' – albeit never absolutely new by his own clarification – mode of thinking. Now for Hodge these projects are, although indissociable, developed around two differing commitments. The first of these is of course to 'truth', to 'telling it how it is', and is thereby metaphysical; whilst the second marks an ethical commitment to 'an open-ended project of thinking'.[6]

Now it is possible to read these indissociable but contrasting commitments as giving rise to a certain ambiguity or ambivalence

---

5   Heidegger stresses the inseparability of the 'what' and 'how' of thinking in
     the second volume of his extensive discussion of Nietzsche (1991b: 119)
6   Joanna Hodge makes this claim in *Heidegger and Ethics* (1995: 150, 149).

within Heidegger's work.[7] And indeed it is perhaps on the basis of this ambiguity that Derrida and Caputo both stress the non-coincidence of the ethical potentiality disclosed by Heidegger's methodology of *de-struktive* interpretation with what they consider Heidegger's delimiting – that is, metaphysical – commitment to the 'proper', his desired revealing of originary truth. On my part, although I agree with this suggestion regarding Heidegger's doubled focus, I argue that if the inextricability of the 'what' and 'how' of his thinking is taken into account, then he can be seen overall to be opening and projecting a method of interpretation that is, at least potentially, informed by an ethical commitment. On this basis, one way that we can look at what Derrida and Caputo do in their interpretations of Heidegger is to say that they open and sustain this ethical commitment. They, in other words, want to 'demythologise' Heidegger,[8] and it is this move that I believe shows us how Heideggerian interpretation can point towards a post-metaphysical potentiality which perhaps escapes the vicious circling of metaphysics seen as impasse.

The Instantiating of Undecidability

– What would a path be without aporia? Would there be a way [*voie*] without what clears the way there where the way is not opened, whether it is blocked or still buried in the nonway? I cannot think the notion of the way without the necessity of deciding there where the decision seems impossi-

---

7   This ambiguity is also marked by Simon Critchley who writes: 'Heidegger's thinking moves relentlessly between two borders, the metaphysical and the nonmetaphysical, alternately striking both edges and producing a dissonant resonance' (Critchley, 1993: 94).

8   Caputo comments in a note to his *Demythologizing Heidegger* that at the same time that his work was appearing, Thomas Sheehan concluded a piece for *The New York Review of Books* – 'Heidegger and the Nazis' (June 16, 1988: 38–47) – saying that what was needed was 'not to stop reading Heidegger but to start demythologising him' (cited in Caputo, 1993b: 215n4).

ble. Nor can I think the decision and thus the responsibility there where the decision is already possible and programmable. And would one speak, could one only speak of this thing? Would there be a voice [*voix*] for that? A name? (Derrida, 1995b: 83).

To assess these possibilities, we need to return to how Derrida and Caputo see them as being instantiated. We already know that they configure the ethical potentiality of Heideggerian interpretation as an irrecusable undecidability, where undecidability marks a repeated non-coincidence, the interruption of every closed circularity or exchange. We do however also need to keep in mind that undecidability does not mean for them illogic or indeterminacy, and that it does not necessarily lead to or affirm any absolute free play or relativism.[9] Further it is configured by them both not as any thinking or discourse that is somehow absolutely other or oppositional to that essential decidability which configures a certain metaphysics. After all, a thinking of undecidability does not itself 'exist somewhere, pure, proper, self-identical'.[10] Rather it marks the condition and consequence of the deconstructive soliciting of self-affirming and self-regulating notions of identity. In other words, undecidability is simply the disclosure of the impossibility of any absolute or clear-cut decidability.

---

9   As discussed previously, Derrida, despite the frequent mis-readings of him by his critics, is consistently careful to dissociate undecidability from indeterminacy and free play and to refute any suggestion that his deconstruction is an instantiation of absolute free play or nihilism (see Derrida, 1995a: 148–149; 1986a: 124; 1991c: 107–108). On a related theme, for an example of Heidegger's responses to charges of 'irresponsible and destructive' nihilism and irrationalism, see his 'Letter on "Humanism"' (Heidegger, 1998: 263–276).

10   Derrida makes this claim for deconstruction in *Limited Inc.* (1995a: 141). Appropriating a strategy of negative theology, Derrida is generally far more explicit in explicating what deconstruction is not as compared to what it is or might be. This is not to say, however, that deconstruction *is* a negative theology, a point that Caputo persuasively argues in *The Prayers and Tears of Jacques Derrida* (e.g. Caputo, 1997b: 1–3, 6–12). For another interesting discussion of Derrida's attitudes towards negative theology, see Harold Coward's *Derrida and Negative Theology*.

With these provisos, then, it is quite clear that undecidability constitutes the repetition and development of Heidegger's 'logic of anxiety'. As we remember, this showed us how relations are not at all a clear-cut link between one thing and another, but how they rather encompass the uncanny holding together of non-coincidence. In its turn, undecidability both repeats and develops this irrecusable non-coincidence. However it also takes another step – it rethinks this non-coincidence as the basic question of judgement and justice.[11] That is, it highlights the non-coincidence of the structural (and ethical) conditions through which any judgement is made possible. As Derrida puts it, it is the irrecusability of undecidability that makes clear to us the irreducible excess of any 'order of ethical-political responsibility'. At the same time though it is the necessary condition for all 'structures of decisions and of responsibilities' (Derrida, 1995a: 116, 149; cf. 1992a). In other words, the 'logic of anxiety' is repeated by Derrida and Caputo as a passion for justice.

How does this work? In what way does this interlacing of undecidability and potentiality point to an ethics or to justice? Furthermore, given its instantiation as a passion for justice, we are told that the deconstructive thinking of undecidability shows us a justice that is always yet to come. And what, then, does this mean? To start with, although we might have innumerable laws and regulations telling us what and how to decide, such decision-making for Derrida is not necessarily just. In such cases, after all, we're simply following pre-set rules, and we would probably want to agree that justice and the ethical cannot quite be reduced to the results of following such rules. After all, as Derrida reminds us, 'the call for justice is never, never fully answered' (1997b: 17). Indeed this instantiation of undecidability, jus-

---

11   Interestingly, it is with this same question and promise of justice that Caputo considers Derrida to have most clearly diverged from Heidegger (e.g. Caputo, 1997b: 348n5). Whilst I agree with Caputo's basic point here, I nonetheless want to stress that Derrida's promise of justice is informed by Heidegger's 'logic of anxiety'. Derrida's projection of the possibility and promise of justice is, as such, made possible through his repetition of this logic.

tice and potentiality marks that non-coincidence which deconstruction per se both is and sustains. It marks, for instance, the non-coincidence of the *promise* of justice with the *system* of law. And it is from this that we can derive that exemplary ethical ordeal and strategy which marks the need for a promise to what is not yet and cannot be presented, to what is other, always already in difference and constitutively undecidable. Indeed, it is actually this moment of suspense where we suspend the rules in the name of justice that makes not only jewgreek justice but deconstruction possible.

Hence it is this series of instantiations – of interpretation as deconstruction, of non-coincidence as undecidability as (a passion for) justice – which now needs to be further clarified. That is, deconstruction's very depiction of itself as the interlacing of potentiality, undecidability and justice needs further elaboration.[12] Also needing further clarification is the idea that as potentiality, justice and the ethical are, in fact, unachievable in any final sense, they are also undeconstructible.[13] Now this will also entail delineating the different interlacings of this series as it is respectively instantiated within Derrida's and Caputo's work.[14] As I have previously stressed, it is imperative to

---

12   As Derrida writes in 'Force of law', 'The "sufferance" of deconstruction, what makes it suffer and what makes those it torments suffer, is perhaps the absence of rules, of norms, and definitive criteria that would allow one to distinguish unequivocally between *droit* [law] and justice' (Derrida, 1992a: 4). Other distinctions Derrida makes are also based on this imperative and impossibility of distinguishing – albeit never absolutely – the undecidable (that is, the promise) from the decidable (the system). In *Specters of Marx*, for example, Derrida distinguishes what he terms the specter [sic], spectrality, a spectral logic and hauntology from the logic of either living or not living, from, that is, ontological decidability.

13   Derrida makes this claim in 'Force of law'. He writes: 'Justice in itself, if such a thing exists, outside or beyond law, is not deconstructible. No more than deconstruction itself, if such a thing exists. Deconstruction is justice'. (1992a: 14–15). Caputo extensively glosses this 'scandalous' claim in, for instance, his *Against Ethics* (1993a: 86–87), *Demythologizing Heidegger* (1993b: 192–208), and 'Deconstruction in a nutshell' (1997a: 131–134).

14   This series could also be a 'sheaf' in Derrida's usage of the term in 'Différance': 'the word *sheaf* seems to mark [...] appropriately that the assem-

avoid conflating Caputo's work with Derrida's too quickly. As Derrida comments, 'in reading [Caputo] I am not simply looking at the reflection of my text in his. We write very different texts'.[15] Not only, then, do they not absolutely coincide, but they both work to question the possibility of any such absolute coincidence.

It is at this point, then, that it becomes necessary to start to unfold Caputo from Derrida. We need to consider how Caputo himself is repeating Derrida (and Heidegger). This will further help to illustrate how Derrida and Caputo interlace (and substantiate) potentiality, undecidability and justice somewhat differently. Thus it is here where Caputo is so closely involved with repeating, glossing and, indeed, defending Derrida – assuming the 'task and vocation' of a 'supplementary clerk' or *Extra-Skriver*[16] – that I want to tease out some of the divergences between their instantiations. Indeed, as both Derrida and Caputo stress, my only starting point *can* be here where they are both already involved. So with this advice, let us now look at some of the turns that constitute this an-economic exchange, this post-metaphysical narrative of undecidability and justice that is set out as a possible ethics by and between Derrida and Caputo (and, of course, Heidegger).

---

blage to be proposed has the complex structure of a weaving, an interlacing which permits the different threads and different lines of meaning – or of force – to go off again in different directions, just as it is always ready to tie itself up with others' (Derrida, 1982a: 3).

15   Derrida makes this comment in an interview with Mark Dooley: 'The becoming possible of the impossible: an interview with Jacques Derrida' in *A Passion for the Impossible* (2003: 22).

16   This is Caputo's own description of his work from *Against Ethics* (1993a: 20–21).

Repeating Undecidability and Justice

> Undecidability [...] is not a sentence that a decision can leave behind. The crucial experience of the *perhaps* imposed by the undecidable – that is to say, the condition of decision – is not a moment to be exceeded, forgotten, or suppressed. It continues to constitute the decision as such; it can never again be separated from it; it produces it *qua* decision *in and through* the undecidable; there is no other decision than this one: decision in the matter and form of the undecidable. An undecidable that persists and repeats itself through the decision *made* so as to safeguard its decisional essence or virtue as such. (Derrida, 1997a: 219).

To begin wherever we are, is to begin with undecidability. Every decision, after all, marks a foray into the realm of potentiality, undecidability and justice. And, of course, the other. After all, if we begin in undecidability, we also begin with the other. Our decision-making is always about the other insofar as we don't need to make decisions about what is same to us. So on this basis every decision affirms both a passion for the impossible and an openness to the other which is not to be a taking account of the other.[17] It is a decision-making that Derrida thereby configures in terms of the gift, the promise, the secret, hospitality, faith, and a certain thought of the messianic. In all of these configurations, the aim is to refrain from delimiting the opened potentiality and otherness sustained and repeated through undecidability. Hence – structured as a promise, as an experience of the impossible, of the aporia, and always *à venir* – neither undecidability, deconstruction itself, nor justice *can* be configured as any given and thereby de-

---

17   This other, which is considered by Derrida through the phrase '*tout autre est tout autre*' (Derrida, 1995b: 76; cf. 1995d: 82–115), is configured as irreducibly other whilst not being transcendentalised as absolutely other or Other, as is the tendency in Levinas's formulations. As Derrida writes elsewhere, it is a '*tout autre* that cannot be confused with the God or Man of onto-theo-logy or with any of the figures of the configuration (the subject, consciousness, the unconscious, the self, man or woman, and so on)' (1989c: 61).

constructible system or programme.[18] Neither fully present nor determined as such, they are and remain undecidable, unprogrammable, undeconstructible and, apparently, thereby ethical.

How does this work? One starting point for Derrida's delineation of these ethical implications of undecidability is his depiction of deconstruction as having a 'messianic structure'.[19] By this he does not mean that deconstruction or ethics should be counted as one of the concrete, historical or determined messianisms such as the Muslim, Judaic or Christian religions – despite its being possible, by Derrida's reckoning, 'to see deconstruction as being produced in a space where the prophets are not far away' (1986a: 119). For such religious messianisms, as with the messianism apparent in Marxism, say, the point is to wait for a Messiah or future of known characteristics. We wait for a foreseeable future with foreseeable consequences. Further, this foreseeable future can be used to regulate the present, to make an easier time of our progress to this anticipated and particular future. In contrast, given its openness to the coming and/or interruption of the *tout autre*, its undecidability, deconstruction is informed by a messianic without any messianism, a messianic with no pre-determined or expected futural characteristics.

As such, deconstruction *is* that 'thinking of the messianic and emancipatory promise *as promise*: as *promise* and not as onto-theological or teleo-eschatological program or design' (1994: 75, first

---

18   It is with regards to this point that Simon Critchley is compelled to ask whether, whilst deconstruction 'can certainly be employed as a powerful means of political analysis', it can provide an 'adequate account of political life?' (Critchley, 1993: 101, 102). This question is certainly answered in the negative by, among others, Richard Rorty and Mark Lilla. I will consider these issues in detail in the following chapter.

19   Derrida discusses deconstruction as having a messianic structure in, for instance, 'The Villanova roundtable' (Derrida, 1997b: 22–25); *Archive Fever* (1996a: 72); *Specters of Marx* (1994: 59); 'Faith and knowledge' (1998: 17–18). Jack Reynolds in 'Derrida and Deleuze on time, the future, and politics' also stresses the unforeseeable characteristics of the messianic.

emphasis mine).[20] It is a promise that Derrida sees as portrayed through the instance and experience of the interruption by the undecidable, the *tout autre*. It is a promise made to an undecidable future (other, Messiah), rather than a known one. And it is under this formulation that deconstruction describes itself as an ethical non-appropriative interpretation of and address to the other.[21] Deconstruction, as Caputo sums it up, sees itself and justice *as* being on the 'lookout' for the other, for 'something unforeseeable, something new' (Caputo, 1997a: 42). It demands and exemplifies both a 'hospitality' and perhaps a 'friendship' offered in the face and midst of undecidability and the *tout autre*.[22] Indeed it is as its promise of hospitality to undecidability and the *tout autre est tout autre* that deconstruction can be seen as having a profoundly ethical force.[23]

---

20 As Derrida comments parenthetically in *Archive Fever*, he prefers the 'to-come of the *avenir* rather than the *futur* so as to point toward the coming of an event rather than toward some future present' as this former does not constitute a 'positive thesis'. Rather 'it is the condition of all promises or of all hope, of all awaiting, of all performativity, of all opening toward the future' (Derrida, 1996a: 68; cf. 1979: 99).

21 It is at this point that Derrida distinguishes his formulation of deconstructive interpretation from Heidegger's, insisting that his has no – or, rather, only minimal – resonances of 'gathering' or 'appropriation'. As he states in 'The Villanova roundtable', 'one of the recurrent critiques or deconstructive questions I pose to Heidegger has to do with the privilege Heidegger grants to what he calls *Versammlung*, gathering' (Derrida, 1997b: 14). Continuing, Derrida comments that unlike Heidegger he privileges dissociation. Derrida is careful not to say, however, that this privileging entails the destruction of the other, stressing that any purity as such 'is a synonym of death' (13). Elsewhere Derrida suggests that deconstruction instantiates an impulse towards 'a thought of friendship which could never thrive in that "gathering" (*Versammlung*) which prevails over everything' (1997a: 244).

22 Derrida explicitly addresses the notions of 'hospitality' throughout, for instance, *Of Hospitality* and within *Aporias* (1993a: 33–34) and *Adieu to Emmanuel Levinas* (1999a: 41–42, 111), and 'friendship' in his *Politics of Friendship*.

23 As Caputo stresses here, it is far too simple 'to think that deconstruction cannot oppose cruelty or oppression' (Caputo, 1993a: 119). Niall Lucy, in his *Debating Derrida* and more recent *A Derrida Dictionary*, also argues

Instantiated *as* its messianic structure and promise, deconstruction gives us a careful and indeed rigorous dis-closure, dissemination and repetition of the irrecusable potentiality and undecidability within the names of justice and the *tout autre*. It is in gifting us with undecidability that deconstruction is an ethical dis-closure[24] and promise that works to solicit delimitation. It shows us an idea of justice that remains irreducible to law programmes and textbooks. Now this is nothing radical, it is, after all, quite clearly set out by Derrida himself. What I want to say in addition, however, is that when configured in terms of the 'logic of anxiety' gifted by Heidegger, this overcoming of the closed economies of gratitude, calculation and the law shows deconstruction as a development of post-metaphysics.[25] In other words, deconstruction develops the potentially ethical commitment that in-

---

this point. Although Derrida's own remarks regarding a possible deconstructive political praxis vary (see, for instance, 'Deconstruction and the other' (1986a: 119–120) as compared to the positions formulated in *Limited Inc* and 'Force of law'), he nonetheless argues that deconstruction in no way authorises or legitimates any hesitation in response or decision, and 'should never lead either to relativism or to any sort of indeterminism' (Derrida, 1995a: 148). Rather it, informed by undecidability, 'defines a task and a responsibility' which is that 'we must think, know, represent for ourselves, formalize, judge the possible complicity between [... our ...] discourses and the worst (here the final solution)' (1992a: 63).

24   An interesting point of non-coincidence between Derrida and Heidegger concerns the workings of ethical dis-closure. Whilst Heidegger delineates this possibility through the metaphor of the circle or spiral and the necessity of entering into the circle in another way, Derrida discusses ethical disclosure through such tropes as the 'gift'. The working of the gift, as Derrida stresses, is beyond any notion of any economic circularity, rather it works only as it is given without anticipated return (see Derrida, 1997b: 18–19; cf. 1992a: 25), it is – along with the secret and the promise – a messianic structure.

25   This overcoming, however, by its constitution, neither instantiates nor desires any unbreachable division between a metaphysical circularity of exchange and this post-metaphysical dissemination without expected return (see, for example, Derrida, 1991d: 30). As discussed earlier, the desire for and instantiation of such a distinction fits far more readily with the configurations of the 'Post' delineated by Deleuze (and Guattari) and Levinas.

forms Heidegger's counter-metaphysical methodology and thinking. At the same time, however, by doing this along with deconstructing the determinacy of any actual ethics or messianism, it puts forward the undecidability of the messianic structure as the basis for a post-metaphysical ethics.

It is at this nexus of hospitality, the undeconstructible, and deconstruction's interlacing of potentiality, undecidability and justice as a post-metaphysical ethics that Caputo must be seen as already involved. Repeating Derridean deconstruction, Caputo in turn both deconstructs and supplements it. A self-designated *Extra-Skriver*, Caputo instigates an an-economic exchange with deconstruction, repeating and supplementing Derridean and Heideggerian narratives,[26] enfleshing them. Specifically Caputo sees Derrida (and Heidegger) as still a little too abstract, concerned with singularities and facticity perhaps, but afraid to ask their names. And it is on this basis that Caputo interlaces talk of justice, potentiality and undecidability with talk of 'flesh'. Basically, as Caputo sees it, flesh both grounds and discloses that ethical commitment and imperative which constitutes and conditions deconstruction. Indeed it stresses the non-originary and non-pure ground for this ethical imperative, being in no way able to ground any ethical imperative as a transcendental absolute. Flesh, after all, is resistant to all metaphysical attempts at delimitation and explication. It is irreducible to the project of knowledge, instantiating rather a project of justice that has no option but to continue in the midst of undecidability. For Caputo, then, to begin wherever we are can only mean to begin within the eventality and facticity of flesh. And it is this non-originary beginning that conditions the call for that justice which arises from and responds to the singularity and enfleshment of others.

So, whilst Derrida claims that deconstruction inspires a justice through its undeconstructible and messianic structure – where justice

---

26   Caputo stresses throughout his work that he is aiming to supplement the deconstructions opened by Derrida and Heidegger. Indeed he subtitles his *Against Ethics* as *Contributions to a Poetics of Obligation with Constant Reference to Deconstruction*, a move that further stresses his role as *Extra-Skriver*.

is that promise and gift given in the name of undecidability – Caputo argues for a justice through highlighting the facticity and fragility of flesh. The site of both the other and a post-metaphysical ethical commitment, flesh supplements the messianic structure of deconstruction. And it is in supplementing deconstruction, that Caputo fleshes it out, adding in names and bodies (and, later, prayers and tears) to its projection of a post-metaphysical thinking of obligation and justice.[27] As Caputo argues, the justice which is developed through deconstruction cannot be dissociated from the enfleshed condition of bodies.

In other words, we can see Caputo as not only fleshing out and so supplementing certain of Derrida's formulations, but as thereby developing a kind of deconstructive narrative with deconstruction itself. For instance, whilst delineating Derridean deconstruction as a narrative informed by a passion for the *tout autre*, justice and the impossible, Caputo also works to enflesh it. So, for instance, Caputo's *The Prayers and Tears of Jacques Derrida* enfleshes Derrida, whilst his *Against Ethics* reads as an extended enfleshment of deconstruction itself. Caputo fleshes out Derrida's concern for the *tout autre* into a concern for disasters, for the fate and flesh of proper names, for what he calls 'the disadvantaged, the differends, the losers, leftovers, the little bits and fragments' (Caputo, 1993a: 87). Supplemented by Caputo, the narrative of deconstruction comes to read as a narrative of the problems, conditions and commitments informing first singularity and enfleshment, and secondly obligation and justice. After all, as Caputo reminds us, the 'poetics of obligation is a poetics of flesh' (149). Caputo's enfleshment of deconstruction initiates, then, an ongoing exchange with Derrida. Their interlaced instantiations of deconstruction constitute a narrative where it becomes increasingly difficult

---

27   Caputo is also interested in the enfleshment of Derrida himself. In his recent work on Derrida – *The Prayers and Tears of Jacques Derrida* – Caputo puts forward a portrait of Derrida gleaned from his recent turn to a more autobiographical writing as circumcised, with eyes blinded and swollen with tears, confessing and praying. In a similar vein, also see Derrida's *Circumfession*, written in conjunction with Geoffrey Bennington.

to determine 'which one quotes the other'.[28] This narrative of deconstruction itself remains open, without clear-cut or decidable borders, oriented to the *tout autre*.

Repeating the Abrahamic Narratives

> Each 'story' [...] is part of the other, makes the other a part (of itself), each 'story' is at once larger and smaller than itself, includes itself without including (or comprehending) itself, identifies itself with itself even as it remains utterly different [...] (Derrida, 1979: 99–100).

One exemplary moment or event within this narrative of deconstruction as a post-metaphysical ethics unfolds with Derrida's and Caputo's various supplements to and glosses of the story of Abraham and Isaac. A supplementing in which, it must be stressed, both Derrida and Caputo take as their starting point, Kierkegaard's own non-originary interpretation of the story of Abraham.[29] Exemplifying both a disclo-

---

28   See Derrida's 'Living on: borderlines' (1979: 99). Both Caputo and Derrida discuss this narrative exchange in detail in *A Passion for the Impossible*.

29   Dealt with by Derrida in *The Gift of Death*, Kierkegaard's interpretation of the story of Abraham and Isaac (in *Fear and Trembling*) is also, prior to Derrida's version above, referred to and repeated constantly by Caputo in his *Against Ethics* and, more recently, throughout the essays in *A Passion for the Impossible*. These include, in the former, an extended version of it signed by one Johanna de Silentio (Caputo, 1993a: 139–143) which Caputo then – as designated *Extra-Skriver* – further glosses (143–146). Further, all these stories of Abraham inform Caputo's reading of Derrida in *The Prayers and Tears of Jacques Derrida*. For example, Caputo there works to situate Derrida's work (and, further, 'religion') as 'more prophetic that apophatic, more in touch with Jewish prophets than with Christian Neoplatonists, more messianic and more eschatological than mystical. His writing is more inscribed by the promise, by circumcision, and by the mark of father Abraham than by mystical transports' (1997b: xxiv). Lastly, Caputo discusses Derrida's telling of the story in *More Radical Hermeneutics* (2000: 144–147).

sure of the '*un*-decon', as Caputo puts it, and a possible site for the enfleshing of a jewgreek justice,[30] these various repetitions all make up a narrative of undecidability. Indeed, repeated and supplemented several times over in the narrative of deconstruction, the story of Abraham and Isaac highlights the ethical imperative and problematic of that undecidability where decisions are both necessary but constitutively ungrounded. Specifically this story stresses the undecidability, impossibility, paradox and madness that constitute the time of the decision – where, for instance, a decision is simply not made from knowledge. Decisions rather occur in the suspension of all structures such as time, knowledge, calculation, reason, language and, finally, even law. They are necessarily secret, unable to be sensibly shared, communicated or even justified.

Overall, then, these stories and repetitions all revolve around the structure and moment of decision, its instant.[31] In their enfleshing of this instant, however, these stories also demand its renegotiation. For instance, as Derrida notes in *The Gift of Death*, there is a very real absence of women in the Abrahamic stories. And it is this absence that also marks Caputo's repetitions of this story. He thus unfolds in one instance 'The story of Sarah' as told by one Johanna de Silentio.[32]

---

30   As Derrida notes, Levinas also uses Kierkegaard's gloss of the story of Abraham to situate an ethical possibility where 'there is an appeal to the uniqueness of the subject and sense is given to life in defiance of death' (Levinas, 1976: 113, cited in Derrida: 1995d: 78*n*6, translated by David Wills).

31   Derrida discusses the 'instant' of the decision in *The Gift of Death*, arguing that the decision 'remains irreducible to presence or to presentation, it demands a temporality of the instant without ever constituting a present' (1995d: 65). Furthermore, the instant of the decision can be 'neither guided nor controlled by knowledge [...] It structurally breaches knowledge and is thus destined to nonmanifestation; a decision is, in the end, always secret' (77). An interesting discussion of Derrida's focus on and gloss of such Kierkegaardian themes can be found in David Goicoechea's 'The moment of responsibility (Derrida and Kierkegaard)'.

32   'The story of Sarah' can be found in Caputo's *Against Ethics* (1993a: 139–146).

Here, despite the title, the story is retold from Isaac's point of view, an Isaac who, believing that the 'Lord was served by justice, not by the blood of the ram', wished that 'the God of Sarah could be a little more important' (1993a: 140). Focused on the story and flesh of Isaac and the absence of Sarah, 'The Story of Sarah' renegotiates the scandal of Abraham's decision, showing us that at no instant is it possible to make any judgement or decision that is 'somehow or another above or beyond the flux of interpretation (*hermeneia*)' (144, 145). Hence the story and decisions of Abraham requires a renegotiation of those structures of difference and identity that open and situate ethical relations.

The significance of this is clear. After all, far from taking place in 'a world without others, without words', obligation can only operate 'face to face, flesh to flesh' (142). So insofar as Abrahamic obligation is instantiated in the space of the absolute separation, the abyss, of Abraham's non-relations with the Lord and with others, it needs to be renegotiated at the level of flesh. In 'The Story of Sarah', on the other hand, such structures are questioned, and obligation is rather desired and situated at the level of relations of flesh, insofar as Isaac, the ram and any/every other are flesh. Hence, at the moment of sacrifice – supposedly an event configured in the abyss of the instant and decision of Abrahamic obligation, and beyond the problematics of mediation – Abraham and Isaac must nonetheless be depicted as 'man to man, face to face, flesh to flesh' (142). This suggested replacement of obligation at the level of flesh disrupts Abraham's acceptance of obligation as, ostensibly, an abyssal structure that is outside of mediation. In reifying an absolute (hierarchising) separation – 'this was no finite voice, no mortal call' (141) – which would always override the mediated bonds of flesh to flesh, 'Abraham's obligation becomes an idiolect incomprehensible to himself and to anyone else' (143).

Once renegotiated in terms of flesh, however, the structure and event of obligation is opened from an essentially prescriptive configuration (one *to* the Other) to one of mediation (one *with* others). Inextricable from the plurality of the demands of flesh, of being *with* others,[33] obligation is instantiated through a practice of mediation rather than distinction. It is the recognition that the hierarchical distinctions required by Abrahamic obligation are neither so clear-cut nor so absolute as to override the obligations before flesh. Further, it is the demand that flesh not be overridden or subsumed in the heeding of any 'one incommutable command' or prescription spoken with 'absolute authority' (141). As Johanna de Silentio and Isaac (and Caputo and Derrida) recognise, Abraham misses this possibility completely:

> Yet even after so terrible a lesson, even after the madness of the blood economy had been so painfully visited upon him, Abraham still insisted on spilling the blood of the innocent ram caught in a thicket [...] (Caputo, 1993a: 142).

> Isaac, who was faithful to his father all the days of his life, knew that he had [only] been saved by the Lord, that the countenance of the Lord had somehow stayed his father's hand. He resolved henceforth that while he would always obey his father it was the soft voice and gentle caress of Sarah that he would keep in his heart. (Caputo, 1993a: 143).

Repeated by jewgreek justice, Abraham's decision constitutes a scandal. Seen through jewgreek justice, the story of Abraham is a refusal and rejection of the stories (and flesh, and claims) of Isaac and Sarah, of the ram, and of any/every other. Jewgreek justice is thus a call for the opening of the story of Abraham, demanding the renegotiation of its ethical relations and structures of distinction. Nonetheless, in suggesting that obligation should come down to 'the sparing of flesh, to the lesser evil and the least violence' (Caputo, 1993a: 145), jewgreek

---

33   As can be seen, I here want to retrieve the Heideggerian relation of being with others from both Levinas's critique of it as too ontological and his development of it into the 'face to face' relation constituting ethics as first philosophy. This last relation, I suggest, is itself too metaphysical. Instead, I want to suggest that being with others can exemplify that uncanny being together, constitutive of jewgreek justice, which does not configure the relation with the other in terms of appropriation or delimitation, but concern (Heidegger, 1996: 110–118; 1995a: 153–163).

justice is also constituted as its awareness of the 'precariousness of its effect' (Derrida, 1979: 102). Responsibility, after all, is irresponsibility, and obligation is always and already also sacrifice. There is, Derrida reminds us, no way of justifying responsibility to one rather than another, no way of justifying the sacrifice resultant on any/every decision. Obligation and responsibility, in other words, are 'condemned a priori to paradox, scandal and aporia' (1995d: 68; cf. 1999a: 34–35). Hence, decisions are not only structured as contingent upon the eventality and facticity of flesh, but upon their ownmost unjustifiability. They are, as such, constituted only in the form of a promise.

Exemplified in practice by its repetition of the story of Abraham, jewgreek justice thus opens the space and possibility – further, the promise – for a renegotiation of the site, structure and eventality of obligation. Inscribing it both within the facticity of flesh and the structure of the promise *as* promise, jewgreek justice situates and unfolds obligation not in terms of the separation and (hierarchical) distinction underpinning the Abrahamic decision, but in terms of a relational possibility of a 'face to face, flesh to flesh'. Being 'flesh to flesh' is the promise and demand for an ethical inter-relatedness that needs to be renegotiated at each and every instant without consideration for either return or the instantiation of prescriptive ethical certainties. A being with others, obligation can only be contextual, contingent and particular – indeed, enfleshed and in-between – despite being conditioned by what are, in effect, the quasi-transcendental and universal structure of, for instance, the promise *as* promise.[34] The singularity, impossibility and enfleshed condition of Abraham's decision, then, is the singularity, impossibility and condition of any/every decision. Jewgreek jus-

---

34   Working against absolute distinction, Derrida stresses in 'The Villanova roundtable' that 'attention' to singularity is not an opposition to universality: 'I would try to keep the two together' (Derrida, 1997b: 22). Caputo adds in a corresponding footnote here that Derrida on occasion 'speaks of messianic justice as a "universalizable culture of singularities"' (Caputo, 1997b: 22*n*19, citing Derrida, 1998: 18). This disclosure of a justice within the relation of singularity with the universal is discussed by Diane Perpich in 'A singular justice: ethics and politics between Levinas and Derrida'.

tice thus writes and rewrites the story of Abraham, supplementing and enfleshing it with stories of Isaac and Sarah and any/every other, and in this way highlights both the enfleshment and the an-economic structures of decision-making, suspension and justice.

The Sparing of Flesh

Jewgreek justice thus remains both imperative and essentially unjustifiable, unconditioned by any transcendental absolutes. Unable to instantiate itself through either any absolute ethical or empirical commands or prescriptions, jewgreek justice opens and structures itself as that promise situating and responding to obligations within the eventality of an enfleshed inter-relatedness and undecidability. Deconstructing the Abrahamic assumption of absolute difference, separation and authority underpinning a prescriptive obligation, jewgreek justice instead delineates obligation in terms of a promise for an ethical negotiation that is to be 'sparing' of flesh. After all, as Caputo sees it, obligation only happens in 'the event of someone, of something personal' in the midst of an 'inarticulate hum' (Caputo, 1993a: 246). It is an operation aimed at recognising, negotiating and responding to this event ethically, at keeping it in question and neither discarding nor subsuming it under any invocation of or demand for universalisable or legitimisable criteria. Situating obligation not in the frame of an absolute or a corresponding abyss but in terms of a relational and responsive undecidability, jewgreek justice thus promises the renegotiation of difference and identity with regard to the obligation of flesh and the in-between: being with others. Further, it is through its renegotiations of difference and identity, along with that of obligation itself, that jewgreek justice substantiates its own structure as an open possibility and promise. It is, however, these promises of renegotiation that need further explication. Not only must it be unfolded how such a renegotiation of obligation promises a 'sparing' of flesh, and how this in turn involves a renegotiation of difference and identity, but, in addition, it must be asked whether and how these various renegotiations do in fact substantiate my claim that jewgreek justice does exemplify the promise and possibility of a post-metaphysical ethics.

Our starting point here, then, is that this promise and obligation for a 'sparing' of flesh is overall enabled by the turn from the metaphysical logic of distinction and delimitation to a 'logic' of undecidability. Unfolded through deconstruction *as* jewgreek justice, this (ethical) turn marks a renegotiation of the structures of prescription, difference and identity underpinning obligation. That is, these structures and economies of prescription, difference and identity are reconfigured in terms of the possibility of an ethical being *with* others which cannot be determined either by any economies of identity or return or, even, reason, or else by any structures of absolute unbreachable difference. Further, it is a being *with* others that must extend beyond the face to face relation of one to *an other*, to the mediation and renegotiation necessitated by a consideration also of plural others and obligations.[35] Being with others thus shows us that obligation which remains not simply haunted by undecidability, but irreducible to '*all determinate community, all positive religion, every onto-anthropo-theological horizon*' (Derrida, 1998: 16, emphasis original). It is irreducible, that is, to *all* positive structures of determinate and determined difference and identity. Jewgreek justice, in other words, tells us that being with others not only cannot be constrained via any sys-

---

35   This is a point which Robert Manning stresses in his reading of Derridean deconstruction in his 'Openings: Derrida, *différance*, and the production of justice'. In this paper Manning suggests that Caputo's reading of Derrida and deconstruction as concerned primarily with singularities misses the point. Derrida is rather concerned, Manning argues, with a thinking of 'ethics and justice through other others, through many others' that extends 'into the realm where my obligation to the singular one is crossed by my obligations to other others' (Manning, 1996: 411). Regarding this overt concern with 'other others', an interesting point is raised by Derrida in '"Eating well," or the calculation of the subject', where he questions the Heideggerian and Levinasian depictions of the other as 'the other man: man as other, the other as man' (Derrida, 1991c: 113).

tem of ethical prescription, but also cannot be either constrained by or dissociated from the facticity of the socio-political.

Specifically, in describing that being *with* others traced through a 'logic' of undecidability, the eventality of jewgreek justice – and, indeed, flesh – is effectively spectralised. That is, this being *with* other others constitutively extends beyond 'all living present' (Derrida, 1994: xix). The jewgreek promise is not a promise that only holds for certain others[36] – that is, presenced or presentable others. Rather, it must extend to *other* others, to a being *with* other others, with ghosts:

> It is necessary to speak *of the* ghost, indeed *to the* ghost and *with* it, from the moment that no ethics, no politics, whether revolutionary or not, seems possible and thinkable and *just* that does not recognize in its principle the respect for those others who are no longer or for those others who are not yet *there*, presently living, whether they are already dead or not yet born. No justice – let us say no law and once again we are not speaking here of laws – seems possible or thinkable without the principle of some *responsibility*, beyond all living present, within that which disjoins the living present, before the ghosts of those who are not yet born or who are already dead [...] (Derrida, 1994: xix).

Flesh, then, is itself spectralised and undecidable. It is not only 'both male and female, and neither male nor female' and both 'human and nonhuman' (Caputo, 1993a: 209, 210), but 'between life and death' (Derrida, 1994: xviii). The eventality of flesh and the jewgreek promise for the sparing of flesh are as such undelimitable. Not only is the eventality of flesh that which 'we will not hasten to determine as self,

---

36   This opening – that is, spectralising – of the promise before others, marks Derrida's (and Caputo's) radicalising of the Heideggerian (and Levinasian) relation of the *being with*. Whereas Derrida and Caputo open this relation to 'other others', both Heidegger and Levinas constrain it to be a relation of Dasein before Dasein, where Dasein seems to be translated in terms of a solely human reality. Levinas, in particular, delineates this relation as human – and, further, as perhaps specifically masculine – in *Totality and Infinity*. Derrida discusses this sort of reduction in 'The ends of man', *Of Spirit*, and '"Eating well"'.

subject, person, consciousness, spirit, and so forth', but the jewgreek promise of justice extends 'beyond the living present in general' (7, xx).

In other words, jewgreek justice effects its renegotiations of obligation, difference and identity through its constitution as that promise which cannot be constrained by the living present. Constituted *as* that promise which cannot hold *any* expectation of its positive or final instantiation, jewgreek justice shows us an ethical potentiality and trajectory of what Derrida has called 'another type of responsibility'.[37] Consequently, it is *this* seriasure of the messianic and spectralised promise, obligation, jewgreek justice and deconstruction that exemplifies the possibility of a post-metaphysical ethical thinking. That is to say, instead of determining some absolutely new – as such, non-metaphysical – possibility, such thinking rather unfolds as the renegotiation of underlying structures of prescription, obligation, difference and identity in terms of undecidability and an enfleshed yet spectralised being with others. Situated, then, *within* the eventality and spectralised facticity of flesh, jewgreek justice exemplifies – and, further, *meets* – the promise and trajectory of a post-metaphysical ethics, a trajectory disclosed by the narrative projected between Derrida and Caputo. Finally, however, we need to remember that the narrative of jewgreek justice also repeats and harbours within itself at least one essential ghost, that of a certain Heidegger.

---

37   Derrida makes this claim in '"Eating well"' (1991c: 104). Specifically, he affirms this notion of responsibility as needing to be excessive – as that 'surplus of responsibility that summons the deconstructive gesture or that the deconstructive gesture [...] calls forth' – against that 'limited, measured, calculable, rationally distributed responsibility' which he sees as configuring 'models of traditional morality and right' (Derrida, 1991c: 117, 118, 117). He also discusses an 'infinite responsibility' in 'Remarks on deconstruction and pragmatism' (1996b: 86).

No Future without Repetition

This is one of the things that should now be very clear to us. Not only are we unable to ever completely surpass the past, but repetition itself needs to also encompass an openness to the future. Whatever we do, however we decide, and wherever we begin, we need to keep an eye out for ghosts from both before and ahead of us. And it is in this way that the narratives of deconstruction and justice are haunted. In particular, and given that I have argued that deconstruction exemplifies the development of both that ethical potentiality opened by Heidegger through a 'logic of anxiety', and my question 'What is post-metaphysics?', we need to look at Heidegger's spectral 'presence' here. Obviously, given my argument, I do not believe that Heidegger's presence within this post-metaphysical narrative of jewgreek justice can be overstated. Heidegger, or at least a certain demythologised Heidegger, is undeniably lodged within deconstruction's narrative of justice. And his presence works to keep the possibility of jewgreek justice both open and in question, deconstructing its hopes or assurances of certitude. This is because Heidegger's presence is perhaps problematic. The Heideggerian ghost, after all, brings with it the question and spectre of a metaphysics and politics associated with Nazism.[38] If the law of six degrees of separation also counts ghosts,

---

38   Although the question of the relation of Heidegger's hermeneutic methodology and fundamental ontology to a metaphysics and politics associated with Nazism is beyond the scope of this work, it is a question which is of major importance and should be neither ignored nor answered once and for all (for instance, as Victor Farias sets out to do in his *Heidegger and Nazism*). Rather it is a question which, working to keep Heidegger's disclosures *in* question, has the possible consequence of both instigating and sustaining a critical interrogation of that (ethical) potentiality opened by Heidegger and developed in contemporary non- and post-metaphysical configurations. For Derrida's main investigation into the relation of certain of Heidegger's disclosures to the question of (his) Nazism, see his *Of Spirit*. Other discussions of Heidegger and Nazism include Lyotard's *Heidegger and 'the jews'*, Philippe Lacoue-Labarthe's *Heidegger, Art and Politics*, Pi-

should we see a deconstructive post-metaphysical ethics as also haunted by Nazism? On this basis, a questioning interpretation of the spectre of Heidegger would seem imperative for all contemporary non- and post-metaphysical projections.

Now in one sense at least this questioning is simply wrong-headed, given that it might simply end up repeating a rather tired move of essentialist thinking. At the same time, though, we could say that such questioning is imperative, given that the irrecusability of Heidegger's presence informs Derrida's and Caputo's attempts to de-mythologise him. Certainly the repetition and presence of even a de-mythologised Heidegger must itself still remain under scrutiny despite the unavoidability of such a repetition. Conditioning contemporary non- and post-metaphysical projects, Heidegger as such both informs and haunts Derrida's and Caputo's deconstructive project of jewgreek justice, stressing its constitutive undecidability. Repeated and spec-trally present, Heidegger marks deconstruction and jewgreek justice as irreducibly open, as a question and possibility. We could also say that Heidegger's presence marks the danger of undecidability, where we cannot avoid the risk that decisions may work to close things down rather than open them up, and that this risk is itself inextricable from the narrative of justice.

Overall, then, the deconstructive narrative of jewgreek justice instantiated between Derrida and Caputo – as an interlacing of Derrida and Caputo – can be seen not only as an open development of Hei-degger's thinking, but as a possible projection of a post-metaphysical ethics. Narrating between themselves the possibility of a jewgreek

---

erre Bourdieu's *The Political Ontology of Martin Heidegger*, and Günther Neske and Emil Kettering's *Martin Heidegger and National Socialism*. Giv-ing rise to much of the recent debate over what has become known as the Heidegger controversy or affair is Victor Farías's work *Heidegger and Na-zism*. This inflammatory work has been critiqued extensively in all of the works mentioned above and elsewhere. For some of Heidegger's own comments concerning his association with Nazism, see his 'Political texts, 1933–1934', 'The Rectorate 1933/34: facts and thoughts', 'The self-assertion of the German university', and his 'Der Spiegel interview'.

justice, Derrida and Caputo have in effect reawakened Heidegger's question of post-metaphysics *as* a question of justice. Reawakened through what can only be a possibility – or, as Caputo prefers to discuss jewgreek justice, an impossibility – the question 'What is post-metaphysics?' is neither answered nor stifled. Rather, repeating Heidegger's radicalising development of interpretation as a releasement of 'strangeness, darkness, [and] insecurity' (Heidegger, 1987: 39), jewgreek justice exemplifies a being – and response – without any regulated or given answers or solutions. It is a response and hospitality that is both offered before any guarantees, and highly dubious of any guarantees.[39]

So, reawakened, the question 'What is post-metaphysics?' shows us the possibility of a thinking no longer caught or lodged in the impasse of metaphysics. As we need to keep in mind, however, this does not imply that such thinking has escaped metaphysics as such, but rather that it works to keep metaphysics at a minimum, to, in effect, demythologise it.[40] Indeed, seeing post-metaphysics as a demy-

---

39   Caputo discusses this in his *Against Ethics* as constituting the 'feminine operation' – ascribed to Derrida (Caputo, 1993a: 209) – which he here discusses as being not so much 'a question of finding an answer to the night of truth but of sitting up with one another through the night, of dividing the abyss in half in a companionship that is its own meaning' (244). It is, he stresses, a 'listening to the alarms that are sounded by other flesh' (242). By this Caputo (and Derrida) mean an operation which is focused not on the ascertaining or the prescribing of 'acts of reason and phallogocentric lucidity', but on 'being there for the other, for someone who calls out for help' (242–243, 244). Carefully stressed as non-reductionist, Caputo situates the 'feminine operation' – an 'operation of flesh, not of empirical women', wherein flesh itself is an undecidable, 'both male and female, and neither male nor female' (209) – as being concerned not with the arche of absolute knowledge but with faith, with proper names rather than with either any absolute or 'the anonymous' (244–246). Indeed, for Caputo, the 'feminine operation' *is* obligation. Elsewhere Caputo also describes this operation as a 'healing gesture' (2000: 38).

40   Caputo, in projecting his demythologising of Heidegger, asks 'Who is Heidegger demythologised, made to answer to another responsibility? Would that not be another Heidegger, a Heidegger against Heidegger, a Heidegger

thologised metaphysics stresses not only the irrecusability of metaphysics – that it cannot be either absolutely escaped or abandoned – but that it *can* (further, imperatively must) be deconstructed and kept to a minimum. So configured, such thinking is the asking of – and affirmation of in responding to – the question of what is and matters despite the lack of any reassuring metaphysical grounding or regulation. Finally, unfolding such a response *as* jewgreek justice, Derrida and Caputo explicate that which, remaining essentially open, constitutes the possibility and task of a post-metaphysics – that is, a demythologised metaphysics which is, indeed, a provisional instantiation of the ethical potentiality of metaphysics itself.

---

who represents all that Heidegger fought against?' (Caputo, 1993b: 214). A demythologised metaphysics, then, would be a metaphysics unable either to absolutely affirm or escape itself, constituted and remaining rather *in* (its) deconstruction.

7. Questions and Relations

> [C]an one take into account the necessity of [Heidegger's] existential ana-
> lytic and what it shatters [...] and turn towards an ethics, a politics (are these
> words still appropriate?), indeed an 'other' democracy (would it still be a
> democracy?), in any case towards another type of responsibility that safe-
> guards against what a moment ago I very quickly called the 'worst?' Don't
> expect from me an answer in the way of a formula. I think there are a cer-
> tain number of us who are working for just this, and it can only take place
> by way of a long and slow trajectory. It cannot depend on a speculative de-
> cree, even less an opinion. Perhaps not even on philosophical discursivity.
> (Derrida, 1991c: 104).

Concerned with the problematic links between Heidegger's project
and subsequent configurations of the 'Post',[1] the above passage highlights the same types of questions that have been the focus of my last
chapters. These questions are also concerned with my explication of
Heideggerian questioning as an opening of an ethical potentiality. Indeed I suggest that it is a particular engagement with these questions
that constitutes and develops the 'long and slow trajectory' of what I
have termed a demythologised metaphysics or post-metaphysical ethics. Specifically, this is an engagement that keeps these questions open
as questions. On this view, then, Derrida's questions above are, indeed, what need to be thought and rethought.

---

1   As Heidegger reminds us, 'The thinking attempted in *Being and Time*
    (1927) sets out on the way to prepare an overcoming of metaphysics [...]
    That, however, which sets such thinking on its way can only be that which
    is to be thought'. It is, as Heidegger adds in an attached note (from the fifth
    edition, 1949), what '*calls for* thinking' (Heidegger, 1998: 279). As seen
    previously, it is with regard to such clarifying points that I argue that Hei-
    degger never aims to fully abandon metaphysics, and is rather focused upon
    rethinking – interpretatively repeating – metaphysics.

So, regarding these questions and the relations they both pre-suppose and question, it is clear that their interplay constitutes that trajectory which I have set out as Derrida's and Caputo's joint development of the question of a post-metaphysical ethics. However it also becomes clear that, in outlining this development and the conditions of its possibility, I have passed over – or, rather, assumed – the workings of its 'logic' too expediently. It is thus time to fully unpack this logic and the part it plays in the development of that demythologised and demythologising interpretation or post-metaphysical ethics that is informed by an affirmation of responsibility and obligation. Now so far it might seem that I've discussed this development as if it were an unproblematic relation of succession or evolution. In such a relation this affirmation of obligation (and, further, difference) would simply result from that methodological demythologising of metaphysical thinking exemplified by Heideggerian interpretation or Derridean deconstruction. Such a view, of course, has the benefit of straightforwardness and appeals to our commonsense idea of progress – restrictive metaphysics is gradually replaced by a much more easy going ethics. However this narrative is far too simple. Instead, this affirmation of obligation is itself somehow older than that questioning which paradoxically both presupposes and affirms it.[2] This, however, is not to suggest either that this affirmation *is* the simple origin or *arche* of this questioning. The relation, on the contrary, is that of a double in-

---

2   Derrida asserts that this affirmation is older than questioning in his long footnote in *Of Spirit* and, further, remarks that this anteriority of affirmation is '*marked*' in Heidegger's work (1989b: 129n5). These points and the note in question are considered in many of the papers discussing Derrida's *Of Spirit* included in *Of Derrida, Heidegger, and Spirit*. These include, for example, David Farrell Krell's 'Spiriting Heidegger', Simon Critchley's 'The question of the question: an ethico-political response to a note in Derrida's *De l'esprit*', and John Sallis's 'Flight of spirit'. Interestingly, Derrida's description of this affirmation as older echoes his early description of 'dif-férance': '*différance*, in a certain and very strange way, (is) "older" than the ontological difference or than the truth of Being. When it has this age it can be called the play of the trace [...] which no longer belongs to the horizon of Being [...] which has no meaning and is not' (Derrida, 1982a: 22).

scribing or interplay, and has to do with the necessarily undecidable configuration of this affirmation. After all, this affirmation is, on the one hand, 'always anterior and presupposed', whilst, on the other, it is never itself present in any 'experience' or 'speech act' (Derrida, 1989b: 129n5).

In other words, it is the logic of this relation – a double relation; hence a double logic – which marks that logic of anxiety and undecidability through which I have traced the possibility of an open post-metaphysical thinking. Consequently it is *this* interplay between affirmation and questioning which needs to be briefly explicated before I can begin to really clarify the possibility and implications of the demythologised metaphysics proposed in the previous chapters. Such clarification will also confirm my claim that the only possible formulation of a post-metaphysics is in the form of a provisional and nonpositive outline. After all, as Derrida reminds us, such thinking cannot depend upon any 'speculative decree' or even on any 'philosophical discursivity' (1991c: 104). Rather it has to do, as he states elsewhere, with the *'experience and experiment of the undecidable'* (1995a: 116).

On this basis, before I begin my own provisional outline of some of the possibilities and implications of what I have called jew-greek justice, I will briefly discuss this anteriority of affirmation and how it subtends the openness and focus of a demythologised metaphysics. In addition to further unpacking my claim that it is Heidegger's projection of interpretation which, both encompassing and releasing a certain ethical potentiality, is taken up and developed by Derrida and Caputo into a post-metaphysical thinking of deconstruction *as* justice, I will argue that this potentiality is conditioned by this affirmation which is posited as always and already anterior to – although not, of course, absolutely outside of – the basic functioning of questioning and interpretation.[3] However, on the subject of this always

---

3   It seems possible at first sight that the relation of this always already anterior affirmation to the ethical potentiality of a questioning interpretation corresponds to the relation outlined by Heidegger in *Being and Time* (1996: 139–144; 1995a: 188–195) between a pre-conceptual understanding and the processes and structure of that interpretation 'grounded existentially in un-

already anterior affirmation, it is clear that we cannot simply develop any analytic of the 'yes' in the same way I have here put forward an analytic firstly of Heideggerian interpretation and its various repetitions within the 'Post' and, secondly, of how Derrida's and Caputo's repetitions of the ethical potentiality of this interpretation constitute a demythologised metaphysics. After all, as Caputo reminds us, 'an analytic is supposed to resolve into simples, to come back to simple conditions', whilst 'to come back to the yes is to come back to something that is already doubled within itself, structurally' (1997b: 65). Described as encompassing both the 'archi-yes' of an unpresented anteriority and that promise to the future which 'promises to keep the memory of the first yes and confirm it, to repeat it' (65), this affirmation or 'yes, yes' thus seems to enable and affirm what is to come into question. It affirms what, in Heidegger's terms, is to be thought.

This affirmation, then, is what Derrida calls the 'gage' or 'engage'. It is a 'sort of pre-originary pledge'[4] that functions behind, substantiating and supplementing, both Heidegger's and his and Caputo's post-metaphysical projects. As a doubled, always already anterior pledge, the 'yes, yes' constitutes, in effect, the non-simple condition of possibility for both questioning itself and its ethical potentiality. Nevertheless, we need to remember first off that the doubled 'yes,

---

derstanding' (1995a: 188). That is, the relation of the fore-structure to the as-structure. Indeed, writing with reference to Dasein's relation to being, Heidegger stresses that 'Inquiry, as a kind of seeking, *must be guided beforehand* by what is sought' (1995a: 25 my emphasis; cf. 1971a: 71). The as-structure of interpretation is grounded in and conditioned and guided by the fore-structure of understanding. However, Heidegger sets out understanding here in positive terms, as a positive phenomena, with interpretation being the 'working out of [those] possibilities projected in understanding' (1995a: 189) – possibilities projected by and present, no matter in how vague a form, within Dasein's understanding. As such, this relation differs from that of this anterior affirmation – outlined in non-positive terms – as the condition for that ethical potentiality of a re-figured interpretation which informs jewgreek justice.

4   Derrida discusses this in *Of Spirit* (1989b: 130n5; cf. 1997b: 27; 1991c: 100).

yes' is itself neither constitutive of nor pregnant with any question or ethical potentiality – although, of course, Derrida argues that the single 'yes' expects and requires its confirmation. As he puts it, 'You cannot say "yes" without saying "yes, yes"'. One 'yes' requires 'to be repeated and repeated immediately' (1997b: 27, 27–28). We also need to remember that the 'yes, yes' in no way represents any 'hidden, virtual or potential' presence (1982a: 20). Rather, being merely the pledge of and for the question, and having no being as such, it is empty.[5]

What this tells us, then, is that this doubled affirmation cannot be thought of as a pointer towards any originary or pure position or plenitude. Rather, as Derrida argues, it is through its *non*-presence that it is able to act on the one hand as the empty condition for interpretative questioning and its ethical potentiality and, on the other, as supplementary to it. Now another way that both Heidegger and Derrida describe this situation is that this sort of affirmation also functions as the promise and memory of language itself. As Heidegger puts it:

> What do we experience when we consider the matter sufficiently? That questioning [*das Fragen*] is not the appropriate gesture of thinking [*nicht die eigentliche Gebärde des Denkens ist*]; rather, [the appropriate gesture is] hearing the affirmation of what is to come into question [*sondern – das Hören der Zusage dessen, was in die Frage kommen soll*]. (Heidegger, 1959: 175, cited and translated by Krell, 1993: 31).[6]

---

5   Also describing 'différance' as an effectively empty condition Derrida remarks that 'it (is) that which not only could never be appropriated in the *as such* of its name or its appearing, but also that which threatens the authority of the *as such* in general' (Derrida, 1982a: 25; cf. 1973: 158).

6   This passage is from a series of three lectures bearing the title 'The nature of language' and is translated by Peter Hertz and published in English in *On the Way to Language* (Heidegger, 1971a: 57–108) by the following: 'What do we discover when we give sufficient thought to the matter? This, that the authentic attitude of thinking is not a putting of questions – rather, it is a listening to the grant, the promise of what is to be put in question' (1971a: 71). I have deliberately used David Farrell Krell's translation above rather than Hertz's because of Krell's use of 'appropriate' for *eigentliche* as opposed to Hertz's 'authentic'. Hertz's translation suggests too many metaphysical

It must be emphasised, however, that Heidegger does not configure this anterior grant of language as the grant of its (or any) essential being in full and complete essence or plenitude. It is never, in other words, the grant or promise *of* any full and originary presence. Rather, 'language holds back its own origin and so denies its being to our usual notions' (Heidegger, 1971a: 81). At the same time though, given that language has always and already been granted as this withholding, it already requires a response. Such a grant, then, is not only the affirmation, but the supplement to and condition of questioning.

It is in this way, then, that this affirmation or grant makes possible a questioning which is both response to and an opening of ethical potentiality. Older than questioning and engaging us in questioning, this affirmation thus sustains a spectral presence within questioning, having always already infiltrated it and repeating it as its (ethical) potentiality. Asking the 'question of the question' (Derrida, 1989b: 129n5), this affirmation substantiates the ethical potentiality of interpretation and deconstruction, enabling their repetition as jewgreek justice. That is, it sustains that 'dimension of responsibility' which cannot be presented simply as the ontological questioning of metaphysics (Critchley, 1993: 99).[7]

Hence, with language as grant and affirmation – that is, both 'persist[ing] as this [its] avowal' and 'active as this [its] promise',[8] yes, *and* yes – the disclosure of questioning is never over with once and for all. Enabled and configured through the memory and promise of this doubled structure of affirmation, questioning and deconstruc-

---

connotations which, I believe, would tend to edge the import of this passage more in the direction of Heidegger's metaphysical project rather than to his ethical project where I believe it should be situated.

7   As Simon Critchley writes, 'The question and the questioning stance of philosophy is always a response to and a responsibility for that which is prior and over which the question has no priority' (Critchley, 1993: 97).

8   Heidegger makes these claims in 'The nature of language' in *On the Way to Language* (1971a: 76). In his turn Derrida discusses these two assertions – translations of the same line: '*Die Sprache west als dieser Zuspruch*' (Heidegger, 1959: 180–181) – in *Of Spirit* (Derrida, 1989b: 135n5).

tive interpretation is, in its turn, the open repetition of this structure. That is, it is both a repeated affirmation of what is always already anterior to it – and, therefore, other to at least some extent – and a response and promise to that which, although other, remains traced within it. Whilst the relation between affirmation and questioning inscribes affirmation as the condition of possibility for a questioning interpretation, it is a condition which – empty and non-simple – remains inscribed within and supplementing that which it enables. The interplay of this doubled inscription, then, not only describes a certain logic of supplementarity but a 'hermeneutic circularity' familiar in a form of transcendental reasoning:

> There is of course a 'hermeneutic' circularity in arguments establishing transcendental principles in that any transcendental condition has the 'peculiar character that it makes possible the very experience that is its own ground [...] and that in this experience it must itself always be presupposed.' (Ruthrof, 1998: 209, citing Kant, 1973: A737/B765).

On the one hand, then, this doubled affirmation can be seen to function as a sort of transcendental condition. That is, it is arrived at and functions as the 'necessary inference' and 'most general condition' (Ruthrof, 1998: 206, 219) of the potentially ethical trajectory of jew-greek justice. However, although the doubled affirmation of the 'yes, yes' functions, within Derrida's and Caputo's formulations, as such a condition of possibility, it is a condition which is also inscribed *within* interpretation. It is thus as more of a *quasi*-transcendental condition[9] that this doubled affirmation enables and situates the disclosure of a

---

9   Although Horst Ruthrof argues that under Kant's formulation, there is no 'direct bond between the transcendental deduction as procedure and the metaphysic from which it emerged' and that the transcendental therefore need entail no 'promise of access to presence' (Ruthrof, 1998: 219), I here prefer Rodolphe Gasché's terminology. In unpacking the (at least) doubled structure of what he terms Derrida's 'infrastructures' – for example, différance, arche-trace, iterability, supplementarity – Gasché argues that they 'are not *strictu sensu* transcendentals of conditions or possibilities' (Gasché, 1986: 224), but rather 'quasi-transcendentals'.

questioning and deconstructive interpretation as its potentially ethical trajectory. It must, however, be stressed that although this doubled affirmation acts as the most general condition of such a post-metaphysical thinking, it nonetheless remains not only uninvested with any presence or being as such, but, further, undecidable. Indeed the relation between this always already anterior and doubled affirmation and the processes of ethical interpretation it subtends is constitutively undecidable. Such a relation thus makes no promise of either any access to presence or positive ethical instantiations.

In other words, this affirmation also functions as the supplement to that ethical trajectory disclosed through deconstruction. And it is as supplement that this affirmation operates also as a 'sort of blind spot', as 'the not-seen that opens and limits visibility' (Derrida, 1976: 163). After all, the supplement, Derrida stresses, constitutes both a lack and an exorbitance which is not only maddening and dangerous but which also – deconstructive not only of the ideal of the transcendental condition as simple origin but of itself as *simple exteriority* (167) – deconstructs the possibility that the 'yes, yes' can function as any simple condition for a presentable jewgreek justice. As exorbitant, then, and as always already engaged, this affirmation 'overwhelms the question'. Now this is, of course, a risky manoeuvre. Certainly if this affirmation 'answers before even being able to formulate a question' (Derrida, 1991c: 100), it presents us with a post-metaphysical ethics

> that can only exceed (and *must* exceed) the order of theoretical determination, of knowledge, certainty, judgment [...] in other words, more generally and essentially, the order of the *present* or of *presentation*. (Derrida, 1992d: 81).

Indeed it would present us with a post-metaphysical ethics that is 'out of joint' with the orders of the present, and as we know

> To be 'out of joint,' whether it be present Being or present time, can do harm and do evil, it is no doubt the very possibility of evil. But without the opening of this possibility, there remains, perhaps, beyond good and evil,

only the necessity of the worst. (Derrida, 1994: 29; cf. 1999a: 34–35; 1983: 19).

Interpretation, Comportment and Jewgreek Justice

So what should be apparent by now, then, is that it is the possibility or potentiality that counts as far as jewgreek justice goes. Certainly it is clear that neither deconstruction nor jewgreek justice can be seen as constituting or developing any future present or realisable program or state.[10] They neither set out any blueprint for any program, nor develop any list of principles, prescriptions or commandments by which such a program might be devised. However, given that Heidegger has cautioned us that to focus on answers rather than on the question *as question* is to close the question down, I do not see this as a full-scale problem. Although, on the one hand, jewgreek justice does not disclose or affirm any particular model for ethico-political interpretation, on the other the *asking* of this – and other, related – questions, not only works to keep jewgreek justice open, but affirms its minimal in-

---

10   This is, of course, one of the points that marks a divergence between the jewgreek (and deconstructive) notion and negotiation of the ethico-political, and those notions of the political – although not, I argue, the ethical – which have been discerned within Heidegger's work. On the one hand, jewgreek justice instantiates a certain deconstructive repetition of the ethical potentiality opened by a Heideggerian methodology, further developing this methodology to substantiate an ethico-political interpretation and negotiation which is always open and provisional. Heidegger's notions and explications of the political, on the other hand, have been massively critiqued (especially from the Farías text onwards) for essentialist and regulative, not to mention fascist, tendencies. Of any number of works on the question of Heidegger and politics, *The Heidegger Case*, edited by Tom Rockmore and Joseph Margolis, comprises a range of differing responses. Another interesting discussion of this question is to be found in Miguel de Beistegui's *Heidegger and the Political*.

stantiation as both question and interpretation. As, in other words, a type of ongoing engagement or negotiation. Indeed one way we could clarify this rather hazy conception of jewgreek justice might be to think about it by way of Heidegger's delineation of interpretation as a form of comportment.

Now, as we know from previous chapters, there are a number of points that go to inform Heidegger's methodology of interpretation. First of all we know that Heidegger instantiates interpretation as the substantiation and negotiation of potentiality. In other words, it is as an attunement to potentiality that interpretation affirms 'that there is *constantly something still to be settled*' (Heidegger, 1995a: 279). It is outlined, then, as that mode of *being* which neither closes over nor dims down the possible, nor tranquillises itself with the actual. In addition, interpretation marks that mode of being-there that comprises an attuned and non-delimitative 'being there with one another' (1995b: 66). And it is on this basis, then, that interpretation exemplifies what Heidegger has elsewhere explicated as comportment – a mode of being there and being *towards* which can also be delineated in terms of the openness informing *Gelassenheit* (releasement and/or letting be).[11]

A further point of import here is that Heidegger's disclosure of interpretation as comportment is instantiated within the horizon of facticity. As he puts it, the basic experience of facticity is far from a 'mere background for interpreting' (Heidegger, 1991e: 70), instead situating the very project of interpretation as a non-delimitative comportment. Comportment, after all, is inextricable from the opened being thereness of factical existence, of being with other others – experiences that are constitutively informed by potentiality and inscribed within facticity and undecidability. Indeed, under Heidegger's formulation, the very possibility of comportment and interpretation rests

---

11   I have discussed this projection of *Gelassenheit* earlier in Chapter 2. I would also suggest that Heidegger delineates this mode and possibility of interpretation or comportment in terms of 'dif-ference', *Ereignis* etc.

upon the condition of facticity.[12] Furthermore, if seen as conditioned by facticity, interpretation is irrecusable. As Heidegger puts it, it 'belongs to the being of the there' (Heidegger, 1996: 135; 1995a: 184). Consequently, the attunement of interpretation to potentiality (and thus undecidability), and its constitution as comportment, marks the instantiation of what Heidegger has called a 'hermeneutics of facticity' (see Kisiel, 1995: 274–275). Hence, the instantiation of Heideggerian interpretation as comportment, needs to be seen as 'a way of comporting ourselves in our necessarily finite engagements' (Wood, 1999: 117).[13]

What this means with regards to seeing jewgreek justice as a form of comportment, then, is that it too is inscribed within this experience of facticity. However, what I do need to stress here is that facticity is in no way a simple correlation to any particular given. Just as for Heidegger facticity is inscribed with potentiality and uncanniness, for jewgreek justice it features undecidability, difference and potentiality. Indeed, it is on this very basis that we can see jewgreek justice as comprising an opened comportment rather than a delimitative appropriation. And, as comportment, that it remains ungrounded and unsubstantiated except by the non-simple conditions of its instantiation: facticity and undecidability, flesh and obligation – conditions which, as we know, are actually anterior, unpresentable and, furthermore, quasi-transcendental. The experience of facticity and flesh thus not only constitutes the condition for jewgreek justice,[14] but also in-

12   For discussion of the emphasis Heidegger accords to facticity in his work up to *Being and Time*, see Theodore Kisiel's *The Genesis of Heidegger's Being and Time*.

13   Arguing a similar point to David Wood, Caputo is careful in his *More Radical Hermeneutics* to stress that what I have termed the jewgreek configuration of facticity should not be conflated with that finitude which presupposes and is made sense of through an infinitude, a criticism which he directs at Gadamerian finitude which he explicates as a 'transcendental' or 'edifying' finitude (see Caputo, 2000: 50, 54).

14   David Wood argues in 'The experience of the ethical' that 'experience' – both 'as a *concept* and as an *openness*' – exemplifies the 'condition for philosophy's productive intercourse with what lies outside of itself'. As he con-

forms and substantiates its constitutively provisional formulation as comportment and interpretation.

At this point, however, it still remains to be considered just how jewgreek justice develops its instantiation as comportment into an ethico-political negotiation of facticity. Furthermore, the question is how such a negotiation remains itself only a question, rather than rigidifying into an enframed and enframing answer, a realisable future present.[15] Now, one possibility that I have touched on earlier is that jewgreek justice can only be instantiated within the risk of its collapse. That is, jewgreek justice cannot be instantiated as the trajectory of a post-metaphysical ethics – as an ungrounded and unsponsored ethico-political negotiation of facticity – without the ongoing risk of (non-) metaphysics. Hence, jewgreek justice can only exemplify an ethico-political negotiation of facticity if it is also concurrently in danger of instantiating and affirming a particular representation of that facticity. Consequently, jewgreek justice instantiates an effective post-metaphysical and ethico-political questioning interpretation of facticity only when it *is* a question and possibility at risk of closure. In pragmatic terms, this means that the jewgreek projection of justice, inscribed by and within the facticity of flesh and undecidability, can

---

tinues here, if 'negotiation with alterity is the locus of the ethical, "experience" is the essentially contested marker of that site' (Wood, 1999: 109).

15   In her 'Fate and fortune: Derrida on facing the future', Genevieve Lloyd stresses that Derrida, with reference to his *Politics of Friendship*, is 'trying to make visible something different from that "*order of good sense*" which "goes from the possible to the real"' (Lloyd, 2000: 11, citing Derrida, 1997a: 18). This 'something', Lloyd continues, is 'what Derrida calls "the experience of the *perhaps*"', where '[t]his "perhaps" is not a modifier on presence', rather evoking 'an orientation towards a future which is not to be understood in terms of a future present' (Lloyd, 2000: 11). As Derrida writes in *Politics of Friendship*: 'What is going to come, *perhaps*, is not only this or that; it is at last the thought of the *perhaps*, the *perhaps* itself. [...] Unheard-of, totally new, that very experience which no metaphysician might yet have dared to think' (Derrida, 1997a: 29, cited by Lloyd, 2000: 11).

only be instantiated as a promise and interpretation without possibility of 'proper' or full actualisation:

> The call of justice [can only cultivate] the possible as possible. The future towards which it calls us is not definite, not future-actual, which would reduce it to a matter of prediction and of working towards a preset goal, of reaching a mark which we set for ourselves, an articulated *telos* towards which we need only strain our wills [...] This call maintains itself resolutely in the sphere of the possible, of radical openness and flexibility [...] It is not a call for chaos, but a call to stay open to the frailty and fragility of the future, to refuse to be taken in by the enormous prestige of accumulated actuality. (Caputo, 1991: 18; cf. 2000: 119).

Indeed, as jewgreek justice demonstrates, the (non-)metaphysical grounding and dream of a 'proper' institution or of the instantiation of a specific future present, is itself constitutively problematic.

In other words, jewgreek justice negotiates the im/possibility of a reinterpretation of facticity which is informed by undecidability and difference rather than by identity or the ideal. As such, opening up, spectralising and supplementing every metaphysical or empirical economy or dream, the ethico-political negotiation of post-metaphysics not only does not project any realisable institution but also does not 'make the mistake of thinking *the* impossible is real' or of treating it as 'foreseeable regulative ideal' (Caputo, 1997b: 170; cf. 1997a: 133). It is 'impassioned' neither by any 'faith in a non-empirical ideal which exceeds the limits of experience and science' nor by any future present which 'establishes an ideal horizon of expectation' (1997b: 170). In this way, jewgreek justice instantiates a comportment towards facticity as a post-metaphysical and ethico-political negotiation, which, critical rather than predictive, is sustained as question rather than answer.

As I have stressed, then, it is its minimal constitution that distinguishes jewgreek justice from 'proper' institutions of both metaphysical and empirical justice. These latter institutions can in fact be known by their dependence upon a desired correlation of metaphysical ideals and prescriptions with empirical conditions. We could also say that, insofar as jewgreek justice can be seen to be projected minimally as that comportment open to the undecidability and ethical potentiality of being with other others – that is, configuring flesh as obligation – 'proper' institutions of justice aim, on the other hand, to realise some futural possibility which is configured in terms of very specific ideals and parameters. It is in the same way, then, that the Levinasian dream of a pure ethical empiricism is configured and constrained by the absolute height and infinitude of the other as Other – an other which must thereby fit certain specifications to be Other. Similarly, Rorty's pragmatism[16] depends upon and is configured in terms of an affirmation not only of a certain 'natural attitude' (borrowing from Husserl (Caputo: 2000: 86, 88)), but also of particular ideal forms of 'community' and 'consensus'. These latter forms are themselves dependent upon and configured in terms of both an unquestioned attachment towards 'the classical liberal subject and to individual, subjective *autonomy*' and the perceived desirability (and interchangeability) of both 'America' and 'democracy' (102, 116).[17]

Overall, then, in delineating the trajectory of jewgreek justice as coming to rest in neither metaphysical nor empirical ideals or dreams, what needs to be stressed is that it opens and traces a way *between* – as both and neither – metaphysics and empiricism, *between* ethical relativism and prescriptivism. That is, in configuring itself minimally as comportment and sustaining itself as promise, it avoids its instantiation (and delimitation) within any of the above extremes.

---

16   Caputo discusses Rorty's pragmatism under the name of 'Yankee Hermeneutics' in his *More Radical Hermeneutics* (2000: 84–124). Although Caputo here discusses the parallels between Rorty's, Derrida's and his own work – all of which, he argues, are engaged in a certain 'de-capitalization' (85) – he nevertheless describes Rorty's work as ultimately not deconstructive enough.

17   Chantal Mouffe also criticises Rorty's conflation of democracy, capitalism and both economic and political liberalism under 'the term *liberalism*': 'one is driven [...] to a pure and simple apology for the "institutions and practices of the rich North Atlantic democracies", which leaves no room for a critique (not even an immanent critique) that would enable us to transform them' (Mouffe, 1993: 10, citing Rorty, 1983: 585).

However, what nonetheless needs to be kept in mind is that jewgreek justice is constitutively inscribed within the risk, danger and temptation of these extremes: the risk of 'being reduced once again to juridical-moral rules, norms, or representation, within an inevitable totalizing horizon' (Derrida, 1994: 28). Indeed, it is *as* this risk – the risk of 'the return of precisely that which it would deconstruct' (McNeill, 1993: 104) – that jewgreek justice traces and sustains its way *between* these extremes.

Risk and the Way Between

> Does there not come a moment when deconstructive questioning must itself withdraw from the scene? And how are we to interpret *this* withdrawal? In particular, does not such questioning inevitably risk appearing as the master discourse, the authoritative discourse, the authority on all possible authority – and thereby risk the return of precisely that which it would deconstruct. (McNeill, 1993: 104).

What has become apparent at this point, then, is that jewgreek justice as a post-metaphysical ethics shows us the potentiality and risk in itself, (non-)metaphysics and ethics. It thereby traces a way which lies *between* the horns of the dilemma, a way which *is* 'the experience of the nonpassage' and '*necessitates* doing the impossible' (Derrida, 1993a: 12; 1995b: 59). However it is also clear that it is in its opening of the between as the 'nonpassage', that jewgreek justice constitutes a model for an ethico-political interpretation and negotiation. And it is this instantiation of jewgreek justice as a model for an ethico-political negotiation of risk, potentiality and the between which now needs to be considered. Certainly, jewgreek justice sustains the ethical promise and potentiality – and of course the risk – in post-metaphysical undecidability. Nevertheless this, of course, might itself appear as a problem. If it sustains undecidability and doesn't shirk the risk of its collapse, how effective can it be in any institution of socio-political effects?

Jewgreek Justice and the Socio-Political

> If [...] the ethical moment in deconstruction asks the question of the question, the primacy of responsibility to the Other, then is there not also a necessary moment of questioning that would be directly related to politics? Is not politics precisely the domain of questioning, that is, of contestation, antagonism, struggle, conflict, and dissension? What is the relation [...] between the rigorous and responsible undecidability of deconstruct[ion] [...] and the necessity for political decisions and political critique? (Critchley, 1993: 101; cf. 1992: 189–190).[18]

Although his focus is specifically on deconstruction here, Critchley does seem to pinpoint a problem with post-metaphysical ethics. Certainly, if such an ethics sustains undecidability in the face of the given, then it would seem to remain forever distant from the sorts of 'political decisions and political critique' Critchley is concerned with. And on that note, then, my use of an 'and' to connect 'jewgreek justice' with the 'socio-political' would seem to be a mistake. However, it must be remembered that I have previously argued that jewgreek justice is constitutively situated not only within the experience of undecidability but also within the facticity and eventality of flesh and the instants and events of decision-making. And it is on this basis that we can now start to consider how and to what extent jewgreek justice is

---

18   Similar questions are put to Derrida directly in, for instance, the dialogue entitled 'Hospitality, justice and responsibility'. The questions asked to start off this dialogue include: '[A]fter deconstruction, what is to be done? How do we act?' and '[H]ow do we make a decision on the basis of undecidability?' (Derrida, 1999b: 65).

able to function as a socio-political as well as an ethical possibility and strategy.[19]

It is the consideration of this question, then, that informs the remainder of this chapter. Hence, the final sections of this chapter will encompass an outline of my argument that jewgreek justice sets in place and utilises a notion of a socio-political that is simply irreducible to any economy of exchange, return or calculation. As such, this outline will consider how jewgreek justice can function within the factic domain of contestation, obligation and inter-relatedness. Such an outline will further work to disclose the parameters of jewgreek justice, setting forth the field of its eventality and effect as not only an ethical promise and strategy but a socio-political one.[20]

However, before I begin my discussion of the instantiation of jewgreek justice in terms of the socio-political, several points need to be clarified. These concern the question of whether, in embarking upon such an explication, what is being unfolded corresponds to a desire or demand for some delimitation of jewgreek justice. Does this sort of explication demand that jewgreek justice must either be able to be held accountable within the socio-political domain for the produc-

---

19　Simon Critchley considers such questions in, for instance, *The Ethics of Deconstruction*, 'The question of the question: an ethico-political response to a note in Derrida's *De l'esprit*', and 'Deconstruction and pragmatism – is Derrida a private ironist or a public liberal?'. A contrasting discussion of the relation between deconstruction and the political can be found in Ernesto Laclau's 'Deconstruction, pragmatism, hegemony'.

20　These issues are also taken up by Robert Manning who stresses that for deconstruction the point can never be to 'refrain from taking a position, but [rather] "to do it more often and better, that is, to do it otherwise"' (Manning, 1996: 415, citing Derrida, 1984). This doing it 'otherwise' Manning then explicates as the 'opening up' of 'possible' and 'additional ways of thinking and understanding' (415). Indeed, as Derrida also stresses, deconstruction is never '*neutral*. It *intervenes*' (Derrida, 1982b: 93). Such statements of course frame Derrida's own stands taken with regard to apartheid, racism, feminism, carnophallogocentrism etc. Good discussions of these stands can be found in the work of Niall Lucy, particularly his *Debating Derrida* and *A Derrida Dictionary*.

tion of an 'adequate account of political life' (Critchley, 1993: 102), or else admit to its inadequacy within and/or irreconcilability with the socio-political domain? On this issue, then, we need to think about whether such a demand does in fact exemplify a delimitation and, if so, whether it then conflicts with the instantiation of jewgreek justice as an impossible, imperative and undelimitable hospitality and friendship. After all, as Derrida asks, who could 'ever determine the proper extent of a[ny] thematization so as to judge it finally adequate? And is there any worse violence than that which consists in calling for the response, demanding that one *give an account of* everything, and preferably *thematically?*' (Derrida, 1995b: 25). Or, to be even more blunt, do Critchley's questions correspond to a desire for a delimitation of deconstruction in demanding its full accounting of and accountability in the political arena? And would this be at odds with the instantiation of jewgreek justice?

Now such questions are considered, for example, by Morag Patrick who argues that Critchley's thesis that deconstruction – *without* help from a Levinasian formulation – results in an impasse from its 'inadequate thematization of politics as a space of questioning' (Patrick, 1997: 171), stems from a basic misreading of the deconstructive project. Rather than deconstruction requiring some 'political supplement [...] which would make good the deconstructive deficit of accounts' where it fails to 'account for the activity of political judgement, political critique, and the political decision' (Patrick, 1997: 170, citing Critchley, 1992: 190), Patrick argues that any such project remains 'irreconcilable with Derrida's concerns insofar as it is conclusive of the figures of the undecidable in Derrida that these figures *cannot be called to account*' (Patrick, 1997: 170, my emphasis). In other words, Patrick suggests that Critchley, in demanding that Derridean deconstruction must become accountable in its move from undecidability to the decision, is, in effect, acting to delimit and undermine the deconstructive project itself.[21] Consequently, Patrick argues

---

21   Morag Patrick argues that all such demands that deconstruction 'exhibit its
      political significance by accounting for the necessity of political decision

that the question and possibility of the ethico-political instantiation of the deconstructive project should (and, indeed, *can only*) be unfolded with regard to the notion of excessive responsibility and the messianic structure and promise which informs it.

At this point, then, with such questions arising around the proper functioning and instantiation of jewgreek justice within the political, it also needs to be asked how this notion of the political can (and should) be delineated. Now, it is certainly the case here that we can dismiss out of hand any definitions of the political that simply correlate it to any given structure or system. This is, of course, the approach taken by Philippe Lacoue-Labarthe and Jean-Luc Nancy who argue that the political simply cannot be treated as a 'distinct and autonomous domain (or, and this does not make much difference, one tied up with or subordinated to another such empirical or regional domain)' (1997: 109). The political, they say, instead exemplifies that concept opened *as question* which 'does not itself produce a[ny] political position; it is the very position of the political' (110). As this position *of question*, then, the political is far from representative of any particular economy of exchange or return. Repeating the impossibility of *any* post-metaphysical substantiation of identity politics, the question or field of such a possibility can in no way solely exemplify nor be legitimated by any given or produced political position or positivity.[22] Indeed, opened as a question, this possibility solicits its instantiation as and/or legitimation by any of its determinate possibili-

---

and critique' are reflective not only of 'traditional presuppositions about the possibility of politics and the space in which it takes place' but also of a 'limited understanding of the nature of deconstructive writing' (Patrick, 1997: 172). With respect to Critchley's critique of Derridean deconstruction, Patrick suggests that 'politically supplementing Derrida's work with features drawn from Levinas's [...] is unhelpful' and, further, mistaken (174).

22   Honi Fern Haber argues in her take on postmodern politics that a political theory is only 'viable to the extent to which it is able to construct itself to pay attention to difference'. Politics, she also says, 'is always potentially, and even inherently, oppositional' (1994: 2) – a view that both Simon Critchley and indeed Chantal Mouffe would be in accord with.

ties – as, for instance, any political theory or science or, indeed, even as the well known overarching determination of everything being political.[23] As Derrida notes, it is just such an opening up of the political that makes possible a 're-politicization' and, further, 'another concept of the political' (Derrida, 1994: 75).[24]

Now, when considered with regards to my instantiation of jewgreek justice, it becomes apparent that such a 're-politicization' of the political cannot be fully dissociated from the ethical promise that informs it. We know, after all, that jewgreek justice is not only informed by the deconstructive notions of undecidability and excessive responsibility, but also that it is driven by its always already anterior affirmation and instantiation of a promise to spare flesh – a promise which is necessarily fragile and contingent in its instantiation. Hence, jewgreek justice operates not only in terms of its ethical promise, but

---

23   Philippe Lacoue-Labarthe discusses this latter possibility – the 'domination of the "everything is political"' – as exemplifying a kind of 'intimidation' which 'forces anyone whatsoever [...] to be accountable, to show their hand, to intervene, to commit themselves, etc' (Lacoue-Labarthe & Nancy, 1997: 97). Such a position is, in effect, a type of positivity and absolute prescription which can be (and has been) used to charge an instantiation such as deconstruction with nihilism, irresponsibility and, what Caputo has called, 'apolitical aestheticism' (Caputo, 1997a: 125). For example, as Caputo so wryly puts it, from the stronghold of any such position, '[i]t is not uncommon to portray Derrida as the devil himself, a street-corner anarchist, a relativist, or subjectivist, or nihilist, out to destroy our traditions and institutions, our beliefs and values, to mock philosophy and truth itself, to undo everything the Enlightenment has done – and to replace all this with wild nonsense and irresponsible play' (36). Along with Caputo, then, I argue against any such portrayal of deconstruction and jewgreek justice.

24   Caputo stresses the socio-political focus of what I have termed jewgreek justice when he discusses Derrida's *Politics of Friendship* as suggesting 'a post-metaphysical way of thinking about politics' (Caputo, 2000: 115): 'It proceeds without pretension to being a full-blown political *philosophy* with a "theory" of human nature or the state, or a comprehensive political program [...] [However, the] *Politics of Friendship* serves public purposes, concerns social and political structures, and addresses public issues' (115–116).

220

as its socio-political instantiation. And I also want to suggest here that this socio-political instantiation is its disclosure of an open being with. Jewgreek justice, in other words, exemplifies a ceaseless ethical attention, negotiation and questioning at the level of a facticity and flesh which cannot be reduced to any determinate possibility or domain. Indeed, both promised and instantiated at the level of the eventality and undecidability of flesh and obligations, jewgreek justice requires the shift from any one to one, face to face, reciprocated (and reciprocatable) relation, to an inter-relatedness and a being with other others, with multiple others. It exemplifies a friendship and hospitality which is irreducible to any/every economy of reciprocity or presence.

In other words, jewgreek justice exemplifies a resituating of both the ethical and the political. For instance, the ethical relation is opened *from* being grounded in or by absolutes – for instance, any idea of an absolute Otherness either interior or exterior to a simple ethical relation of reciprocated obligation – *to* being situated in contingency, flesh and facticity, in the socio-political.[25] Secondly, the idea and possibility of the political is opened from its instantiation as determinate form or practice, to encompassing the strategic negotiation of this ethical promise. The question and possibility of the socio-political is, then, for jewgreek justice, far from having been aban-

---

25   Michael Zimmerman considers this opening of the ethical in his discussion of Caputo, 'John D. Caputo: a postmodern, prophetic, liberal American in Paris'. Here, however, Zimmerman argues that Caputo's instantiation of moral obligation *in* 'the sheer fact of suffering flesh' is problematic. As he comments, 'Is does not imply ought': 'factical, ontical givenness *cannot* impose moral obligation' (Zimmerman, 1998: 205). Concerning this problem in his response to Zimmerman – 'Michael Zimmerman's very acute and penetrating observations about risking a "fleshly-ontical immanentism"' – Caputo states that he 'would say that the "is" of the flesh is also and already an "ought," its *Sein* is always already a *Sollen*, so long as the flesh is understood in all of its phenomenological robustness and not reduced to an empiricist shadow of itself' (Caputo, 1998: 219). In other words, what I think Caputo is saying here is that flesh needs to be understood not only in regards to its empirical givenness, but also in terms of its ownmost undecidability and potentiality and need.

doned to either nihilism or relativism or, as Critchley suggests, the double bind or aporia of that undecidability indistinguishable from indecision. Rather, the eventality of jewgreek justice *asks* the question and possibility of the socio-political along with that of the ethical.

So, just as it cannot be dissociated from a questioning of the ethical, jewgreek justice is also constitutively instantiated through its questioning of the political. Consequently, regarding its instantiation and affirmation of the ethical and messianic promise *as promise* but within the level of the facticity (and spectrality) of flesh and decisions, and *as* a necessitated mediation and renegotiation, jewgreek justice initially appears to be the counter to those questions asked by Critchley and cited at the beginning of this section. Not only does jewgreek justice open and sustain a non-determinate space for the asking of both ethical and socio-political questions, but it substantiates a possibility for a being with others which is neither totalising nor pre-scriptive. Furthermore, in outlining jewgreek justice as an ethically driven renegotiation and reinterpretation of structures, economies and relations of difference, identity, prescription and obligation, I have already instantiated it as situated within that non-determinate space Critchley outlines as the political – within, for instance, the factical 'field of antagonism, decision, dissension and struggle' (Critchley, 1993: 102).

What this means, then, is that in instantiating and negotiating the eventality, facticity and irrecusability of decisions and obligations at the level of the inter-relatedness and fragility of flesh, jewgreek justice unfolds and highlights the socio-political through its promise of an ethically opened decision-making, rather than as any *actual* (pre-scribed and/or legitimated) decisions and practices. That is, the notion and function of this socio-political instantiates and sustains the ethical promise of jewgreek justice in its ceaseless attention to the eventality, facticity and differends of flesh. Furthermore, it is its instantiation within and renegotiation of the socio-political which keeps jewgreek justice on the lookout for those instances and differends of obligation that accompany every coming of and being with other others. In its obligation, promise and decision to spare flesh, then, jewgreek justice does indeed highlight the imperative for an open socio-political decision-making which is itself a rigorously ethical attentiveness to difference, to any/every other, to other others, to flesh, etc. It perhaps marks, in other words, what Caputo has called an 'ethics-becoming-politics' (Caputo, 2000: 64).

At this point, then, Critchley's concerns of 'the ethical moment in deconstruction' – instantiated, I have argued, as the promise informing jewgreek justice – being, perhaps, 'too formalistic and abstract at the level of undecidability, or too contingent and empty at the level of the decision' (Critchley, 1993: 101, 102), seem to somehow miss the point. However, there is one obvious point which is pertinent here – namely, that Critchley is concerned solely with Derridean deconstruction and not with the possibility of that jewgreek justice which I have suggested is opened by (and between) the work of both Derrida and Caputo. Hence I could perhaps suggest that Caputo's particular interpretative repetition of deconstruction – his enfleshing of it – itself answers Critchley's concerns. That is, in his work to enflesh the possibilities of that undecidability opened by deconstruction, Caputo has in fact situated it within the facticity of flesh and obligation – a domain that would seem to correspond to the political domain as configured by Critchley. After all, just as Critchley stresses the unavoidable 'necessity for political decisions and political critique' (Critchley, 1993: 101), so Caputo stresses that flesh does not and cannot wait and that obligation happens without why. Thus, although the instant (and instance) of the decision *is* inscribed within undecidability and madness, it is also inscribed within the basic facticity and interrelatedness of flesh and obligations. It is, furthermore, in no way prescriptive or tolerant of indecision. Consequently, it is *as* inscribed within and by obligations, *as* inscribed and informed by the needs of flesh in its facticity, that jewgreek justice is instantiated within and through the socio-political, and is inextricable from Critchley's notion of political decisions and critique.

Nonetheless, Critchley's concerns still linger. Can the jewgreek instantiation of friendship equate to what Critchley would consider an effective political strategy or adequate account of political decisions and life? Our question now, then, is whether Critchley's designations of the political as the domain of 'contestation, antagonism, struggle, conflict, and dissension' (Critchley, 1993: 101) – an agonistics – relate to the instantiation of jewgreek justice as friendship and hospitality. In other words, is there a disparity here between a political agonistics and jewgreek friendship? And, if this is the case, would that mean that any such instantiation of jewgreek justice perhaps cannot account for Critchley's concerns? In other words, although this agonistics and projected friendship both recognise the essential undecidability informing decision-making, and although they both work to 're-peatedly interrupt all attempts at totalization' (Critchley, 1992: 223), and are both instantiated within and as a certain factic eventality, the question remains as to whether they do, in fact, designate the same domain. And it is the answer to this question that will perhaps finally determine a response to Critchley's concerns as to whether any instantiation of jewgreek justice can constitute an adequate account of the political.

What we now need to do, then, is determine whether there is in fact a disparity between Critchley's projection of the political in terms of agonistics and the jewgreek instantiation of it in terms of friendship and unconditional hospitality. However, before we turn to this question, it's important to note that any particular difference could not concern the conditions, processes or desires informing these delineations of the political. After all, both Critchley's and the jewgreek instantiation of the political are concerned with that decision-making which is both enabled by undecidability, and yet is still imperative. On this basis, any difference or disparity could only reside in the actual instantiation of the political by each of these delineations.

Now, of these instantiations, Critchley's seems to want to de-limit undecidability via a demand for accountability – it sees (and sets) a difference and therefore a differend between undecidability and the socio-political domain. In response to this, however, I would argue that instantiating the political through such a move marks a return firstly to that logic of reciprocity which institutes an economy of exchange and return, and which thereby curtails the ethical potentiality of undecidability through a demand for accountability. Secondly, it marks a return to a logic of difference which, driven by ideas of irreconcilability and the differend, assumes the non-existence of 'hauntological movements and effects' (Lucy, 1997: 150).[26] Jewgreek justice on the other hand – instantiating the socio-political as the possibility for a friendship and unconditional hospitality based on undecidability – is careful to keep undecidability open, informing all decision-making. As a result of this difference in instantiation, then, it is perhaps Critchley's delineation of the political which is unable to account for the jewgreek projection of friendship.

One last series of points which can be seen as arising from Critchley's challenge to deconstruction, also concern his assertions that the deconstructive logic of undecidability needs to be supplemented so as to be able to engage in political decision-making – assertions which clearly indicate an alignment with a logic of irreconcilable difference and the differend over that of undecidability and spectrality. These points disclose a series of problems similar to ones encountered previously with regards to the attempted instantiation of a non-metaphysics. First of all, to suggest that jewgreek justice as the possibility of friendship is perhaps irreconcilable with any political agonistics is to suggest that jewgreek justice (along with the political) has a proper or positive instantiation. That is, that jewgreek justice (and the political) should be instantiated not as a strategic possibility, but as a determined and decidable presence – an instantiation which would forget and delimit its ownmost structure of undecidability. Secondly, if irreconcilable with both the instantiation of the political and the operation of decision-making within this agonistics, the instantiation of jewgreek justice would mark and sustain a clear distinction between ethical and political decisions and processes of decision-making – a distinction which could also be neither substantiated nor legitimated in

---

26   Niall Lucy convincingly argues that 'the differend – any differend – is a consequence of not thinking through "the ghost", of re-ontologizing "difference" instead of seeing its hauntological movements and effects' (1997: 150).

that, as deconstruction stresses, all decisions are informed by unde-cidability. In other words, given that the sustaining of any such dis-tinctions is rendered at the least problematic, jewgreek justice cannot be instantiated as any purely or positively ethical configuration which is reduced to indecision before the facticity of the socio-political. Af-ter all, as Caputo repeatedly stresses, 'we are' always already 'up to our ears in historical, political, social, religious, sexual, and who knows what other sorts of structures and networks' (2000: 12).

Being with Others

> I would like to speak of another 'community' (a word I never much liked, because of its connotation of participation, indeed fusion, identification: I see in it as many threats as promises), of another being-together than this one here, of another gathering-together of singularities, of another friend-ship, even though that friendship no doubt owes the essential to being- or gathering-together. (Derrida, 1995b: 46).

At this point, then, I want to approach some of the questions I have opened in the previous section in a slightly different way. Specifically I want to further explore how jewgreek justice informs our being with others. Now I have of course already discussed this possibility in terms of comportment, our rigorous and responsive attention to the eventality and inter-relatedness of spectralised obligations and flesh. However, given the jewgreek focus on ethics as also becoming poli-tics, it is now necessary to unpack this being-together so as to explore its possible instantiation as what Derrida has called 'another "commu-nity"'. To begin with, having been set out by Derrida and Caputo in terms, for example, of friendship, hospitality, tolerance and obligation, we know that this being with others takes the form of an inter-related and interactive responsiveness and responsibility which is irreducible to any prescribed or totalising economy or community. In this mode it would rather constitute what Derrida has earlier delineated as that 'community of the question [...] when the question is not yet determined enough for the hypocrisy of an[y] answer' (1978b: 80):

> A community of decision, of initiative [...] but also a threatened community, in which the question has not yet found the language it has decided to seek, is not yet sure of its own possibility within the community. A community of the question about the possibility of the question. This is very little – almost nothing – but within it, today, is sheltered and encapsulated an unbreachable dignity and duty of decision. An unbreachable responsibility. (Derrida, 1978b: 80).

Such a community or being-together would thus not be based on any given answers or prescriptions. It would not be founded or sustained by way of any given or prescribed truth, expectation or invitation. Rather, negotiated *through* undecidability and in terms of unconditional hospitality and unbreachable responsibility, jewgreek justice unfolds a being with others – that is, *with* any/every other, and *with* other others – which demands the dissociation of hospitality, firstly, from any concept of invitation and, secondly, from any expectation of return or exchange. This being with others is rather to be instantiated upon surprise and unconditional hospitality, and constituted in terms of a promised attentiveness to the flesh, eventality and spectrality of singularities, to obligations and to other others. It aims, as such, to open up the parameters and possibilities of the social rather than to close them down. Neither prescribing nor delineating any full community, jewgreek justice asks the question of and unfolds the possibility for a 'sort of minimal community' or 'another friendship'.[27] Indeed, it suggests an inter-relatedness where '[w]hat is meant by community and institution must be rethought' (Derrida, 1983: 16).

---

27   Derrida discusses this possibility of a 'minimal community' in *Politics of Friendship* (1997a: 236), and 'another friendship' in *On the Name* (1995d: 46).

Afterword: Projections and Possibilities

> One of the most tormenting realities of contemporary social thought is the fact that many thinkers devoted to the cause of emancipation unwittingly embrace philosophical positions with totalitarian consequences. (Steiner, 2003: 93).

> What is called for today – at a time when the democratic ideal seems finally to be catching on worldwide – is not a thoughtless rejection of modern humanism but, rather, a postmodern, postmetaphysical rearticulation of it. (Madison, 2001: 254).

As I indicated at the end of the previous chapter, in renegotiating and interlacing a notion of the ethical inextricably within the political and the social, jewgreek justice unfolds itself as a post-metaphysical promise of a 'new' community. That is, it seems to open the possibility for new forms of not only the ethical and the political, but the social. However, before I embark on exploring these new forms, and some of their possible implications, what is required is a brief summing up of both their grounds and possible trajectories. Now my argument overall has been that jewgreek justice marks an instantiation of a post-metaphysical ethics which neither settles into nor legitimates any absolute relativism or prescriptivism. Configured, rather, as comportment (and risk), jewgreek justice substantiates both undecidability and an ethical potentiality, sustaining an openness towards undecidability, alterity and difference. In other words, jewgreek justice asks and engages with questions of the post-metaphysical, ethics, and the socio-political, *as questions*.

Now if this is so, it is now time to clarify what this actually entails. First of all, what might these new forms actually look like? One suggestion provided to us by Derrida is that of a new form of democracy, what he calls democracy to come. Specifically, instantiated through the provisional interlacing and interpretation of the ethical, political and social possibilities carried out by jewgreek justice, this democracy to come exemplifies no 'new concept of democracy, but a new determination of the given concept of democracy, in the tradition of the concept of democracy' (Derrida, 1997b: 12). Neither seeking to instantiate itself as absolutely new, nor to be instantiated absolutely,[1] this promise of a democracy always to come thus shows jewgreek justice to be a possible ethico-political model which perhaps opens up thought and practice, giving it over to another (demythologised) responsibility. Similarly we could so describe other promises of jewgreek justice: hospitality, friendship, and so forth.

Another way to look at this which I see as particularly useful here, however, is to see jewgreek justice as carrying out a post-metaphysical retrieval and reconfiguration of the Enlightenment.[2] That is, structured around such quasi-transcendental motifs or messianic promises as democracy to come, hospitality, friendship and a minimal community, jewgreek justice retrieves and repeats certain aspects of the discourse of the Enlightenment. And it is this process that, I would suggest, concurrently develops the possibility and trajectory for a 'new Enlightenment' (Derrida, 1989a: 75). Now, if we look at it in this way, jewgreek justice can very clearly be described as the deconstructive development and enfleshment of the Enlightenment project,

---

1   Derrida writes in *Politics of Friendship* that 'democracy remains to come; this is its essence in so far as it remains [...] [B]elonging to the time of the promise, it will always remain, in each of its future times, to come: even when there is democracy, it never exists, it is never present, it remains the theme of a non-presentable concept' (Derrida, 1997a: 306; cf. 1996b: 83).

2   Both Derrida and Caputo directly explicate their work in terms of a 'new' Enlightenment. For instance, as Caputo notes in his 'Deconstruction in a nutshell', Derrida 'would contend' that deconstruction 'is a continuation of what is best about the Enlightenment, but by another means', further suggesting that 'it may be that what the Enlightenment seeks cannot be found on the basis that the Enlightenment lays' (Caputo, 1997a: 54; cf. 59–60). For some of Derrida's calls for and explications of deconstruction as a 'new Enlightenment' (Derrida, 1989a: 75), see, for example, 'The principle of reason: the university in the eyes of its pupils' (1983: 5, 19), *Points ... Interviews, 1974–1994* (1995c: 400, 428), and *Specters of Marx* (1994: 88).

or, more minimally, of a certain 'spirit of the Enlightenment' (1994: 88) which must not be renounced.[3] Certainly this delineation of jewgreek justice can be seen as putting forward a 'new' or alternative trajectory, methodology and epistemological framework for emancipatory politics in general.

Now this is important for several reasons. Firstly, attempts to reconfigure and develop the Enlightenment project – to return, in the view of some theorists and commentators, to reason – are becoming increasingly important (and prevalent). And this is due, at least partly, to some of the challenges and questions raised by the 'Post'. That is, with the deconstruction by the 'Post' of the traditional epistemological framework of the Enlightenment, attempts are currently being made to either reground its political project (e.g. Mouffe and Rorty), or rehabilitate its epistemological framework (e.g. Habermas). Secondly, the highlighting of what can be considered actual and pragmatic implications and possibilities of jewgreek justice further discredits the widely accepted belief that projects of the 'Post' have neither efficacy nor relevance in the face of the factic, socio-political domain. In my discussion of some of the trajectories and implications of jewgreek justice, then, I am asserting not only that a 'Post' can be instantiated which is able to engage within the socio-political domain, but that a post-metaphysical ethics can also inform and supplement the devel-

---

3   In *Specters of Marx*, Derrida projects his 'New International' in terms of an interpretative repetition, a radicalisation, of 'at least one of the spirits of Marx or of Marxism', where a 'fidelity to the inheritance of a certain Marxist *spirit* would remain a duty' (Derrida, 1994: 86, 87). Rorty of course questions the need for this sort of fidelity in *Against Bosses, Against Oligarchies* (2002: 17–21). Nevertheless such a retrieval of or fidelity to a certain spirit is exemplary not only of the relation of jewgreek justice to the Enlightenment but, I argue, of that mode of opened repetition instituted by Heidegger. That is, Heidegger would argue the need for fidelity towards the 'guiding question' of metaphysics rather than towards what he sees as its traditional (and rigid) formulations.

opment of 'new' socio-political projects and alternative epistemologies.[4]

Before I can begin this discussion, however, there are some preliminary remarks to be made. First of all, it is *as* its projection of itself as a post-metaphysical and demythologised 'ethics-becoming-politics', that jewgreek justice is able to instantiate itself in the name of a 'new Enlightenment'. Specifically, jewgreek justice can be seen to comprise a repetition of what Chantal Mouffe has called the 'democratic project' of the Enlightenment (Mouffe, 1996: 1).[5] However, such an instantiation, as we know from Derrida, cannot depend on any 'speculative decree' and '[p]erhaps not even on philosophical discursivity' (Derrida, 1991c: 104). What therefore needs to be considered is how and to what extent the trajectory of jewgreek justice *is* that of a new Enlightenment? And what does such an instantiation actually comprise? Also to be considered is the possible development of a new methodological and epistemological framework which might, in turn, hold implications for other socio-political projects which are desirous of retrieving and extending certain Enlightenment ideals whilst taking at least some account of the 'Post'.[6] Such projects – aimed at re-

---

4   A related view is taken by Gary Brent Madison in *The Politics of Postmodernity: Essays in Applied Hermeneutics*. In his words, 'Not only is a post-metaphysical use of theory possible, it is also […] crucial to the improvement (the "cultivation") of our practices and to the advancement of that form of social praxis known as democracy' (Madison, 2001: 5).

5   Following Rorty, Chantal Mouffe distinguishes between 'the political project of the Enlightenment and its epistemological aspects'. As she states, 'Once we acknowledge that there is no necessary relation between these two aspects, we are in the position of being able to defend the political project while abandoning [deconstructing] the notion that it must be based on a specific form of rationality' (Mouffe, 1993: 9, 10).

6   For instance, unlike many of those concerned with the attempt to reground and develop certain aspects of the Enlightenment project, both Mouffe and Rorty, in their developments of radical (Mouffe) and liberal (Rorty) democracy, stress the importance of the problematising of the 'Post' for emancipatory politics. In Mouffe's words, albeit with regards to her own project: 'far from seeing the development of postmodern philosophy as a threat, radical democracy welcomes it as an indispensable instrument in the accomplish-

grounding democracy and emancipatory politics, and developing new epistemological frameworks for them – are, after all, the focus of a wide range of positions. They include, for instance, not just deconstruction and jewgreek justice, but feminism, ecological and anti-racist movements, and post-colonialism. Despite their disparate contexts, many of these projects can be seen as concerned to suggest or develop – at the least, call for – new instantiations of democracy or emancipation. That is, they are concerned, in varying ways, to *answer* the question of democracy as posed by the 'Post' through its deconstruction of the epistemological framework of the Enlightenment. In other words, the focus for many of these projects is to find and substantiate a mode by which the question of *how* a democracy or community can now be instantiated and maintained can be answered. What I suggest, then, is that *if* jewgreek justice can be shown to comprise a reconfiguration of – or, at least, another way of talking about – both the Enlightenment and its epistemological framework, it might thereby work to effectively and critically supplement other attempted reconfigurations of Enlightenment ideals.

In the Name of a New Enlightenment

> I do not see how one can pose the question of ethics if one renounces the motifs of emancipation and the messianic. (Derrida, 1996b: 82).

Before I turn to discussing the jewgreek retrieval and reconfiguration of justice (and democracy) from the Enlightenment tradition, and what it perhaps entails, it is necessary to briefly consider the Enlightenment

---

ment of its goals' (Mouffe, 1993: 21). Similarly Rorty starts from and argues for a liberal – indeed, utopian – democracy on the basis of an 'anti-foundationalism' and a 'post-Philosophical culture' (Rorty, 1998a). This recognition of the importance of the 'Post' for attempts to develop certain Enlightenment ideals is, notoriously, absent in the work of Habermas.

project itself.[7] Although it is far beyond the confines of this work to comprehensively outline this project, there are several points that need mentioning. Briefly, the Enlightenment project is comprised of a loosely unified set of doctrines[8] which assert that 'the source of all human misery is ignorance, especially superstition', and that only 'knowledge, reason, and science can destroy ignorance and superstition and help improve the human condition' (Hollinger, 1994: 2). This set of doctrines can further be expressed as the idea that only 'a society based on science and universal values' – which are assented to and accepted by all rational (human) beings – can be 'truly free' and 'happy' (7).[9] In other words, the Enlightenment project bases justice – as the promise of emancipation – upon reasoned and universal values, and the assumption of a possible and positive 'endless human progress' (7). Hence, as Kant stresses, the instantiation of 'an *age of enlightenment*' necessarily presumes and entails that 'the obstacles to general enlightenment [...] are gradually being reduced'.[10]

With justice instantiated, for instance, in terms of the Enlightenment goal of realising 'a society based exclusively on knowledge

---

7   See Peter Gay's works for a comprehensive analysis and discussion of the central themes of the Enlightenment: *The Enlightenment: The Rise of Modern Paganism* and *The Enlightenment: The Science of Freedom*. Also see *The Philosophy of the Enlightenment* by Ernst Cassirer.

8   Peter Gay, for instance, describes the Enlightenment as comprising a 'single army with a single banner, with a large central corps, a right and a left wing, daring scouts, and lame stragglers' (Gay, 1995: 7–8).

9   Claire Colebrook notes that the 'demand of enlightenment in its revolutionary and political manifestations began as an internalisation of law: authority ought not be seen as imposed from without but should be generated from human reason' (Colebrook, 1999: 47). See Kant's *Foundations of the Metaphysics of Morals* for clear formulations of the Enlightenment vision of ethics and justice being based on reason and freedom.

10   Kant makes this claim in *Foundations of the Metaphysics of Morals* (1987: 90–91). This optimistic attitude is characteristic of the majority of Enlightenment thinkers. Edward Gibbon, for instance, writes that 'We cannot determine to what height the human species may aspire in their advances towards perfection but it may safely be presumed that no people [...] will relapse into their original barbarism' (Gibbon, cited in Gay, 1996: 98).

that liberates people from oppression' (Hollinger, 1994: 13), it is clear that it operates as both a metaphysical and empirical ideal. In other words, as a metaphysical idea – an a priori, necessarily universal and unconditioned principle – justice grounds and frames the possibility of its empirical institution. The Enlightenment idea of justice thus constitutes and functions as a regulative ideal, a *telos*, which orders and prescribes the 'proper' empirical. That is, it discloses a proper goal and framework for the empirical which is, at least potentially, realisable and actualisable. Acting as the formal condition for the empirical possibility of justice (formulated, in Kant's terms, as the moral law of the categorical imperative which is to ground and organise practical behaviour), this idea of justice – based on universalised values of reason and unconditional freedom – affirms a metaphysical logic. That is, it relies on that logic which Heidegger considers to be constitutively metaphysical, effecting in itself an a priori 'staking out of the field and [as] the establishment of the goal' (Heidegger, 1991b: 194). It is this metaphysical logic, then, that drives and determines – indeed, promises – the empirical institution of justice and emancipation in terms of a dream of endless and positive human progress and enlightenment. The Enlightenment's promise of justice and emancipation thus has its proper instantiation in terms of such a teleological dream and/or given.

On the other hand, jewgreek justice and democracy is inscribed within the doubled logic and undecidability of flesh and the ghost. Indeed, its projection of a democracy to come is constitutively spectral, the 'theme of a non-presentable concept' (Derrida, 1997a: 306) and a promise *without* possibility of proper or full actualisation. It is a projection which, instantiated through a logic of undecidability, is supplemented by both the contingency and facticity of flesh, and the movements and effects of spectrality. Democracy to come, far from representing, demanding or promising any positive (or, indeed, negative) given institution, is rather indicative of the deconstructive repetition and questioning interpretation of this metaphysical drive and dream of the Enlightenment. Indeed, repeated in terms of that spectralised being with others which is the jewgreek promise of a new community, this new form of democracy or the Enlightenment cannot be seen as founded upon any universalised, regulative or prescriptive ideals. Indicative of 'an alliance without institution' (Derrida, 1994: 86), this democracy to come, for instance, cannot be considered as able to be instantiated through the operation and dream of any such metaphysical ideal. Rather, such post-metaphysical interpretations of the Enlightenment dream and promise exemplify a promise for an impossible justice, a messianic justice.[11]

In other words, jewgreek justice comprises the acknowledgement of both 'the failure of the Enlightenment's sociopolitical project' and the 'continuing influence of the ideas constituting the political and ethical force of Enlightenment thought' (Racevskis, 1993: 76). Indeed:

> [T]he thread that may connect us with the Enlightenment is not faithfulness to [its] doctrinal elements, but rather the permanent reactivation of an attitude [...] that could be described as a permanent critique of our historical era. (Foucault, 1984b: 42).[12]

As the retrieval and reactivation of such an attitude – or 'ethos' as Foucault also calls it here – the jewgreek promise of justice is not only constitutively open and in question, undecidable, but also constitutively critical. It functions 'like a kind of *white light* to hold against

---

11   Derrida, for example, outlines ten 'plagues of the "new world order"' in *Specters of Marx*, stressing that the dream and promise of the Enlightenment have not been (and, perhaps, cannot be) realised (see 1994: 81–85). He further distinguishes two (at least) differing interpretations of these plagues – first, that of seeing them as operating in an '*idealist* logic' where the aim is to 'reduce the gap *as much as possible*' between the negative 'empirical reality and a regulating ideal' (86). Secondly, Derrida suggests an interpretation which would 'obey another logic', which would bring into question the 'very concept of the said ideal' (86, 87). Democracy or the 'New International' is, Derrida stresses, not a realisable goal per se, but rather a questioning of both ideal and reality which entwines and supplements both interpretations.

12   An interesting discussion of Foucault's relation to and retrieval of the Enlightenment, with reference to certain Heideggerian themes, is Benjamin Pryor's 'Counter-remembering the Enlightenment'.

the flesh of the present' exposing 'the blemishes of the current age' (Caputo, 2000: 119). What this jewgreek reconfiguration demonstrates, along with questioning and supplementing the metaphysical and epistemological foundations and dreams of the Enlightenment, is that it can never be simply a question of deciding either for or against the Enlightenment. After all, as Derrida puts it, 'it is sometimes in the name of [...] a new Enlightenment that I deconstruct a given Enlightenment' (Derrida, 1989a: 75; cf. 1995c: 428).

What this means, then, is that jewgreek justice functions as a sustained interpretation, where Enlightenment ideals and maxims are repeated as the opened questions and ethical and socio-political potentialities of a new Enlightenment. These questions and potentialities are, as such, never able to be fully instantiated, as to do so would be to substantiate the totalising dreams of either metaphysics or empiricism, or, indeed, the 'old' Enlightenment.[13] In other words, the trajectory of jewgreek justice as a new Enlightenment is its way (and methodology) of critically interpreting – that is, of opening and supplementing – Enlightenment ideals. Hence, for jewgreek justice, the Enlightenment ideals of justice, emancipation and democracy represent not any possible empirical future present as such, but guiding questions which inform (rather than legitimate) that long and slow trajectory of a post-metaphysics which is itself unable to legitimate or be inscribed within any determinate ethics or metaphysics, or given empirical institution.[14] Such ideals, then, are opened to undecidability and alterity, and to dif-

---

13   Caputo distinguishes between an 'old' and a 'new' Enlightenment in *The Prayers and Tears of Jacques Derrida* (1997b: 353n5).

14   Derrida unfolds such an interpretation of an Enlightenment ideal as question when he stresses the constitutive and necessary openness of, for instance, emancipation: 'I believe that there is an enormous amount to do today for emancipation, in all domains and all the areas of the world and society. Even if I would not wish to inscribe the discourse of emancipation into a teleology, a metaphysics, an eschatology, or even a classical messianism, I none the less believe that there is no ethico-political decision or gesture without what I would call a "Yes" to emancipation, to the discourse of emancipation' (Derrida, 1996b: 82).

ference and the future. In other words, the jewgreek questioning of justice, emancipation, democracy and community not only marks a retrieval and repetition of the Enlightenment project, but its effective reconfiguration by way of the logic of undecidability.

Repeating the Democratic Project

> Deconstruction [...] permits us to think the political and think the democratic by granting us the space necessary in order not to be enclosed in the latter. (Derrida, 1996b: 85).

> [This deconstructive] ethical conception of justice can never be fully instantiated in the public realm, nor can it be divorced from the latter; rather justice regulates public space, making politics critical, utopian and radically democratic. (Critchley, 1996: 36).

To best explore this reconfiguration of the Enlightenment project, I will consider in more detail one aspect of the jewgreek repetition of it, specifically its delineation of democracy to come. Now as I have already stressed, this is projected by jewgreek justice in the form of a messianic promise which is configured as always yet to come, *à-venir*. It substantiates, as both Derrida and Caputo emphasise, no ideal or empirical institution or possibility, unfolding rather as a questioning comportment that constitutes and is informed by – saying 'yes, yes' to – a sustained 'engagement with regard to democracy' (Derrida, 1996b: 83). This critical engagement thus opens up democracy and democratic structures to 'the possibility of something presently unforeseeable within the settings of their current horizons' (Caputo, 2000: 118).

Democracy to come, then, is informed *not* by the possibility and requirements of its own realisation, but affirms, as a promise, something which not only exceeds but supplements the context-specific institutions of democracy. It affirms something which is not transcendental but quasi-transcendental, and which is inscribed within and by undecidability and flesh. In other words, the jewgreek projection of democracy operates not in the terms of either the given or the possible, or, even, as Rorty suggests as a 'question of efficiency' (Rorty, 1998b: 172). Rather it is supplemented by an excessive and ethical promise and responsibility, the undecidable logic and promise of an 'ethics-becoming-politics'.[15] And it is in this way that democracy to come comprises an enfleshed messianic promise to a spectralised community, where not only the institution of this promise but the 'we' of this community must be regarded with 'the greatest suspicion' (Caputo, 2000: 121): 'Are we Greeks? Are we Jews? But who, we?' (Derrida, 1978b: 153).

Democracy is thus repeated and sustained *as a question*. Furthermore, it is through being sustained as a question that democracy to come keeps its instantiations from ending up in or as determinate – and, indeed, complacent – democratic future presents. In other words, it is this repetition of the democratic institution and community as a question and as an impossibility, as a democracy to come, which distinguishes it from other attempted retrievals and reconfigurations of democracy and the Enlightenment project. For example, although both Mouffe and Rorty both work to resubstantiate democracy in terms of contingent and context-specific relations and practices,[16] they nonetheless aim to instantiate some positive or possible formulation of democracy within particular parameters. Specifically, they aim to instantiate democracy without reference to any other ideal than itself. That is, democracy – whether radical and inscribed within an irrecusable agonistic pluralism (Mouffe), or liberal and utopian (Rorty) – is effectively to legitimate itself, to substantiate itself without reference to any

---

15   Simon Critchley stresses the openness of this projection of democracy and justice when he comments that although 'deconstruction is pragmatist', it is '*not pragmatist all the way down*. At the basis of deconstruction is a non-pragmatist (or at least non-Rortian) foundational commitment to justice as something that cannot be relativized' (Critchley, 1996: 37).

16   See, for instance, Mouffe's 'Deconstruction, pragmatism and the politics of democracy' (1996: 5) and *The Return of the Political* (1993: 8, 69) and Rorty's 'Remarks on deconstruction and pragmatism' (1996g: 17).

(even quasi-transcendental and post-metaphysical) conceptions of the ethical. Such a picture reveals a certain complacency concerning the telos, institute and the 'we' of democracy, wherein all of these are to be automatically disclosed within and determined through the institution of the democratic future present.[17]

Contrary to this picture, jewgreek justice projects its development of democracy and of the Enlightenment by way of that logic of undecidability and anxiety which itself also substantiates jewgreek justice as a post-metaphysics. Indeed, it is through its instantiation by way of the logic of undecidability that jewgreek justice can be considered to implicate not just a new Enlightenment but a new epistemological framework for this Enlightenment, and, potentially, for emancipatory politics in general. That is, explicated as a questioning comportment, this new jewgreek Enlightenment is constitutively unenframable by traditional epistemological grounds of 'rationalism, individualism and universalism' (Mouffe, 1993: 7). For jewgreek justice – as the possibility and trajectory of this new Enlightenment – there is, in Mouffe's words, 'no longer a role to be played' by the 'epistemological perspective of the Enlightenment' (10). Indeed, such an epistemological perspective or framework is at odds with jewgreek justice. Whilst the methodological and epistemological framework of the 'old' Enlightenment could be seen to be the grounding and substantiating of a correlation – that is, a transcendentally ordered relation – between its metaphysical and empirical ideals, jewgreek justice dis-

---

17   For instance, as I have noted, Rortian democracy highlights and unfolds along one particular liberal utopian trajectory – the 'institutions and practices of the rich North Atlantic democracies' (Rorty, 1983: 585), that is, a 'sentimental education' (1998b: 176) – by which all other conversations and communities must be measured and, eventually, subsumed. Similarly, Mouffe's radical democracy also proposes and takes a particular trajectory, that of a provisional hegemony – a 'we' – of what she calls articulated 'democratic equivalences' and a 'new "common sense"' (Mouffe, 1993: 19), comprised specifically against and in terms of the agonistic pluralism of the socio-political. Mouffe's vision of democracy, then, is developed in terms of conflict. Indeed, she goes so far as to stress that without conflict there can be no democracy (e.g. 1993: 4, 8, 18; cf. 1996: 8).

closes an epistemological framework which is informed by a logic of undecidability. In other words, the form of jewgreek justice as a new Enlightenment does not need to be either positively grounded or constituted. Instead it must remain spectralised through and through, and opened to the undecidability and facticity of the hermeneutical situation.

Provisional Conclusions

What I have suggested, then, is that although jewgreek justice is constitutively unable to present or legitimate any formula for democracy, emancipation, justice or even community, what it does project is the possibility of a methodology and epistemology able to substantiate the opening and deconstruction of such Enlightenment ideals as the trajectory of a new Enlightenment. Furthermore, informed by the jewgreek logic of undecidability and anxiety, such a projection is perhaps able to critically inform and supplement other projects concerned with the further development of emancipatory politics. In other words, I am suggesting that this jewgreek reconfiguration of the Enlightenment project – its reconfiguration of Enlightenment ideals and certainties as the guiding questions of a post-metaphysical ethics – is able to take effect in and supplement not only the undecidability of the hermeneutical situation, but the complacency of other projected trajectories of emancipatory politics. That is, insofar as other ethical or socio-political projects affirm specific – given or possible – institutions or future presents, they are interrupted and questioned by jewgreek justice. In other words, in affirming a possible non-positive trajectory for a new Enlightenment and for emancipatory politics – a being with or being together which is neither determined by nor irreducible to any given or possible ideal or future present of democracy, justice or community – jewgreek justice is potentially able to question other, positive answers to and projections of the Enlightenment, exposing them to undecidability and the alterity of other others.

Now, having delineated and developed this possibility throughout the previous chapters, culminating in the disclosure of a possible trajectory for a new Enlightenment, the time has come to consider some of the provisional conclusions and implications of my argument. My delineation of jewgreek justice, then, as an opened and sustained post-metaphysical ethics – that is, as a constitutively critical and ethical mode of interpretation informed by the logics of anxiety and undecidability disclosed by Heidegger and Derrida (and Caputo) respectively – exemplifies not only a certain retrieval of the 'Post', but a delineation of this 'Post' as ethical. For example, with much of the rhetoric of and about the 'Post' widely seen as stymied by charges of paradox, relativism, and inefficacy in the face of the socio-political domain, my delineation of jewgreek justice suggests a way and methodology for thinking about ethics and the 'Post', and about the socio-political, which is not dependent on or inscribed within what Heidegger calls fundamental metaphysical positions. It is through its shift from the development of prescriptive formulas to the sustaining of an opened and ethical comportment, along with its development of such a comportment, then, that I argue that jewgreek justice develops and instantiates a new trajectory for ethics. That is, it instantiates a post-metaphysical 'ethics-becoming-politics' which configures the possibility and trajectory for a new Enlightenment. Furthermore, it is an ethical possibility and trajectory able to critically and effectively engage within – that is, supplement – the socio-political domain of both the hermeneutical situation and emancipatory politics.

Overall, then, the provisional conclusions of this book can be summed up as follows. First of all, although much of the discourse of and about the 'Post' is caught in paradox and at an impasse, there can be configured a constitutively open model of the 'Post'. Developed from within the horizon of Heideggerian interpretation and its overcoming of metaphysics, and instantiated by Derrida and Caputo as jewgreek justice, such a 'Post' is also, I argue, constitutively ethical – comprising, as such, a post-metaphysical ethics. However, informed by a logic of undecidability and anxiety, this jewgreek justice is also constitutively unable to develop or legitimate any positive delineation of ethics as such. Nevertheless, this does not entail that this post-metaphysical ethics leads only to relativism, nihilism or paradox. Rather, I have demonstrated that it comprises and develops the possibility and methodology of an openness and a comportment towards undecidability, difference and alterity, a comportment which is, furthermore, constitutively inscribed within facticity and the hermeneutical situation.

Such a comportment, I have then suggested, can in turn be seen as the possible trajectory and methodology for a sustained and critical engagement within the socio-political domain, an engagement which can itself be configured as a new Enlightenment. Furthermore, I have suggested that the delineation of jewgreek justice as a new Enlightenment has resounding implications for emancipatory politics in general, not only critically opening and questioning, but supplementing, its various projected institutions, structures and formulas. Such possibilities and implications are, then, I suggest, relevant for all those who are concerned with the possibilities and trajectories opened for ethics and emancipatory politics by the 'Post'. That is, they are relevant for all those who are looking (albeit, non-absolutely) beyond the 'Post' and who are, with Derrida, asking about and working for 'an ethics, a politics (are these words still appropriate?)' which 'cannot depend on a[ny] speculative decree, even less on an opinion' (Derrida, 1991c: 104).

Bibliography

Baugh, Bruce (1992) 'Transcendental empiricism: Deleuze's response to Hegel', *Man and World* 25, 138–148.

Benso, Silvia (1994) 'On the way to ontological ethics', *Research in Phenomenology* 24, 159–188.

Bogue, Ronald (1996) 'Deleuze's style', *Man and World* 29(3), 251–268.

Bourdieu, Pierre (1996) *The Political Ontology of Martin Heidegger*, trans. Peter Collier. Cambridge: Polity Press.

Calcagno, Antonio (1995) 'Interface: modernity and post-modernity: the possibility of enthusiasm according to Immanuel Kant and Jean-Francois Lyotard', *Philosophy Today* 39(4), 358–370.

Caputo, John D. (2000) *More Radical Hermeneutics*. Bloomington & Indianapolis: Indiana University Press.

_____. (1998) 'An American and a liberal: John D. Caputo's response to Michael Zimmerman', *Continental Philosophy Review* 31, 215–220.

_____. (1997a) 'A commentary: deconstruction in a nutshell'. In John D. Caputo (ed), *Deconstruction in a Nutshell*. New York: Fordham University Press, 31–202.

_____. (1997b) *The Prayers and Tears of Jacques Derrida: Religion without Religion*. Bloomington and Indianapolis: Indiana University Press.

_____. (1996) 'A community without truth: Derrida and the impossible community', *Research in Phenomenology* 26, 25–37.

_____. (1993a) *Against Ethics*. Bloomington and Indianapolis: Indiana University Press.

_____. (1993b) *Demythologizing Heidegger*. Bloomington and Indianapolis: Indiana University Press.

_____. (1991) 'Hyperbolic justice: deconstruction, myth, and politics', *Research in Phenomenology* 21, 3–20.

_____. (1987) *Radical Hermeneutics*. Bloomington and Indianapolis: Indiana University Press.

Carroll, David (1989) *Paraesthetics*. New York and London: Routledge.

Cassirer, Ernst (1979) *The Philosophy of the Enlightenment*. Princeton, New Jersey: Princeton University Press.

Colebrook, Claire (1999) *Ethics and Representation: From Kant to Post-structuralism*. Edinburgh: Edinburgh University Press.

_____. (1998) 'The future-to-come: Derrida and the ethics of historicity', *Philosophy Today* 42(4), 347–360.

Cooper, Simon (1997) 'Beyond enframing', *Arena* 9, 23–56.

Coward, Harold G. (1992) *Derrida and Negative Theology*. Albany: SUNY Press.

Critchley, Simon (1996) 'Deconstruction and pragmatism – is Derrida a private ironist or a public liberal?' In Chantal Mouffe (ed), *Deconstruction and Pragmatism*. New York and London: Routledge, 19–40.

_____. (1993) 'The Question of the question: an ethico-political response to a note in Derrida's *De L'esprit'*. In David Wood (ed), *Of Derrida, Heidegger, and Spirit*. Evanston, Illinois: Northwestern University Press, 93–102.

_____. (1992) *The Ethics of Deconstruction*. Oxford: Blackwell.

De Beistegui, Miguel (1998) *Heidegger and the Political: Dystopias*. New York and London: Routledge.

Deleuze, Gilles (1995) *Negotiations*, trans. Martin Joughin. New York: Columbia University Press.

_____. (1990) *The Logic of Sense*, trans. Mark Lester and Charles Stivale. New York: Columbia University Press.

_____. (1988) *Spinoza: Practical Philosophy*, trans. Robert Hurley. San Francisco: City Lights Books.

Deleuze, Gilles and Félix Guattari (1994) *What is Philosophy?*, trans. Graham Burchell and Hugh Tomlinson. New York and London: Verso.

_____. (1987a) *A Thousand Plateaus*, trans. Brian Massumi. Minneapolis: University of Minnesota Press.

_____. (1984) *Anti-Oedipus*, trans. Robert Hurley, Mark Seem, and Helen R. Lane. London: Athlone Press.

Deleuze, Gilles and Claire Parnet (1987b) *Dialogues*, trans. Hugh Tomlinson and Barbara Habberjam. New York: Columbia University Press.

Derrida, Jacques (2003) 'The becoming possible of the impossible: an interview with Jacques Derrida'. In Mark Dooley (ed), *A Passion for the Impossible: John D. Caputo in Focus*. New York: State University of New York Press, 21–33.

_____. (2002) *Ethics, Institutions, and the Right to Philosophy*, trans. Peter Pericles Trifonas. Lanham, Boulder, New York and Oxford: Rowman and Littlefield.

_____. (2000) *Of Hospitality: Anne Dufourmantelle Invites Jacques Derrida to Respond*, trans. Rachel Bowlby. Stanford California: Stanford University Press.

_____. (1999a) *Adieu to Emmanuel Levinas*, trans. Pascale-Anne Brault and Michael Naas. Stanford, California: Stanford University Press.

_____. (1999b) 'Hospitality, justice and responsibility: a dialogue with Jacques Derrida'. In Richard Kearney and Mark Dooley (eds), *Questioning Ethics: Contemporary Debates in Philosophy*. New York and London: Routledge, 65–83.

_____. (1998) 'Faith and knowledge: the two sources of "religion" at the limits of reason alone'. In Jacques Derrida and Gianni Vattimo (eds), *Religion*. Stanford, California: Stanford University Press, 1–78.

_____. (1997a) *Politics of Friendship*, trans. George Collins. London and New York: Verso.

_____. (1997b) 'The Villanova roundtable: a conversation with Jacques Derrida'. In John D. Caputo (ed), *Deconstruction in a Nutshell*. New York: Fordham University Press, 3–28.

_____. (1996a) *Archive Fever: A Freudian Impression*, trans. Eric Prenowitz. Chicago and London: University of Chicago Press.

_____. (1996b) 'Remarks on deconstruction and pragmatism'. In Chantal Mouffe (ed), *Deconstruction and Pragmatism*. New York and London: Routledge, 77–88.

_____. (1995a) *Limited Inc.*, trans. Samuel Weber. Evanston: Northwestern University Press.

_____. (1995b) *On the Name*, trans. David Wood, John P. Leavey, Jr., and Ian McLeod. Stanford: Stanford University Press.

_____. (1995c) *Points . . . Interviews 1974–1994*, ed. Elisabeth Weber. Stanford: Stanford University Press.

_____. (1995d) *The Gift of Death*, trans. David Willis. Chicago and London: University of Chicago Press.

_____. (1994) *Specters of Marx*, trans. Peggy Kamuf. New York and London: Routledge.

_____. (1993a) *Aporias*, trans. Thomas Dutoit. Stanford California: Stanford University Press.

_____. (1993b) 'Circumfession', trans. Geoffrey Bennington. In Geoffrey Bennington and Jacques Derrida (eds), *Jacques Derrida*. Chicago and London: University of Chicago Press.

_____. (1992a) 'Force of law: the "mystical foundation of authority"', trans. Mary Quaintance. In Drucilla Cornell, Michel Rosenfeld, and David Gray Carlson (eds), *Deconstruction and the Possibility of Justice*. New York and London: Routledge, 3–67.

_____. (1992b) 'Given time: the time of the King', trans. Peggy Kamuf, *Critical Inquiry* 18, 161–187.

_____. (1992c) *Jacques Derrida: Acts of Literature*, ed. Derek Attridge. New York: Routledge.

_____. (1992d) *The Other Heading: Memories, Responses, and Responsibilities*, trans. Pascale-Anne Brault and Michael B. Naas. Bloomington and Indianapolis: Indiana University Press.

_____. (1991a) 'At this very moment in this work here I Am' (selections), trans. Ruben Berezdivin. In Peggy Kamuf (ed), *A Derrida Reader: Between the Blinds*. New York: Columbia University Press, 405–439.

_____. (1991b) *Cinders*, trans. Ned Lukacher. Lincoln: University of Nebraska Press.

_____. (1991c) '"Eating well," or the calculation of the subject: an interview with Jacques Derrida', trans. Peter Connor and Avital Ronell. In Eduardo Cadava, Peter Connor, and Jean-Luc Nancy (eds), *Who Comes After the Subject?* New York and London, Routledge: 96–119.

_____. (1991d) *Given Time, I: Counterfeit Money*, trans. Peggy Kamuf. Chicago: University of Chicago Press.

_____. (1989a) 'Jacques Derrida in conversation with Christopher Norris'. In Andreas Papadakis et al. (eds), *Deconstruction Omnibus Volume*. New York: Rizzoli.

_____. (1989b) *Of Spirit: Heidegger and the Question*, trans. Geoffrey Bennington and Rachel Bowlby. Chicago and London: University of Chicago Press.

_____. (1989c) 'Psyche: inventions of the other', trans. Catherine Porter. In Wlad Godzich and Lindsay Waters (eds), *Reading de Man Reading*. Minneapolis: University of Minnesota Press, 25–65.

_____. (1987) *The Truth in Painting*, trans. Geoff Bennington and Ian McLeod. Chicago and London: University of Chicago Press.

_____. (1986a) 'Deconstruction and the other'. In Richard Kearney (ed), *Dialogues with Contemporary Thinkers*. Manchester: Manchester University Press, 107–126.

_____. (1986b) *Memoires: For Paul de Man*, trans. Cecile Lindsay, Jonathan Culler, and Eduardo Cadava. New York: Columbia University Press.

_____. (1984) 'An interview with Jacques Derrida', *Graduate Faculty Philosophy Journal* 10, 5–27.

_____. (1983) 'The principle of reason: the university in the eyes of its pupils', trans. Catherine Porter and Edward P. Morris, *Diacritics*, 3–20.

_____. (1982a) *Margins of Philosophy*, trans. Alan Bass. London: Harvester Wheatsheaf.

_____. (1982b) *Positions*, trans. Alan Bass. Chicago: University of Chicago Press.

_____. (1981) *Dissemination*, trans. Barbara Johnson. Chicago: University of Chicago Press.

_____. (1979) 'Living on: border Lines', trans. James Hulbert. In Harold Bloom et al. (eds), *Deconstruction and Criticism*. New York: Seabury Press, 75–176.

_____. (1978a) 'The retrait of metaphor', trans. F. Gasdner et al, *Enclitic* 2(2), 5–33.

_____. (1978b) *Writing and Difference*, trans. Alan Bass. London: Routledge.

_____. (1976) *Of Grammatology*, trans. Gayatri Chakravorty Spivak. Baltimore and London: John Hopkins University Press.

_____. (1973) *Speech and Phenomena: and Other Essays on Husserl's Theory of Signs*, trans. David. B. Allison. Evanston: Northwestern University Press.

Dooley, Mark (ed.) (2003) *A Passion for the Impossible: John D. Caputo in Focus*. New York: State University of New York Press.

Farías, Victor (1989) *Heidegger and Nazism*, trans. Paul Burrell, Dominic DiBernardi, and Gabriel R. Ricci. Philadelphia: Temple University Press.

Ferry, Luc and Alain Renaut (eds) (1997) *Why We are Not Nietzscheans*, trans. Robert de Loaiza. Chicago and London: University of Chicago Press.

Foucault, Michel (1984a) 'Preface to *Anti-Oedipus*'. In Gilles Deleuze and Félix Guattari (1984) *Anti-Oedipus*, trans. Robert Hurley, Mark Seem, and Helen R. Lane. London: Athlone Press, xi–xiv.

_____. (1984b) 'What is Enlightenment?', trans. Catherine Porter. In Paul Rabinow (ed), *The Foucault Reader*. Penguin, 32–50.

Gasché, Rodolphe (2000) 'Toward an ethics of *Auseinandersetzung*'. In Walter Brogan and James Risser (eds), *American Continental Philosophy: A Reader*. Bloomington and Indianapolis: Indiana University Press, 314–332.

_____. (1995) *Inventions of Difference*. Cambridge, Massachusetts and London, England: Harvard University Press.

_____. (1986) *The Tain of the Mirror: Derrida and the Philosophy of Reflection*, Cambridge, Massachusetts and London, England: Harvard University Press.

Gay, Peter (1996) *The Enlightenment: An Interpretation: The Science of Freedom*. New York and London: Norton.

_____. (1995) *The Enlightenment: An Interpretation: The Rise of Modern Paganism*. New York and London: Norton.

Goicoechea, David (1999) 'The moment of responsibility (Derrida and Kierkegaard)', *Philosophy Today* 43(3), 211–225.

Guattari, Félix (1995) *Chaosmosis: An Ethico-aesthetic Paradigm*, trans. Paul Bains and Julian Pefanis. Sydney: Power Publications.

Haber, Honi Fern (1995) 'Lyotard and the problems of pagan politics', *Philosophy Today* 39(2), 142–156.

_____. (1994) *Beyond Postmodern Politics: Lyotard, Rorty, Foucault*. New York and London: Routledge.

Hatab, Lawrence J. (1995) 'Ethics and finitude: Heideggerian contributions to moral philosophy', *International Philosophical Quarterly* 35(4), 403–417.

Hayden, Patrick (1995) 'From relations to practice in the empiricism of Gilles Deleuze', *Man and World* 28, 283–302.

Heidegger, Martin (1999) *Contributions to Philosophy (from Enowning)*, trans. Parvis Emad and Kenneth Maly. Bloomington: Indiana University Press.

_____. (1998) *Pathmarks*, ed. William McNeill. Cambridge: Cambridge University Press.

_____. (1996) *Being and Time*, trans. Joan Stambaugh. Albany: State University of New York Press.

_____. (1995a) *Being and Time*, trans. John Macquarrie and Edward Robinson. Oxford: Blackwell.

_____. (1995b) *The Fundamental Concepts of Metaphysics*, trans. William McNeill and Nicholas Walker. Bloomington and Indianapolis: Indiana University Press.

_____. (1993) *Martin Heidegger: Basic Writings*, trans. David Farrell Krell. New York: HarperCollins.

_____. (1991a) 'Nihilism'. In *Nietzsche*, Volumes III and IV, trans. David Farrell Krell. San Francisco: HarperCollins.

_____. (1991b) 'The eternal recurrence of the same'. In *Nietzsche*, Volumes I and II, trans. David Farrell Krell. San Francisco: HarperCollins.

_____. (1991c) *The Principle of Reason*, trans. Reginald Lilly. Bloomington and Indianapolis: Indiana University Press.

_____. (1991d) 'The will to power as art'. In *Nietzsche*, Volumes I and II, trans. David Farrell Krell. San Francisco: Harper-Collins.

_____. (1991e) 'The will to power as knowledge and as metaphysics'. In *Nietzsche*, Volumes III and IV, trans. David Farrell Krell. San Francisco: HarperCollins.

_____. (1990a) 'A greeting to the symposium in Beirut in November 1974'. In Günther Neske and Emil Kettering (1990) *Martin Heidegger and National Socialism*, trans. Lisa Harris. New York: Paragon House, 253–254.

_____. (1990b) 'Der Spiegel interview'. In Günther Neske and Emil Kettering (1990) *Martin Heidegger and National Socialism*, trans. Lisa Harris. New York: Paragon House, 41–66.

_____. (1988) 'Political texts, 1933-1934', trans. William S. Lewis, *New German Critique* 45, 96–114.

_____. (1987) *An Introduction to Metaphysics*, trans. Ralph Manheim. New Haven and London: Yale University Press.

_____. (1985a) 'The Rectorate 1933/34: facts and thoughts', trans. Karsten Harries, *Review of Metaphysics* 38, 481–502.

_____. (1985b) 'The self-assertion of the German University: address, delivered on the solemn assumption of the Rectorate of the University Freiburg', trans. Karsten Harries, *Review of Metaphysics* 38, 470–480.

_____. (1984) *The Metaphysical Foundations of Logic*, trans. Michael Heim. Bloomington: Indiana University Press.

_____. (1982) *The Basic Problems of Phenomenology*, trans. Albert Hofstadter. Bloomington: Indiana University Press.

_____. (1978) 'Modern natural science and technology'. In John Sallis (ed), *Radical Phenomenology*. Atlantic Highlands, N.J.: Humanities Press, 3–4.

_____. (1975) *The End of Philosophy*, trans. Joan Stambaugh. London: Souvenir Press.

_____. (1971a) *On the Way to Language*, trans. Peter D. Hertz. New York: Harper and Row.

_____. (1971b) *Poetry, Language, Thought*, trans. Albert Hofstadter. New York: Harper and Row.

_____. (1969) *Identity and Difference*, trans. Joan Stambaugh. New York: Harper and Row.

_____. (1966) *Discourse on Thinking*, trans. John M. Anderson and E. Hans Freund. New York: Harper and Row.

_____. (1959) 'Das Wesen der Sprache', *Unterwegs zur Sprache*, Pfullingen G. Neske, 157–216.

_____. (1958) 'The question of being', *The Question of Being*, trans. Jean T. Wilde and William Kluback. New Haven, Conn.: College and University Press, 32–109.

Hodge, Joanna (1995) *Heidegger and Ethics*. London and New York: Routledge.

Hollinger, Robert (1994) *Postmodernism and the Social Sciences: A Thematic Approach*. Thousand Oaks, London and New Delhi: Sage Publications.

Kant, Immanuel (1987) *Foundations of the Metaphysics of Morals*, trans. Lewis White Beck. New York: Macmillan.

_____. (1973) *Critique of Pure Reason*, trans. Norman Kemp Smith. London: Macmillan.

_____. (1952) *The Critique of Judgement*, trans. James Creed Meredith. Oxford: Clarendon Press

Kierkegaard, Søren (1983) 'Fear and Trembling' and 'Repetition'. In *Kierkegaard's Works* Volume VI, trans H. Hong and E. Hong. Princeton: Princeton University Press.

Kisiel, Theodore (1995) *The Genesis of Heidegger's Being and Time*. Berkeley, Los Angeles and London: University of California Press.

Krell, David Farrell (1993) 'Spiriting Heidegger'. In David Wood (ed), *Of Derrida, Heidegger, and Spirit.* Evanston, Illinois: Northwestern University Press, 11–40.

Laclau, Ernesto (1996) 'Deconstruction, pragmatism, hegemony'. In Chantal Mouffe (ed), *Deconstruction and Pragmatism.* London and New York: Routledge: 47–67.

Laclau, Ernesto and Chantal Mouffe (1985) *Hegemony and Socialist Strategy: Towards a Radical Democratic Politics*, trans. Winston Moore and Paul Cammack. London: Verso.

Lacoue-Labarthe, Philippe and Jean-Luc Nancy (1997) *Retreating the Political.* London and New York: Routledge.

Lacoue-Labarthe, Philippe (1990) *Heidegger, Art and Politics*, trans. Chris Turner. Oxford: Basil Blackwell.

Levinas, Emmanuel (1996a) *Basic Philosophical Writings*, ed. Adriaan Peperzak, Simon Critchley, and Robert Bernasconi. Bloomington and Indianapolis: Indiana University Press.

_____. (1996b) *Totality and Infinity*, trans. Alphonso Lingis. Pittsburgh: Duquesne University Press.

_____. (1995) *Ethics and Infinity: Conversations with Philippe Nemo*, trans. Richard A. Cohen. Pittsburgh: Duquesne University Press.

_____. (1993) *Collected Philosophical Papers*, trans. Alphonso Lingis. Dordrecht, Boston and London: Kluwer Academic Publishers.

_____. (1991) *Otherwise than Being or Beyond Essence*, trans. Alphonso Lingis. Dordrecht, Boston and London: Kluwer Academic Publishers.

_____. (1986) 'Ethics of the infinite'. In Richard Kearney (ed), *Dialogues with Contemporary Continental Thinkers.* Manchester U.K.: Manchester University Press, 47–70.

_____. (1976) *Noms propres*, Montpellier: Fata Morgana.

Lilla, Mark (2001) *The Reckless Mind: Intellectuals in Politics.* New York: New York Review Books.

Lucy, Niall (2004) *A Derrida Dictionary.* Oxford: Blackwell.

_____. (1997) *Postmodern Literary Theory.* Oxford: Blackwell.

_____. (1995) *Debating Derrida*. Melbourne: Melbourne University Press.

Lloyd, Genevieve (2000) 'Fate and fortune: Derrida on facing the future', *Cogito* 1(1), 4–15.

Lyotard, Jean-François (1995) *The Differend: Phrases in Dispute*, trans. Georges Van Den Abbeele. Minneapolis: University of Minnesota Press.

Lyotard, Jean-François and Jean-Loup Thébaud (1994) *Just Gaming*, trans. Wlad Godzich. Minneapolis: University of Minnesota Press.

Lyotard, Jean-François (1993) *Libidinal Economy*, trans. Iain Hamilton Grant. Bloomington and Indianapolis: Indiana University Press.

_____. (1990) *Heidegger and "the jews"*, trans. Andreas Michel and Mark S. Roberts. Minneapolis: University of Minnesota Press.

_____. (1988) 'An interview with Jean-François Lyotard', trans. Roy Boyne, *Theory, Culture and Society* 5(2-3), 277–309.

_____. (1985) 'The sublime and the avant garde', trans. Lisa Liebmann, Geoff Bennington, and Marian Hobson, *Paragraph: The Journal of the Modern Critical Theory Group* 6, 1–18.

_____. (1984a) *Driftworks*, ed. Roger McKeon. New York: Semiotext(e).

_____. (1984b) *The Postmodern Condition: A Report on Knowledge*, trans. Geoff Bennington and Brian Massumi. Minneapolis: University of Minnesota Press.

_____. (1983) 'Presentations', trans. Kathleen McLaughlin. In Alan Montefiore (ed), *Philosophy in France Today*. Cambridge: Cambridge University Press, 116–135.

Macomber, W.B. (1967) *The Anatomy of Disillusion: Martin Heidegger's Notion of Truth*. Evanston: Northwestern University Press.

Madison, Gary Brent (2002) *The Politics of Postmodernity: Essays in Applied Hermeneutics*. Dordrecht, Boston and London: Kluwer Academic Press.

Manning, Robert J.S. (1996) 'Openings: Derrida, *differance*, and the production of justice', *Philosophy Today* 40(3), 405–417.

McCumber, John (1999) *Metaphysics and Oppression: Heidegger's Challenge to Western Philosophy*. Bloomington and Indianapolis: Indiana University Press.

McNeill, Will (1993) 'Spirit's living hand'. In David Wood (ed), *Of Derrida, Heidegger, and Spirit*. Evanston, Illinois: Northwestern University Press, 103–117.

Mouffe, Chantal (1996) 'Deconstruction, pragmatism and the politics of democracy'. In Chantal Mouffe (ed), *Deconstruction and Pragmatism*. London and New York: Routledge: 1–12.

_____. (1993) *The Return of the Political*. London and New York: Verso.

Neske, Günther and Emil Kettering (1990) *Martin Heidegger and National Socialism*, trans. Lisa Harris. New York: Paragon House.

Niznik, Józef and John T. Sanders (eds) (1996) *Debating the State of Philosophy*. Westport, Connecticut: Praeger Publishers.

Patrick, Morag (1997) 'Excess and responsibility: Derrida's ethico-political thinking', *Journal of the British Society for Phenomenology* 28(2), 160–177.

Perpich, Diane (1998) 'A singular justice: ethics and politics between Levinas and Derrida', *Philosophy Today* 42: *Selected Studies in Phenomenological and Existential Philosophy Supplement* 24, 59–70.

Pryor, Benjamin S. (1998) 'Counter-remembering the Enlightenment', *Philosophy Today* 42: *Selected Studies in Phenomenological and Existential Philosophy Supplement* 24, 147–159.

Racevskis, Karlis (1993) *Postmodernism and the Search for Enlightenment*. Charlottesville and London: University Press of Virginia.

Rasch, William (1994) 'In search of the Lyotardian archipelago, or: how to live with paradox and learn to like it', *New German Critique* 61, 55–75.

Reynolds, Jack (2004) 'Derrida and Deleuze on Time, the Future, and Politics', *Borderlands E-Journal* 3(1), http://www.borderlandsejournal.adelaide.edu.au/vol3no1_2004/reynolds_time.htm (accessed 4 June 2004).

Rockmore, Tom and Joseph Margolis (eds) (1992) *The Heidegger Case: On Philosophy and Politics.* Philadelphia: Temple University Press.

Rorty, Richard, Derek Nystrom and Kent Puckett (2002) *Against Bosses, Against Oligarchies.* Chicago: Prickly Paradigm Press.

Rorty, Richard (1999) *Philosophy and Social Hope.* London: Penguin Books.

_____. (1998a) *Achieving our Country: Leftist Thought in Twentieth-Century America.* Cambridge, Mass.: Harvard University Press.

_____. (1998b) *Truth and Progress.* Cambridge: Cambridge University Press.

_____. (1996a) *Consequences of Pragmatism.* Minneapolis: University of Minnesota Press.

_____. (1996b) 'On moral obligation, truth, and common sense'. In Józef Niznik and Sanders, John T. (eds), *Debating the State of Philosophy.* Westport, Connecticut: Praeger Publishers, 48–52.

_____. (1996c) 'Relativism – finding and making'. In Józef Niznik and Sanders, John T. (eds), *Debating the State of Philosophy.* Westport, Connecticut: Praeger Publishers, 31–47.

_____. (1996d) 'Remarks on deconstruction and pragmatism'. In Chantal Mouffe (ed), *Deconstruction and Pragmatism.* London and New York: Routledge, 13–18.

_____. (1996e) 'Response to Ernesto Laclau'. In Chantal Mouffe (ed), *Deconstruction and Pragmatism.* London and New York: Routledge, 69–76.

_____. (1996f) 'Response to Simon Critchley'. In Chantal Mouffe (ed), *Deconstruction and Pragmatism*. London and New York: Routledge, 41–46.

_____. (1983) 'Postmodernist bourgeois liberalism', *Journal of Philosophy* 80, 583–589.

Ruthrof, Horst (1998) *Semantics and the Body: Meaning from Frege to the Postmodern*. Melbourne: Melbourne University Press.

Sallis, John (1993) 'Flight of spirit'. In David Wood (ed), *Of Derrida, Heidegger, and Spirit*. Evanston, Illinois: Northwestern University Press, 118–132.

Santos, Ramón J. (2003) 'Richard Rorty's philosophy of social hope', *Philosophy Today* 47(4), 431–440.

Schrag, Calvin O. (1992) *The Resources of Rationality: A Response to the Postmodern Challenge*. Bloomington and Indianapolis: Indiana University Press.

Scott, Charles E. (1990) *The Question of Ethics: Nietzsche, Foucault, Heidegger*. Bloomington and Indianapolis: Indiana University Press.

Spivak, Gayatri Chakravorty (1976) 'Translator's preface'. Jacques Derrida. In Jacques Derrida (1976) *Of Grammatology*, trans. Gayatri Chakravorty Spivak. Baltimore and London: John Hopkins University Press, ix–lxxxvii.

Steinbock, Anthony J. (1997) 'The origins and crisis of continental philosophy', *Man and World* 30, 199–215.

Steiner, Gary (2003) 'The perils of a total critique of reason: rethinking Heidegger's influence', *Philosophy Today* 47(1), 93–111.

Weber, Samuel (1994) 'Afterword: literature – just making it'. In Jean-François Lyotard and Jean-Loup Thébaud (1994) *Just Gaming*, trans. Wlad Godzich. Minneapolis: University of Minnesota Press, 101–120.

Wittgenstein, Ludwig (1995a) *Philosophical Investigations*, trans. G.E.M. Anscombe. Oxford UK and Cambridge USA: Blackwell.

_____. (1995b) *Tractatus Logico-Philosophicus*, trans. C.K. Ogden. London and New York: Routledge.

Wood, David (2002) *Thinking after Heidegger*. Cambridge: Polity.
_____. (1999) 'The experience of the ethical'. In Richard Kearney and Mark Dooley (eds), *Questioning Ethics: Contemporary Debates in Philosophy*. London and New York: Routledge, 105–119.

Wyschogrod, Edith (2003) 'Without why, without whom: thinking otherwise with John D. Caputo'. In Mark Dooley (ed), *A Passion for the Impossible: John D. Caputo in Focus*. New York: State University of New York Press, 299–310.

Ziarek, Krzysztof (1995) 'The ethos of everydayness: Heidegger on poetry and language', *Man and World* 28, 377–399.

Zimmerman, Michael E. (1998) 'John D. Caputo: a postmodern, prophetic, liberal American in Paris', *Continental Philosophy Review* 31, 195–214.

Index

Ketil Bonaunet

Hermann Cohen's Kantian Philosophy of Religion

Bern, Berlin, Bruxelles, Frankfurt am Main, New York, Oxford, Wien, 2004. 165 pp.
European University Studies: Series 20, Philosophy. Vol. 679
ISBN 3-03910-421-7 / US-ISBN 0-8204-7033-3 pb.
sFr. 54.– / €* 37.20 / €** 34.80 / £ 25.– / US-$ 41.95

* includes VAT – only valid for Germany and Austria ** does not include VAT

This study examines the influence of Kant on Hermann Cohen's philosophy of religion.

A basic tenet in Kantian philosophy of religion is that morality leads ineluctably to religion. But how does morality lead to religion? While Cohen rejected Kant's doctrine of the postulates (of the existence of God and the immortality of the soul) as it is formulated in *Kritik der praktischen Vernunft*, he searched for alternative ways to found a «religion of reason» in ethics.

This book concentrates on two routes from ethics to religion that are central to Cohen's philosophy of religion in his two last works: *Der Begriff der Religion im System der Philosophie* (1915), and *Religion der Vernunft aus den Quellen des Judentums* (posthumous 1919). One route takes compassion towards the «concrete Other», which is complementary to an ethics of universal respect, as its point of departure, and argues that an attitude of compassion and recognition of the Other as a genuine individual presupposes a distinctive religious consciousness. The other route is inspired by Kant's wrestling with the problem of removal of moral guilt in *Religion innerhalb der Grenzen der blossen Vernunft*, and centres around the questions of guilt and liberation from guilt.

Cohen's ideas and their continued relevance are explored in this book in light of some major concerns of twentieth century and contemporary philosophy of religion.

Contents: Hermann Cohen's philosophy of religion as a Kantian philosophy of religion – Compassion and the discovery of the «thou» as complementation of a Kantian ethics of universal respect – Compassion as belonging to a religious consciousness – Moral guilt as a problem in Kantian ethics and philosophy of religion – The problem of the autonomy of religion within a Kantian philosophy of religion.

PETER LANG

Bern · Berlin · Bruxelles · Frankfurt am Main · New York · Oxford · Wien